Anselm
of
Canterbury

Why God Became Man
and
The Virgin Conception
and Original Sin

by
Anselm of Canterbury

Translation, introduction and notes by
Joseph M. Colleran

AGI BOOKS, INC.

33 Buckingham Dr.   Albany, New York 12208

This translation is from the critical edition of the works of St. Anselm of Canterbury by F. S. Schmitt, O.S.B.
Franciscus Salesius Schmitt, O.S.B. (Ed.), S. *Anselmi Cantuariensis Archiepiscopi Opera Omnia* (Edinburgi, apud Thomam Nelson et Filios, copyright MDCCCCXLV1).

Library of Congress Catalog Card Number 71-77166
This softcover edition ISBN 0-87343-025-5
Manufactured and printed in the United States of America by Edwards Brothers, Inc., Ann Arbor, Michigan

A Library bound and sewn edition of this title is also available under ISBN 0-87343-043-3

CONTENTS

PREFACE

To readers of English history, St. Anselm is best known, perhaps, for his opposition to the English kings William Rufus and Henry I, on matters of ecclesiastical rights. By undergraduate students of the history of philosophy, he is best remembered as the author of an argument for the existence of God which appears naive to most twentieth century minds, and which was rejected, for very similar reasons, by thinkers so different from each other as St. Thomas Aquinas and Immanuel Kant. St. Anselm's right to a place in history, however, is based upon much more than his endurance of political opposition and his proposal of an "ontological argument." In the realm of thought he is a titan of theology, a Doctor of the Church. His reflections on the existence and nature of God have contributed greatly to the development of Christian theology and in no small measure to the development of a "natural theology." It is quite likely, though, that his principal claim to fame is his authorship of the book *Cur Deus Homo.*

Even though this work and related writings of the saint are concerned with precise aspects of the incarnation and atonement of Jesus Christ which are no longer central in theological inquiry, and although many of his insights have been further developed and some of his views have lost their vogue after his lifetime, his writings on the role of the God-man constituted a turning point in theological history. By the tone and method of all his writings, Anselm introduced the Scholastic era, and by his Christological treatises he tolled the knell of more than one ancient view and gave birth to new traditions.

As background for the understanding and evaluation of the treatise *Why God Became Man* and its corollary *The Virgin*

vii

Conception and Original Sin, what seems to be the most relevant introductory material is here presented under these headings:

I. The saint's life.

II. His personality and character.

III. His writings.

IV. The *Cur Deus Homo* and *De Conceptu Virginali:*

    A. Circumstances of composition.

    B. Outlines of the two works.

    C. Contemporary background.

    D. Rationalist theology?

    E. Anselm's doctrine of atonement.

    F. Original sin and its transmission.

    G. General evaluation.

Introduction

I. ST. ANSELM'S LIFE

St. Anselm was fortunate in having one of the most competent of medieval biographers and historians to record his career; his name was Eadmer.[1] His *History of Recent Events* [2] and his *Life of Anselm* [3] are our principal sources of knowledge about the saint. Although Eadmer had direct connections with Anselm only during the latter's years as archbishop, from 1093 to 1109, he nevertheless learned of the earlier years from the saint himself. Certain details of Anselm's life and writings are also known from the prologues to some of his works and from his letters.

Anselm was born about 1033 [4] in the Alpine town of Aosta in Piedmont, south of Burgundy and near the St. Bernard Passes. His mother was Ermenberga, a native of Aosta. His father was Gundulf, a Lombard by birth, who adopted the town and possibly the property, of his wife. Eadmer tells us that both parents were wealthy, but were quite different in character. Gundulf, although he entered a monastery shortly before his death, was worldly and prodigal throughout most of his life; Ermenberga was always not only a discreet householder, but also an upright and exemplary mother. Influenced mainly by her conversations, Anselm showed a preoccupation with God and religion even in his childhood.[5]

When he was young, he was put under the tutelage of a relative who was a professional teacher. This man kept him in confinement in his house, so that he would study more diligently, and shielded him from all distractions which he thought would interfere with the boy's desire for study. The chronicler [6] of the story tells us that after some time the boy "almost lost his mind." When he returned home, he was frightened by the family and neighbors to whom he had become unaccustomed; he avoided company and never answered when spoken to. His mother thought she had lost her son for good, but having ob-

1

tained sound counsel, she directed the servants and others to permit him to do whatever he wanted and never to resist him. He gradually came around to his normal mental health. This grim experience taught him to use prudence and kindness with the young, and helped to make him a model of discretion when he became a teacher.

After this episode, he studied with the Benedictines at Aosta. Before he was fifteen, he decided he could best fulfill God's will by becoming a monk. Accordingly, he applied to the abbot of a nearby monastery. The abbot was unwilling to accept the under-aged applicant without his father's permission. Anselm prayed for some disease which would make him acceptable to the abbot as one worthy of dying in the monastery. His prayer was followed by the appearance of a general weakness, which he took as a sign that all his prayers would be answered. The abbot was still afraid of offending Gundulf, however, and refused to accept the boy.[7]

Soon after this, Anselm became less interested in religious life, and even preferred, or seemed to prefer, the "ways of the world." [8] He turned from study to amusements, and was saved from utter worldliness only by the influence of his mother. When she died, "the ship of his heart lost its anchor," [9] and his father developed a deep hostility toward him, finding fault with him not only for any mistakes he made, but also for anything he did right. At length, for fear that something might happen that would bring disgrace upon his father or himself, he renounced his patrimony and his fatherland and left his father's house for good.[10] Accompanied by a cleric who served as companion and servant, he crossed the Alps in 1056.

Three years later, after spending some time in Burgundy and some in France, Anselm appeared in the duchy of Normandy with the intention of studying with the learned and holy Lanfranc,[11] prior of the Benedictine monastery at Bec.[12] Day and night, under the guidance of the celebrated teacher, Anselm devoted himself to literary studies; he also gave lessons to others less advanced than himself. During this time, he began to realize that if he had become a monk, as he once desired, the fatigue and the hardships of cold and hunger which he would have to endure would be no greater than those he was already enduring for the sake of learning. Besides, he would be sure of a supernatural reward of which he could not be so certain in his present state. Making up his mind to become a monk, he thought he should look for a monastery other than the one at Bec, where he was, and other than the even more famous one at Cluny. His reason was that at Cluny the severity of observance and the fullness of schedule would hamper his quest for learning, and if he were at Bec he would be insignificant in comparison with the outstanding Lanfranc. He eventually realized that his motives for entering a monastery were not worthy, and he then chose Bec, precisely because there he would be of low intellectual stature, compared with Lanfranc, and thus he could concentrate on God as the sole object of his contemplation and desire. In his twenty-seventh year, he became a monk at Bec, where Herlwin, the founder of the monastery in 1034, still lived as abbot.

He led an exemplary life as a monk, progressing in sanctity and winning the respect of his confreres. After three years, Lanfranc was called away to be the abbot of a monastery at Caen, and Anselm replaced him as prior in Bec. This was, most probably, in 1063.[13]

As simple monk, and even as prior, Anselm felt monastic life not as a confinement, but as a condition of freedom. For he was able to devote all of his time and all of himself to the service of God. Never before had he been free to do that. This dedication to the service of God took the forms of observance of monastic fasts and prayers and vigils, and of application of his mind to the explanation and development of revealed Christian doctrine. Some of the fruits of his contemplation during these years have been preserved in his earlier writings: his prayers and meditations, his monologue on the rationale of the Faith, and his musings on the existence and attributes of God.[14]

On August 26, 1078, Abbot Herlwin died, and within a few days the community of Bec elected Anselm the abbot. He argued, pleaded and prayed, and even dramatically prostrated himself on the ground before the monks, in an effort to dissuade them from electing him; but with equal importunity and even prostrations, they begged him to acquiesce for the good of the community. He was consecrated in 1079.

Most of the secular business of the monastery he left to its delegated minor officials, and concerned himself with contemplation and with the instruction and guidance of the monks. He also kept a conscientious supervisory watch over the business and especially the lawsuits of the monastery, so that no injustice or trickery would be used by advocates in favor of the monastery and to the harm of others. Within the very year of his consecration, he went to England to examine the properties of the monastery there. Although this was a normal trip for a new abbot, at least an equally strong motive for his journey was to visit his revered master, Lanfranc, who was then the archbishop of Canterbury. Anselm wanted to consult his former teacher and prior on personal matters, and Lanfranc invited him to discourse on ascetical subjects to the canons, monks, nuns and certain laymen living in Canterbury, and to give his opinions on various theological topics.

Lanfranc died in May, 1089. Since the death of King William, on September 9, 1087, and the accession of his son William Rufus, the churches and monasteries of England had been deprived of their revenues and the barons and clergy were excessively taxed, to support the new king's campaigns for the extension of his dominion and the recovery of Normandy. William Rufus postponed the appointment of a new Archbishop of Canterbury and collected the revenues for his own uses. When this proved successful, he did the same with other vacant sees, unless ambitious and unscrupulous clerics offered high enough prices for the bishoprics.[15]

After three years of this oppression, some English nobles wrote to Anselm, inviting and even begging him to come from Bec and help them. The monks of Bec also urged him to go, so Anselm gave in to the requests and arrived at Canterbury on September 7, 1092.[16] He visited and interviewed the king, the earl of Chester, and many of his old monastic friends, such as Gilbert Crispin. When he was in Canterbury, many of the monks and laity acclaimed him as Archbishop, and, in fright and sadness, he left the place the very next day, without waiting to celebrate the feast of the birthday of the Mother of God among them. When Anselm visited the king, William Rufus treated him with respect, but was adamant about keeping the revenues of Canterbury for himself, and he swore that there would never be another archbishop of Canterbury so long as he himself lived.[17]

In March 1093, he became seriously ill, and being fearful of death and prodded by his barons, he promised to rule by law, and gave consent to the appointment of an archbishop, declaring that Anselm was most capable. Both clergy and laity at once gave unanimous approval. When Anselm was told, he objected and resisted, but without success. He was "carried rather than led" into the neighboring church on March 6, 1093, and invested by the king. He was adverse to the appointment, however, and would not accept the episcopal staff, but the bishops present held it against his closed hand. After praying and reflecting, he came to the conclusion that obedience and the need of the archdiocese required his consent. He was consecrated on December 4, 1093.[18]

The good feeling between king and archbishop did not last long. The king, on the advice of his courtiers, asked Anselm for a thousand pounds, as thank-offering for all the munificence that had been accorded to him. In his *Life of Anselm*, Eadmer gives the impression that it was a simoniacal demand of money for a spiritual gift. In his *History of Recent Events*, however, he indicates that the homage of a gift of money was customary and generally recognized, and that the king was seeking the large sum to help cover the expenses of his military attack on Normandy. There is no indication in Anselm's letters that he considered the war unjust and hence not to be supported, but he did think there would be suspicions of simony if the archbishop of Canterbury paid such a large sum right after his consecration. Not objecting to the payment as such, however, he offered five hundred pounds. The king spurned the smaller sum; Anselm at once had it given to the poor.[19]

In 1094 and 1095, the archbishop asked the king to repair the churches which were going to ruin, to revive the knowledge and practice of Christian life in the kingdom, and to permit him to go to Rome to receive the archiepiscopal pallium from Pope Urban. The king became angry and finally said that he did not recognize Urban as pope, and that it was the custom of English kings not to allow anyone in the kingdom to call a person pope whom the king did not approve. At Anselm's suggestion, the matter of recognition of Urban was left to a meeting of the bishops, abbots and barons with the king and archbishop. It occurred in the early part of 1095. Marked by acrimonious dispute from the beginning, it culminated in the rebellion of most of the bishops against Pope Urban and the archbishop of Canterbury. The king swore he would cease to acknowledge Anselm as archbishop unless he renounced allegiance to Urban. Anselm stood firm, and asked for a safe-conduct to leave the kingdom. When the barons asked for a truce, Anselm consented not to leave. The king promised to respect the truce, but soon broke it, harassing and persecuting some of Anselm's supporters and friends. Before Pentecost, however, a legate brought the pallium from Pope Urban to Anselm, and prevailed upon William Rufus to recognize the archbishop. Friendship prevailed between them for a time, "at least," as Eadmer adds, "in appearance." [20]

From 1095 to 1097, there was no public dispute between archbishop and king, and Anselm spent his time administering the affairs of the Church, consecrating bishops, constructing buildings and concluding his book on the relation of the incarnation to the Persons of the Holy Trinity.[21] Most likely, it was also at this time that he commenced his *Why God Became Man*.[22] The king, however, still refused permission to hold an ecclesiastical council, and this was the principal point of contention between the two, but it did not break into public conflict.

When, in 1097, the archbishop asked permission to go to Rome to seek the pope's advice and direction, William refused. Anselm then declared that it was for the good of religion, the health of his own soul, and even for the honor and advantage of the king that he wanted to go to Rome, so he would leave without permission, although he still requested and hoped for the king's consent. The king confronted him with these alternatives: either to stop his requests and swear never to appeal to the pope, or to leave England at once and never hope to return. He added that if Anselm chose to stay, he would still be fined for his impetuosity.[23]

There were delays due to adverse winds and to harassment by the king's henchmen, but eventually, in November 1097, the archbishop set sail for Europe. When William learned he had gone, he ordered all his property confiscated and all his transactions declared null and void.[24] Anselm was in his first exile.

When he arrived in Rome, he went at once to the Lateran, and was warmly received by the Holy Father, who called him "one to be venerated almost as our equal . . . (and) the apostolic patriarch of that other world." [25] The pope was astonished at the troubles in England and promised Anselm his full support.

To escape the extreme summer heat of Rome, the archbishop went with the abbot John of Telese to a village called Sclavia and remained there for some time. Here he could indulge in contemplation and sacred study without distraction and here he finished and published his treatise *Why God Became Man*.

In 1098 the Council of Bari was held. Anselm attended it and took active part in the theological discussions regarding the *Filioque*, of great interest to the Greek bishops in Italy. The address he gave on this occasion was later developed into the book *On The Procession of the Holy Spirit*.[26]

This council denounced the king of England for simony and for oppression of the Church, and very likely would have excommunicated him if Anselm had not pleaded for him. The saint persuaded Pope Urban not to go beyond a threat of excommunication. In 1099, however, the pope held a synod at the Vatican in which excommunication was decreed against laymen who confer investiture on churchmen, and against churchmen who accept it from laymen. Excommunication was also threatened against those who would consecrate an illegitimate appointee and against clerics who paid homage to lay lords.[27]

After the council, Anselm went to Lyons and visited Cluny, Macon and other towns. It was during this time (1099–1100) that he wrote *The Virgin Conception And Original Sin* and *A Meditation On Human Redemption*. While he was in France, Pope Urban died on July 29, 1099. On August 2, 1100, King

William Rufus died, his heart pierced by an arrow while he was hunting.

Henry I was crowned king, succeeding his brother, and, joined by many barons, he sent word to Anselm inviting him to return to England. At the end of September in 1100, Anselm arrived and told the king what had transpired at the synod in Rome. Henry was incensed, and unwilling to cooperate with pope or archbishop. He demanded that Anselm be re-invested and pay homage for his see. Anselm refused, because of the Roman condemnation. Eventually, in the spring of 1103, the king asked Anselm to go to Rome to present the king's case, and Anselm assented, although he insisted he would never advise the pope to do anything that might injure the liberty of the churches or blight his own honor.[28] Thus began Anselm's second exile.

Paschal II was now pope, and he received Anselm cordially. But when the king's envoy, who accompanied the archbishop, asserted that Henry would not submit to the loss of ecclesiastical vesture, even to keep his throne, Paschal retorted that he himself would never permit the king to possess the right of investiture with impunity, even to buy his own freedom. The meeting broke up without either side being satisfied, and later, on the way to Lyons, the legate told Anselm he would not be welcome back in England unless he recognized in Henry all the rights that had been claimed by his father and brother. This did not square with what he had been told in England before the journey, but it was obviously the king's decision. So Anselm settled in Lyons and was happy to be engaged in contemplation and study in its peaceful atmosphere and in the company of his good friend Hugh, archbishop of the city.

When Henry heard that the pope would not change his decision, he took the archbishopric and its possessions into his own hands. For a year and a half there were negotiations between Anselm and Henry. Finally, Anselm left Burgundy and Henry met with him in Normandy. Fearing the archbishop would excommunicate him, the king restored the possessions of the Church to Anselm and gave him his friendship. After more delays, Anselm returned to England in September, 1106. He could take credit for a victory for the freedom of the Church, since the king gave up the custom of his predecessors and neither chose nor invested the heads of dioceses and abbeys thereafter. Anselm, on his part, conceded that English bishops could pay homage to the king for temporal possessions. A sign of warmer and fairer relations between the two was the king's appointment of the archbishop as his regent during an absence in 1108.

Anselm was not so preoccupied with administrative and political matters that he found neither time for, nor interest in, theological study. In 1107 and 1108 he wrote and published *The Harmony Between God's Foreknowledge, Predestination, Grace And Free Choice*.[29]

During Lent of the year 1109, Anselm was seriously ill and extremely weak, and on Palm Sunday some of his monks suggested that he would be attending "the Easter Court of our Lord." It was, in fact, on the Wednesday before Easter, the twenty-first of April, 1109, that his earthly career came to a peaceful end.

While he was called *beatus* by his successor Theobald,[30] and although the monks of Canterbury and of Bec revered his memory for his saintliness, it was left to his successor, Saint Thomas Becket, a year after his consecration in 1162, to make a request to the pope to canonize Anselm. He presented an account of his predecessor's life and miracles, probably not Eadmer's, but a summary of it by John of Salisbury.[31] Pope Alexander III, in 1163, asked that the matter be submitted to a provincial council at Canterbury, but there is no record that it was held. Sometime before Becket's martyrdom on December 29, 1170, however, a calendar from Christ Church, Canterbury, mentions the transference of "St. Anselm the Archbishop" on April seventh, and "the feast of our most glorious Father Anselm, Archbishop and Confessor" on April twenty-first.[32] It seems likely that formal procedures of canonization had been carried out, although no explicit record of them has been found. Anselm was honored as a saint, especially in Canterbury and Bec, but he was eclipsed in general popular devotion by Becket the Martyr. In the fifteenth century, interest in Anselm and devotion to him were resumed, but they were due largely to the attribution to him

of a writing on the institution of the feast of the Immaculate
Conception, which was not his at all. At least since the early
part of the eighteenth century, he was honored as a Doctor of
the Church.[33]

II. ST. ANSELM'S PERSONALITY
AND CHARACTER

After he was chosen archbishop of Canterbury, Anselm became aware that some of the monks of Bec suspected he was
rather attracted toward the post by ambition than forced into
it by obedience. He declared, in a letter, that he knew no way
of persuading them of his good intentions, if his life had not
been sufficient proof to those critics. The criterion he proposes
is particularly apt in his case, for his whole life manifests a
uniformity of attitudes and a consistency of action that show
him to be most admirable as a human being and most imitable
as a monk. He could say, in the same letter: "I have conducted
myself for thirty-three years in the monastic way of life . . .
in such a manner that all the good people who knew me loved
me . . . and those who knew me more intimately, loved me
more." [34] It is still true that the more you know about the saint
from his letters and his biography, and even from his speculative works, the more you admire and value his character.

One of his outstanding natural characteristics was graciousness. He was genial in manner, affable in conversation, benign
in his dealings with the lowly and oppressed. As prior in the
monastery, he patiently put up with the manners and weaknesses
of all, and provided generously for everyone.[35] A similar genial-
ity shows forth in his writings: he takes positions firmly, but
never is bumptious in presenting his views; he combats the
opinions of his opponents (Roscelin and Gaunilon, for example),
but he does not besmirch or ridicule the persons.

In Anselm, as perhaps in every human personality, there come to the fore certain traits and talents that seem to balance and even to oppose one another. Even as a child, he was fond of solitude and of reflection on the God behind the beauties of his native region; later, he pondered becoming a hermit; and whether in the monastery or in the archbishopric, he favored the contemplative way of life. Yet he had such talent for leadership that he was chosen to succeed Lanfranc as prior, his confreres elected him the abbot of Bec, and the English clergy, knights and humble populace clamored for him to become the archbishop of Canterbury. He felt such a repugnance for administrative tasks that such "secular business" as negotiations with the king regarding the properties of the Church gave him great weariness and made him appear seriously sick to his friends.[36] When it was his duty to resist the king's encroachments, however, he could show himself energetic and adamant in claiming his own rights and those of the Church. He had profound respect for the pope, and defended papal rights and papal decisions to the extent of suffering royal antagonism and two exiles. Nevertheless, he courageously protested to Pope Paschal II that if the Holy Father did not sustain him in insisting that Bishop Thomas of York accept Canterbury's primacy, he himself would simply not stay in England, in a divided Church.[37]

It is on a supernatural plane that he found the way to reconcile personal preferences and objective requirements, self-effacement and self-assertion, loyalty to authority and insistence on his own authority and on the submission of others. The moral trait that is most characteristic of him is *rectitude of will*, or "justice" or "righteousness" of which he speaks so frequently, and on which he insists so much, in his writings.[38] Behind all his acts and attitudes, there was a calm reasonableness, and it was a reasonableness that included the principles of supernatural faith as a foundation, and Christ-like charity as the objective of his intentions and actions.

Eadmer admits that he himself shared a common opinion that Anselm went too far in cultivating the virtues and practicing the mode of life of a monk, when he was the primate of so great a people. His humility, patience and abstinence were censured as extreme, and his mildness in regard to recalcitrant subjects appeared to critics to be an approval of rebellion. But when Anselm explained the reasons for any of his actions, as he was always willing to do, the critics, we know on Eadmer's testimony, had to admit the archbishop was right.[39] He thus inculcated reasonableness and an underlying rectitude of will in his friends, as he practiced them himself.

It was his rectitude that made him take so seriously the obligations of his high position, even while he deplored being in that position. In a discourse to monks, he lamented his lack of advancemnt toward perfection, compared to his previous life as a monk, when he found delight in personal contemplation of God and had subjects who listened to his counsels and put them into practice. He compared himself to an owl who is at ease when she is in a hollow with her brood, but is endangered and attacked when with crows and other birds. When he was with monks, he pointed out, he was at home and happy, but when engaged in politics and administration with secular nobles, he was spiritually torn to pieces. He concluded with the seriously pathetic plaint: *Have pity on me, have pity on me, at least you, my friends, because the hand of the Lord has touched me.*[40] Yet he did not confine himself to residence among the monks of Canterbury, because it was his duty to visit the manors that traditionally belonged to the Canterbury See, even though they were spread far and wide. He recognized the dangers to the common people living and working on Church properties, if he did not visit them.[41] It was his sense of rectitude that ruled him in this as in all his affairs.

The same sense can be said to have guided him in the perennial choice between conservatism and progressivism in changing times. He can be said to have remained staunchly conservative in regard to the plan and manners of monastic life, counseling monks to submit to the program and customs of their monasteries, rather than to think, with danger of self-deception, that they could achieve more by changing the monastic rules and practices.[42] Yet he was progressive and even revolutionary in his adoption of the logic of his times and its application to the problems of theology.[43]

As the Holy Spirit calls the foster-father of our Lord "a just man," or an "upright" man,[44] so we can call St. Anselm "a just man" or "a man of rectitude." He lived up to all the implications of the names of monk, cleric, archbishop, theologian, preacher and pastor, but the name that epitomizes them all and eclipses them all is "saint." Eadmer aptly suggests the applicability to him of what was said of St. Martin: "There was always on his lips the name of Christ, and in his heart there was always devotion, and peace and mercy." [45]

III. ST. ANSELM THE WRITER

It was about the year 1070, when he was 37 years old, that St. Anselm began his writing career. Many of his works were commenced, and practically all of them were copied for publication, at the request of his confreres or others for help in understanding and defending the teachings of the faith or for assistance in expressing and developing their devotion.

While all of the works of the saint have an importance and a charm of their own, our purpose in listing and describing them here is simply to enable the reader the better to appreciate the *Cur Deus Homo* and the *De Conceptu Virginali* in the light of Anselm's whole body of theological thought and devotional meditation. The length and detail of description of each work, then, will depend upon the closeness of relation of that work to the two which specially concern us. The chronology, which is not established with absolute certitude in most cases, is the one proposed by Schmitt and followed by most authorities.[46]

1. *Prayers and Meditations*

The writings that first brought Anselm a measure of fame were the copies of his meditations and prayers [47] which were requested by his fellow monks. These were spread around to other monasteries and were paid the homage, sincere in its

intentions but confusing in its results, of being not only literally
copied but also imitated and adapted by others. Through the
decades after the saint's death, the number of devotional works
attributed to him grew considerably, and in the following centuries swelled to seventy-four prayers, twenty-one meditations
and sixteen homilies.[48] A. Wilmart has shown that only nineteen
prayers, three meditations and no homilies are unquestionably
authentic, although some few of the others are still disputable.[49]
Of the authentic ones, the *Meditation on Human Redemption* [50]
was composed in 1099, after the *Cur Deus Homo,* and a few
others are probably attributable to the same decade, but most of
these prayers were composed before Anselm became abbot in
1078.[51]

What is notable about these prayers is that they inaugurate
a change in prayer-style. From the time of Alcuin (735–804)
in the era of Charlemagne (742–814), to the eleventh century,
the private prayers of monks and laity consisted mainly of selections from the psalms, interspersed with specially composed
prayers of petition addressed to God, or, in some cases, to the
blessed virgin Mary and various saints. The prayer formulas
are regularly briefer than the selections from the psalter. In
Anselm's compositions, the personal and original prayers are
longer and more numerous than the quotations. Where previously
a fixed and brief prayer formula prevailed, Anselm introduced
an elaboration of the address to God or a saint by relative clauses
referring to some Scriptural scene or revelation. He also achieved
theological precision in expressing the relation of saints with
God, and he put an emphasis on the part of the will in both God
and man. There is a noticeable display of emotion, and a glow
of purple prose, but underneath the verbal color and fervor
there is a vivid realization of the holiness of God, the desirability
of pleasing God and the heinousness of sin. There is an effusive-
ness in the prayers which is toned down considerably in later
theological works, such as *Why God Became Man.*[52]

2. *The Monologue On The Rationale Of The Faith*

This work was finished probably in 1076.[53] It is certainly prior
to the work *On Truth* because is is cited in the latter.[54]

Anselm had mentioned some of his thoughts on God's essence to certain monks at Bec, in conversation, and they asked him to write out his reflections. He complied, but gave the work no title and did not affix his name as author. As it started to circulate among the monasteries, he entitled it, provisionally: *Exemplum Meditandi De Ratione Fidei—An Example of Meditating On The Rationale of the Faith.* In accordance with the wish of the confreres who requested the book, he made an effort to use rational arguments and analyses, rather than to adduce the authority of Holy Scripture to establish his conclusions. The subject matter is the essence of God and "some other connected themes," notably what have come to be called the "attributes" of God.

When he came to edit it for publication, Anselm renamed it *Monoloquium De Ratione Fidei.* Then, almost immediately, he revised the title to *Monologion,* which is not a hybrid of Greek and Latin, and which is more attractive because of its brevity.[55] The treatise is, indeed, a monologue or soliloquy, in the usual sense of a "talking out with oneself." "Meditation on the rationale of the faith" [56] is a good description of the content of the work. That phrase, in fact, seems to be a fair delineation of any of Anselm's works.

What was new and significant in the method of this book was the effort to convince readers of the truth of his conclusions about God's essence and attributes *by rational arguments,* and not by adducing the authority of Holy Scripture. This was somewhat revolutionary in theological procedure, and was being urged mainly by younger monks and scholars. Anselm went along with the trend wholeheartedly. But his teacher and patron, Lanfranc, to whom he sent a copy for a critique and suggestion of a title, was definitely not enthusiastic about it. Although Anselm apparently did not save Lanfranc's letter on this matter, his own reply indicates that Lanfranc suggested some additions to the work, and especially urged that Holy Scripture be quoted as authority. Anselm asserts that all his statements can be defended from the Bible or from St. Augustine, and that he is only doing what Augustine had done in his *De Trinitate,* and doing it more briefly.[57]

There is no doubt that Anselm's teaching is in harmony with Augustine's, but it is also true that it is a development of Augustine's, in a quite original way. Elsewhere [58] Anselm says, quite correctly, that if he has gone beyond the Fathers in any way, it is only that he has said what they knew and would admit, but did not say. Still, it remains true that no one before him, including Augustine, ever drew up such a tightly constructed compendium of the truths about God—including aspects of the Holy Trinity—which can be known by human reasoning.

3. *An Address—Faith Seeking Understanding*

After he finished the *Monologion,* Anselm began to wonder if he could show, by one single, brief argument, "what we believe and preach about God, that is to say, that He is eternal, unchangeable, all-powerful, totally present everywhere, incomprehensible, just, compassionate, merciful, true—in fact, truth, goodness, justice, and so on; and how all these things are one and the same, in Him." [59] In this work, too, as in the preceding one, he set aside all authority of Holy Scripture.[60]

The treatise was completed, probably, in 1078. At first, he considered it unworthy of a name, but, deciding to publish it, he called it *Fides Quaerens Intellectum—Faith Seeking Understanding.*[61] Then, for brevity, he changed this to *Proslogion,* or *Address,* because, as Eadmer says, "in this work he addresses either himself or God." [62]

In chapters two to four, Anselm presents an argument for the existence of God, which is original and startling; of all his contributions to theological and philosophical lore, this is undoubtedly the most famous. The argument may be summarized: (According to our faith) God is a being than which no greater can be thought. That than which no greater can be thought, however, cannot exist in the understanding alone. For what would exist in reality as well as in understanding would be greater than what exists in understanding alone. So "that than which no greater can be thought" must exist in reality, or it would at the same time be and not be that than which no greater can be thought. Hence God exists in reality.

The author offers this as an argument which even "the fool" who says in his heart "there is no God," [63] would have to accept, because when he hears the name "God" he knows or has in his understanding, the nominal definition "that than which no greater can be thought." He is made to understand, by exposition of this argument, that God necessarily exists in reality as well as in mind.[64]

The bulk of the book (chapters five to twenty-six) treats of the attributes and powers of God. Since these attributes are all discussed in the light of human reason alone, this section has commonly been considered as the first systematic treatise of "natural theology" or the philosophical study of God.

Eadmer, when he mentions the book,[65] says its purpose is to discuss, by reason alone, "what God is"—His nature and attributes. He did not consider the *existence* of God to be a primary and central topic of discussion, although many, both followers and critics, have, in later centuries, fastened attention on this shorter part as the more important.

The argument came to Anselm as an illumination, almost a revelation, after long reflection. Eadmer tells us that the effort to elaborate the argument for this book gave Anselm "great difficulty," and interfered with his eating and sleeping, and—to his great embarrassment—with his prayers and meditations. He decided the whole effort to make a rational presentation was due to the devil's temptation, so he tried to turn it away from his mind. Then, one night during the chanting of matins, the grace of God suddenly shed light on his mind and heart, and he saw the whole plan and line of argumenation for the complete book. Full of joy, he wrote out his thoughts on two wax tablets and committed them to the care of one of the monks. When the tablets were asked for, a few days later, they were nowhere to be found. Anselm wrote another draft, and although these tablets were kept with greater care, they were found broken and scattered on the floor. The bits were pieced together, and the treatise was finally copied on parchment.[66]

Whatever antecedent and initial difficulties the work had to overcome, it surely provoked great controversy subsequent to publication. The so-called "ontological argument" was criticized, politely but very insistently, by Gaunilo, a monk of the abbey of Marmoutier, and Anselm requested that this criticism and his answer to it, should appear with his *Proslogion* in all future copies.[67] The saint was not dissuaded from his conviction of the value of the argument, and Gaunilo could not admit that the fool would be convinced and converted by it. In the intervening centuries, outstanding theologians and philosophers have been ranged on both sides of the controversy.[68]

4. *The Grammarian*

De Grammatico is an introduction to dialectic, written some time between 1080 and 1085, presumably for the benefit of his students. Presented in the form of a dialogue between teacher and student, it raises the question whether "*grammarian* is a substance or a quality." It is, therefore, not a treatise on grammar or grammarians, but is concerned with the logical "categories" of Aristotle and his commentator Boethius, and specifically with how the classifications apply to the term and concept "grammarian." [69]

5. *Truth*

During the same five years Anselm wrote the *Dialogus De Veritate*.[70] Beginning with the demonstration of God's existence by logical truth as presented in the *Monologion*, Anselm asks the meaning of truth, where it is found, and how it differs from objects or realities in which it is found. He treats of logical truth, moral truth (rectitude of will, truth of action) and especially of ontological truth. His conclusion is that there is one supreme Truth which is not a property of anything, but is subsistent, so that we can speak of something being true to the extent that it is in conformity with that first Truth.

6. *Freedom Of Choice*

The truth of action, or moral truth, has raised questions about the will, and Anselm's next work—also written between 1080 and 1085—was *Dialogus De Libero Arbitrio*.[71] He treats of the nature of freedom of choice, and considers it especially in relation to the moral act. He eliminates the view that the power of choosing evil is an element of freedom, and defines freedom as "the power of preserving rectitude of will for the sake of the rectitude itself." [72] He analyzes the way in which freedom exists in God, in angels in the state of trial, and in man both in his present state and in the state of innocence.

7. *The Fall Of The Devil*

The *Dialogus De Casu Diaboli* [73] is closely related to the two preceding works, and was written soon after them; hence, between 1085 and 1090. Anselm is here concerned to show that the possibility of the fall from grace of an angel is explained only by free choice of the angel, as a result of which God withheld from him the grace of perseverance He bestowed on the faithful angels. He shows keen insight into the nature of evil and the relation of free will to an attraction toward good and happiness.

8. *The Incarnation of the Word*

While all the previous works have some relation to the *Cur Deus Homo,* the one which brought up questions most directly connected with the theme of Anselm's masterpiece, and the one which immediately preceded it, was his *Letter on the Incarnation of the Word.* This work was traditionally known as *Liber De Fide Trinitatis Et De Incarnatione Verbi.*[74] Schmitt names it *Epistola De Incarnatione Verbi.*[75] This work underwent several revisions, the first text being written in 1092, and the definitive one in 1094.

Roscelin, a secular priest who became a Canon and teacher in various centres in Europe, asserted that if the three Persons of the Holy Trinity are not conceived as three separate beings, like three angels or three souls, then they are so united that the Father and Holy Spirit as well as the Son became incarnate in Christ.[76] He also referred to Lanfranc and Anselm as approving the view that the relation of the nature of God to the three Persons was at least similar to that of substance to its accidents, such as man to his color and figure. In his first answer to Roscelin, Anselm tries to justify the analogy of substance and accidents, but in his later recension he omits that illustration. He shows that Roscelin's view is heretical and that it involves contradictory positions. With the notions of nature, person, absolute and relative reality, he establishes the common Catholic doctrine.

Despite the title, the Incarnation is not treated here as a topic in itself, but only in relation to the Persons of the Trinity. But the study of this question brought Anselm's inquiring mind on to the subject of Christ and his redemptive act, with which his great work was concerned.

After these eight works there appeared, in the period from 1098 to 1100, the two studies, *Why God Became Man* and *The Virgin Conception And Original Sin,* which are presented in this volume, and also the *Meditation On Human Redemption,* whose theme is closely related to the other two works.

Then, in the last decade of his life, Anselm continued to write and publish. Most important of his latest works are the following:

9. *The Procession Of The Holy Spirit*

At the Council of Bari in October, 1098, Anselm gave a talk, defending the procession of the Holy Spirit from the Son as well as from the Father, contrary to the view of many Greek Christians. The discourse he delivered on this occasion was later developed and amplified. It was published in 1102 under the title *De Processione Spiritus Sancti.*[77]

10. *The Harmony Between God's Foreknowledge, Predestination, Grace, And Free Choice*

In 1107 or 1108, Anselm wrote *De Concordia Praescientiae Et Praedestinationis Et Gratiae Dei Cum Libero Arbitrio.*[78] This work is a discussion, with emphasis on rational argument rather than on texts of Sacred Scripture, of the question of the reconciliation of divine influence and human freedom. It was a problem that agitated many of the Fathers, especially St. Augustine, and was to concern all the Scholastics. Anselm had previously touched on the question in the first recension of his *De Libertate Arbitrii.*

11. *Posthumous Collections*

After the works previously noted, there were other writings on the use of leavened and unleavened bread in sacrifice, and on the Sacraments. But most worthy of note, perhaps, are the collections of the saint's discourses and conversations, made after his death by his friends and followers.

Alexander, a monk of Canterbury, collected and published some portions of the archbishop's sermons and discourses. The collection generally was entitled *Anselmus De Monte Humilitatis,* from the name of the first discourse; it also goes by the title *Dicta Anselmi.*[79]

There is another collection of parts of Anselm's discourses that classify and analyze the various virtues. Because the explanations are made by "likenesses," that is, by analogies, allegories and examples, the anthology gradually came to be called *Liber De Similitudinibus.* Its compiler is unknown, but its influence and popularity have been great, especially in the thirteenth century.[80]

In 1109, when he was told he was dying, Anselm expressed his submission to God's will, but he added that he would welcome the prolongation of his life for a little while, until he could solve the problem of the origin of the soul.[81] It was characteristic of the man that his last thoughts were not about politics nor even about the organization of the Church in England, but about the truths regarding God and His manifestations and His dealings with His creatures. *

IV. THE *CUR DEUS HOMO* AND *DE CONCEPTU VIRGINALI*

A. *Circumstances of Composition*

We know that St. Anselm brought the *Cur Deus Homo* to completion in the mountain village of Sclavia (whose name was changed to "Liberi" in 1860), in the province of Capua. This was during the summer of 1098, before he went to the council of Bari.[82] Eadmer transcribed it for the community of Bec shortly after it was written.[83] Anselm requested the monks of Canterbury to make a copy of it and of the *De Conceptu Virginali Et Peccato Originali,* so that he might send the volume to Pope Paschal II.[84]

It is also certain, on Anselm's own testimony in his preface, that the first and more important work was commenced in England, before his exile, and therefore at the latest in 1097. There is some reason for believing, however, that during the saint's months of leisure in 1094, due to the absence of the king, he began the actual writing of this work so congenial to him.[85]

The treatise is presented in the form of a dialogue between Anselm and his friend Dom Boso.[86] It is not known with certainty how much Boso actually participated in discussion with Anselm, for the dialogue-structure was common in the middle ages, and generally it was the expression of the thought of one person, the author. In his other theological dialogues,[87] however, the disputants are named "Teacher" and "Pupil"; and the express attribution to two real people in the *Cur Deus Homo* may be taken to indicate that there were somewhat similar discussions between the two. Furthermore, Milo Crispin gives the impression that Boso was involved in some actual discussions,[88] and even more lavishly than Eadmer, he attests to the penetrating intelligence of Boso, which would at least make him capable of the theological conversation.[89] At the very least, Boso was, as Anselm acknowledges in the prologue to the *De Conceptu Virginali,*[90] the principal influence upon him of all those who requested him to write on the subject.

In chapter sixteen of the second book of the *Cur Deus Homo,* Anselm discusses how the Redeemer could take human nature from the race of Adam, without being affected by original sin. He gives one answer, but goes on to admit, after some subsidiary discussion of necessity and impossibility as attributed to God, that there is another explanation possible.[91] He takes up that alternative explanation, and the whole topic of original sin and the way it is transmitted to descendants of Adam, in his work: *The Virgin Conception and Original Sin.* Eadmer gives testimony that Anselm wrote this work and also his *Meditatio Redemptionis Humanae,* at Lyons, when he returned there from

Italy, after the council of Bari.[92] This indicates that the two were composed between the summer of 1099 and that of 1100.

Although the smaller work contains great depths of thought on original sin and expresses views of St. Anselm on such topics as the immaculate conception of the mother of Christ, it can be taken as an adjunct to, and almost a third section of, the *Cur Deus Homo*.

It is hoped that an understanding and appreciation of the two treatises will be fostered best by an analysis, in somewhat schematic fashion, of the content of the two works, to be followed by a description of the contemporary theological background and of Anselm's quite significant theological method, and then by an evaluation of his doctrines on atonement, original sin and the Immaculate Conception.

B. *Outlines*

WHY GOD BECAME MAN

A. *The Question:*
Why, and with what necessity, did God become man, and redeem human beings by His death, although He could have accomplished this by other means? (I, 1; II, 18)

B. *Purpose of Inquiry:*
To enable Christians to understand and appreciate the truths of faith, and to refute and convert unbelievers. (Letter to Pope Urban; I, 1)

C. *Principles of Procedure:*
(1) The truths of faith must be believed before we can analyze them by reason. (I, 1) But after one accepts the faith, he is negligent if he does not try to understand the truth.

(2) Certitude in such matters is derived only from the authority of God. (I, 2; I, 18) Probability can be attained by human intelligence regarding the reasons for God's actions. Even the deepest reasoning does not exhaust the profundities of God's truth. (I, 2)

(3) We should seek proofs based on necessity. Reasons of fitness only make more basic reasons more attractive. (I, 4) Yet, regarding God, anything proved unsuitable to Him is thereby shown to be

impossible. And what is fitting for God should be attributed to Him unless a stronger reason opposes it. (I, 10)

(4) Unbelievers seek knowledge of reasons because they have no faith; believers seek it to expand and deepen their faith. (I, 3)

(5) In this work, an attempt is made to show the existence and death of the God-Man to be necessary, methodically leaving aside certainty regarding the actual, historical Incarnation. (I, 10)

D. *Objections:*

(1) Human birth, weakness, etc. are unfitting for God. So the claim that God became man is offensive to God. (I, 3)

Ans.: Rather, the assertion proclaims God's mercy and love. It was fitting that the circumstances of the human fall be paralleled by those of the restoration. It was not fitting that God's plan be frustrated; and it would have been if a God-Man did not liberate man.

(2) It was more fitting that the liberator of the human race be other than a divine person. And it was possible for God to create an angel or a sinless man to liberate the human race.

Ans.: Man would necessarily be subjected to his redeemer. And it is not fitting for man to be subjected to anyone less than God. For if he were subjected to a creature, he would not have been restored to his original dignity. (I, 5)

(3) "Redemption" by God is not reasonable, because man is not in the possession of anyone but God Himself. And if He could not free us without suffering, He lacks power; if He would not, He lacks wisdom, for He suffered what was unbecoming without reason. To say He suffered out of love is convincing only if there were no other way of freeing us and thus showing His love. (I, 6)

Ans. It is certainly to be admitted that God could free us without suffering and even without a divine incarnation. But there is a necessity of congruity with the nature and goodness of God that satisfaction be made for sin, and that it be not remitted by mercy alone. (I, 11–28)

(4) To say that God acted against the devil *through justice* seems to imply that the devil had a claim in justice to the possession of the human race. Christians seem to think the devil has a right to hold man in possession, because it is just for man to be subjected to abuse by the devil, and it is just for God to permit this; they seem to think, then, it is just for the devil to inflict it.

Ans. Although the "rights of the devil" had been admitted fairly commonly by Christian thinkers, this view is here repudiated. It *is* just for God to permit the devil to molest man, and it is just for man to be molested, but there is no justice in the devil's act. There can be no question of a "contract with the devil." (I, 7)

(5) It is impossible that the Most High be lowered in dignity, and that the Almighty act with great effort.

Ans. The divine nature is incapable of suffering and humiliation and need of effort. But the Christian doctrine is that the Redeemer has both a divine and a human nature, united in one Person. Abasement and weakness are manifestations of human nature; glory and power, of the divine nature. It is not that the divine nature is abased, but that the human one is exalted. (I, 8; see also II, 6–9)

(6) Even though abasement is not attributable to the divine nature, yet it is scarcely just and reasonable that the Just One, called "beloved Son" by God, and One who could identify Himself with the Word, be condemned to free the guilty.

Ans. He died, not by any compulsion by the Father, but by His own will. Texts which seem to indicate lack of freedom in Christ, can be explained differently. (I, 8, 9) Texts indicating Christ died by His own will and those indicating He fulfilled the will of His Father, are reconcilable. (I, 9, 10)

(7) It does not seem fitting for such a Father to permit such a Son to be so treated, even though He is willing.

Ans. If the Son consents and wills the salvation of man, and if the latter cannot be attained any other way, then it is most fitting.

(8) Precisely what has to be proved is that the salvation of man cannot be attained any other way, and you have to prove that this way is reasonable and fitting in itself; otherwise the Son could not have willed it nor the Father permitted it.

Ans. This we shall proceed to do, presuming that the Incarnation never occurred, and then trying to prove that it *had* to occur. (I, 10)

E. *Positive Proof of the Reasonableness and Necessity of the Incarnation:*

Even supposing that Christ never actually existed, we can expect common agreement on these propositions:

1. Man was made for happiness, which cannot be possessed in this life. (I, 10)

2. No one can arrive at happiness unless his sins are forgiven. (I, 10)

3. No human person passes through this life without sin, i.e., the refusal of a creature to subject his will to God's, or the refusal to give God due honor. (I, 10, 11)

4. Hence it is necessary that man's sins be forgiven so that he may arrive at bliss. (I, 10) KEY

5. It is necessary that satisfaction be made, i.e., due honor be given to God, making up for insult by going beyond the precise amount refused. (I, 11) Reasons:

(a) Sin causes lack of order. Disorder is unfitting for the Kingdom of God. And order is restored only through satisfaction. (I, 12)

(b) If sin is remitted without satisfaction or punishment, then one who sins is equal before God with one who does not sin; and this would be unseemly for God. Yet this justice is reconcilable with God's mercy and freedom, which cannot compromise His dignity. (I, 12) It is compatible with His command that *we* forgive enemies, because only He may execute justice. (I, 12)

(c) It is intolerable that a creature derogate from the honor of God and not make recompense by restoration or punishment; for it would be a violation of supreme justice. (I, 13) It is not that restoration or punishment adds to God's perfections. But man owes honor to God. He should pay that debt voluntarily, by either avoiding sin or making satisfaction. If man sins and does not repent, God's justice requires that He deprive man of what he possesses or may possess—and this is punishment, which shows that the sinner is still subject to God. (I, 14) Although God requires the preservation of His honor, He permits man to give this honor freely; and if man refuses due honor, God preserves His honor and the order of the universe by requiring either satisfaction or punishment. If there were difformity in the order of the universe, God would be deficient in His Providence—which is inadmissible. (I, 15)

(d) Human beings are to replace fallen angels, in superabundant numbers, so that a perfect number of intelligent creatures may be attained. (I, 16–18) To replace angels, men would have to be in the same condition as the angels originally were—sinless. And without satisfaction, they would not be sinless. (I, 19)

(e) Man ought to be elevated to his original state, or God would either be unable to achieve His end in creating man, or He would be regretting His first intention. The second and third alternatives are unacceptable. (I, 19) And man cannot be restored to his first state without satisfaction. (I, 20) KEY

Hence, man cannot be saved without satisfaction for sin. (I, 19)

6. This satisfaction must be made in proportion to the measure of sin. And sin, even though the physical action is slight, is contrary to the Will of God and surpasses any merely human loss. (I,

21) Besides, man had submitted to the dominion of the devil and had to undo the shame. (I, 22–23)

7. Satisfaction proportionate to sin, then, exceeds human power. (I, 21) No sinner can proportionately satisfy for sin. (II, 4; I, 11–15, 19–24) Yet inability to pay does not excuse man, because it is the result of his own sin. (I, 24)

8. Yet it is to be expected that satisfaction will be made. For rational nature was created in the state of justice, to make it happy by enjoying God. If it cannot actually attain to happiness by loving God, its creation is without purpose. (II, 1) If God does not bring rational nature to completion, it was pointless for Him to create it. Since God's intention cannot be frustrated, human nature must be able to fulfill its end. (II, 4 & I, 4)

9. Since man cannot attain his divinely appointed end without satisfaction for sin, and since man cannot make the satisfaction, God must bring it about. (When we say God "must" or "ought to" bring about human salvation, we do not mean that God is *compelled* to avoid the unsuitable, and thus is acting more for His own sake, and therefore is not worthy of gratitude. Rather, this is a "necessity" which entails greater gratitude, because the reason for God's acting is His own intrinsic, unchangeable honor.) (II, 5)

10. THE MAIN CONCLUSION: Satisfaction for sin can be made only by a God-Man, able, by His divinity, to give something worthy of God, yet able, by His humanity, to represent mankind. (II, 6) In other words, salvation and human happiness are possible only through Christ. (I, 25)

F. *The Characteristics of the God-Man:*

1. It is necessary that two complete natures be joined in one Person. (II, 7)

2. This humanity will have to be derived from a virgin descended from the race of Adam. If the God-Man were not an offspring of Adam, He would not be able to make reparation for Adam's sin, nor to restore men to the dignity they were to have. (II, 8) His mother must be a virgin, because His origin must be more distinguished than that of ordinary human beings (from two parents), and of Adam (who had no human parent) and of Eve (formed from a male alone). (II, 18) To this truth from reason, might be added this "picture" of fitness: As the sin of man began with a woman, the salvation of man should begin with a woman. As a virgin was the occasion of human evil, a virgin should be the occasion of human salvation. (II, 8)

3. It is more congruous, and therefore necessary, that the Person uniting with a human nature be the Word or Son. For (a) otherwise, there would, incongruously, be two Sons in the Trinity; and an equality among the Persons, depending on the relative dignity of birth; (b) it is more fitting for the Son to pray to the Father than for another Person to pray to the Son; (c) man and devil had claimed unwarranted likeness to God and thus had specially sinned against the Son who is the true likeness of the Father. It is primarily for Him, then, to punish or pardon the crime. (II, 9)

4. The God-Man is not obliged to die, for He is sinless; His will cannot go against God's Will. As Adam would not have died except for sinning, so the God-Man should not die. Yet His inability to sin does not prevent His deserving justice by free choice—since He Himself is the source of all the good He possesses. (II, 10)

5. Yet the God-Man is able to die in His human nature, even though human nature is not necessarily mortal. For He can freely take on mortality, and, being almighty, can bring about His own death, whether other human beings intervene or not. It is fitting, and in some sense necessary, that He accept death, because man offended God by complete alienation from Him by human pleasure, and thus owes the most perfect satisfaction, entailing bitter suffering. (II, 11)

Still, His commitment to death does not involve unhappiness, because it is accepted voluntarily, for a known purpose. (II, 12) Ignorance is not possible to Him, for that would not be of any avail in achieving His mission. (II, 13)

6. His death prevails over all sins, because, due to His perfections, the immolation of One who is perfectly good immeasurably outbalances all conceivable evil. (II, 14) His death is of value even to those who slew Him, because they did not have full knowledge of His divinity, and thus did not commit the extreme sin of willing the death of God. (II, 15)

7. The holiness of God would not permit His union with a sinful human nature, and God necessarily has the wisdom and power to unite with sinless human nature. *How* this is accomplished, however, we cannot fully understand. But we can venture this explanation:

The virgin who was this Man's mother was cleansed from sin through faith in Him and in His future saving death, and He was taken from the virgin in the state of purity. (II, 16) This does not mean that the virgin is the *cause* of His sinlessness, since her purity, through which He is pure, comes from Himself; so He is pure or sinless through Himself and by Himself. Nor does it mean that it was necessary for Him to die, for the reason that His virgin mother's purity was required for His sinlessness, and she was pure by reason of His future death. He had the power to preserve His life, although He was unable to will to preserve it so as never to die. And since it was due to Himself that He was unable to will to preserve His life, it was not by necessity but by the power of His freedom that He laid it down. When we say it is necessary that Christ die, we mean only that the divine will has inalterably decided on this. The necessity is consequent to Christ's will. It would be more an inability than an ability if He could change His intention. (II, 16, 17)

8. Christ gave His life for the honor of God and as an example to inspire human beings never to abandon justice, despite the hardships it entails. No other person gave such example because anyone else would be giving up the life he would eventually lose anyway. He gave it without being compelled, without owing it to others. Neither did he owe it by obligation to do the better thing—in the sense that he owed it "by reason of debt." He offered Himself to the Father, or His humanity to (His own) divinity. (II, 18)

9. The principal reason why His death brought about human salvation is this. What the God-Man did by dying deserved a reward. Yet no reward—either gift or remission of something owed—could be worthy of Him. Hence it is necessary that the reward be given to others for whom He willed it, i.e., to other human beings. In other words, His own kinsmen and brethren are necessarily the beneficiaries of what is due Him, but it does not fill any need of His own. God rejects no one who draws near to Him in the name of Christ and by imitating Christ. (II, 19)

10. Hence the final answer to the general and principal question is: God had no need to descend from heaven to conquer the devil and liberate man. The inalterable truth required it, because God required man to conquer the devil and satisfy for sin. Whatever was exacted was due to God, not to the devil, who deserved only punishment. (II, 19)

11. It has seemed (cf. I, 24) that the mercy of God disappeared in such a plan. But mercy is manifested by the Father who gives His Son to be offered by mankind for itself and by the Son who gives Himself for others. (II, 20)

12. This redemption by the God-Man does not reconcile the devil. (cf. I, 17) For as man could be reconciled only by a God-Man, so

fallen angels could be reconciled only by a God-angel who could die. Man had to be saved by someone of the same race. But angels, although of the same nature, are not of a common species and are not descended one from another. Further, as they fell without any-one else tempting them, they ought to rise without external assis-tance. And this is impossible. (II, 21)

13. It is true to say that God's restoration of human nature has been more marvelous than His creation of it, for redemption follows upon sin and makes more manifest the power and mercy of God. (II, 16)

14. It was necessary that Christ's redemption be beneficial not only to His contemporaries, but to *all* human beings, including Adam and Eve. This is not stated explicitly in revelation, but since it is more fitting than its contradictory, it is necessary. For it would be incongruous for God to allow any period or stage of the human race to pass in which there was not one member of the human race head-ing for the goal for which man was created. (II, 16)

15. Man would not be subject to death if he had not sinned. (II, 2) So, if he is to be perfectly restored, he must be restored to a state of immortality—to be happy forever, if he perseveres in jus-tice; miserable forever, if he does not. (II, 3)

Conclusion: By solving the problem undertaken in this book, we confirm the truth of the Old and New Testaments.

THE VIRGIN CONCEPTION AND ORIGINAL SIN

A. *Topic:*
Another explanation (than that of *Why God Became Man,* II, 17; see preceding outline, F, 7) of how God took human nature, without sin, from the sinful human race. (*Preface*)

B. *Introductory Definitions:*
1. "Original sin" is the lack of justice that passes down to human individuals in their origin from human ancestors.
2. "Personal sin" is that committed by the wilful fault of a person.
3. "Original justice" is the state of moral goodness that coincides with the beginning of a person's existence.
4. "Personal justice" is the state of moral goodness that is ac-quired in the course of a person's existence, after he has been with-out it. (Ch. 1)

C. *Propositions:*

1. If Adam and Eve had persevered in original justice, their progeny would have been preserved in justice. But the deliberate personal sin of Adam and Eve brought about a corruption of body and a weakness of soul. Human nature, which existed entirely in them, was, in its entirety, weakened and tainted. It had (a) the obligation of being in the state of undiminished justice, (b) the obligation of making satisfaction for having abandoned justice, (c) a state of corruption incurred by sin. It is propagated, then, in the condition in which it put itself by sinning. Human nature is inherited having the obligation to make satisfaction for the first sin, and the obligation to regain original justice. (Ch. 2)

2. Original sin, or its opposite, justice, cannot exist in an infant until he has a rational soul. For justice is "the rectitude of the will preserved for its own sake," and it is only in a rational soul that the will is found. (God and angels are considered "rational" natures, but there is no question of original sin in either.) (Ch. 3) Only acts of the will can be strictly called just or unjust. Nothing is punished but the will. (Ch. 4)

3. Sin, the lack of due justice or goodness, is, like all evil, non-being. (Ch. 5) Yet this does not mean that punishment for sin is punishment for nothing. For in inflicting punishment on sinners, God is exacting from them, against their will, the honor due Him which they refuse to render willingly. (Ch. 6)

4. Since sin and injustice exist only in the rational will, and since there is no rational soul until some time after physical conception, the infant is not in the state of original sin from the moment of conception. Yet infants can be said to be "of unclean seed" and "conceived in iniquities," in the sense that original sin will be in the rational soul because of the descent of the body from Adam. (Ch. 7)

5. Hence, there could be no stain of sin in the material the Son of God took from the Virgin. For what is derived from parents is without sin. Normally, indeed, the soul is affected by original sin because of the descent of the matter with which the soul is joined. The reason is that human nature is obliged to make satisfaction for the act of Adam, and is unable to make it, and the soul, coming into matter, does not know the state of justice. In the case of Christ, however, because of the union of the divine and human nature, the human nature is exempted from the debt of Adam, and in His case the corruptible body is not a burden to the soul, preventing it from preserving justice. (Ch. 8)

6. Original sin is imputed to Adam rather than to Eve, because
(1) the name of the male stands for the principal person, thus for
the couple; (2) "Adam" can mean either a male or a female human
being; (3) if not Adam, but only Eve, had sinned, not the whole
human race, but only Eve, would have to die. (Ch. 9) Descendants
of Adam bear the burden of his sin, because God put the whole
human race in Adam's power, so that all would be in the state of
justice if he had not sinned, and without justice if he sinned. Human nature was "totally in Adam," and when human nature offended
God, it lost for itself the favors it had received and which it could
have preserved. When it is multiplied by generation, then, it is
transmitted as sinful, subject to penalty. (Ch. 10. See *Why God
Became Man*, II, 1)

7. A man born of a virgin, however, is not affected by original
sin, because, although he is descended from Adam, his existence is
not due to natural power or human will, but to the will of God
alone. He belongs to the order of marvels, not to the purely natural
or the voluntary orders. Thus he is not subject to the laws and
deserts of generation that is natural and voluntary. (Ch. 11) For
Adam, by sin, could lose the justice and happiness originally given
him, only for those whose generation was due to his own power,
subject to his will. He was not able to transmit them to a person,
even though descended from himself, whose generation was not due
to his natural power and free will. And the virgin's Son is not
brought into being by natural power and free will. The virgin's Son
was in Adam in a way different from all the others: He did not
originate through Adam's natural power or will. Adam was not the
natural source of the God-Man's being, as he was of all other human
beings. It was not due to Adam that Christ had being; although
Christ took on Adam's nature, He took it by God's power, not Adam's.
So also, Christ took descent from all his other ancestors, and so was
"in them" but not within their power, only the power of God. He
was "in Adam," but not the way others are in Adam. (Ch. 12 & 23)

8. Even if Christ were not God, He would not contract the debt
or penalty of any human person. For (a) as it was right for God
to make the first human being in the state of justice, so it is right
for Him to constitute in the state of justice One whom He brings
into being by His own will and power. The existence of the Son
of the virgin does not depend upon human generation and human
will, and thus does not contract the debt of human sin. (Ch. 13) The
matter itself is sinless until there is a human soul united to it, and

human seed is called "unclean" because normally it will be sinful when it is united to a human soul. But this applies only to seed conceived with passion, not to the seed of the virgin. (Ch. 14) Then, (b) the sinfulness of the human mass arises from human will; and in a virgin birth, where conception does not arise from human will or natural human power, or human passion, there is no original sin. (Ch. 15) Christ was conceived in a way exceptional to human nature, hence even as man he would not contract original sin, which is attached to that nature. (Ch. 16) Since the Man born of a virgin is divinely generated of a just Father, and humanly generated of a just mother, He possessed original justice. (Ch. 20) (This differs from the argument of *Why God Became Man,* II, 17, which shows that even if sin were in the whole essence of a virgin, still that essence could become pure by faith.) (Ch. 19)

9. Although a merely human person could originate from Adam without original sin by virgin birth, yet it was necessary for God to become man because only a God-Man could redeem others. (Ch. 17)

10. God did not create new and independent human beings to fill up heaven, after the fall of Adam, because if no one produced by natural generation were saved, it would seem that He had created that natural power in Adam without purpose, since Adam's race would be unable to attain happiness. (Ch. 17)

11. God could have taken a body conceived by a sinful parent. But it was fitting that the conception of this man take place in the purest of mothers. Because of her relations to the three Persons, it was fitting that that virgin shine with a purity than which no greater under God can be thought of. (Ch. 18)

12. Christ could not have *personal* sin, because (1) His individual human nature never existed except in union with the divine nature, which excludes all sin; (2) His soul was never affected against His will or otherwise burdened by a corruptible body. The latter is also due to His being a divine Person. (Ch. 21)

13. Infants existed in Adam when he sinned, but causally or materially as in a seed, not personally as actual individuals. Although all human beings are punished for Adam's sin as if all committed it, yet infants are not punished for it in the same way as if each personally committed it. Still, no one is freed from the evil effects of Adam's sin except through satisfaction for that sin. Christ alone can make that satisfaction. Original sin in infants, that is, the lack of justice, is the result not of personal desire, but of a natural destitu-

tion which their nature received from Adam. The nature has existence in persons and is the reason for the persons being sinful. The personal sin of Adam thus passes over into all who are generated from him naturally. While this "original" sin is not the same as personal sin, yet they are alike in this, that both exclude souls from heaven, unless Christ makes satisfaction for them. (Ch. 22 & 23)

14. Sins of closer ancestors do not affect souls as does the sin of Adam, because the closer ancestors have not been able to preserve justice for their descendants (Ch. 24) or to propagate offspring in the state of justice. Thus they do not pass on their injustice. (Ch. 26) Yet ancestors can do injury to the souls of descendants to the extent that the latter may be left in their sins because of the demerits of ancestors; in this way, sins may be visited on descendants "unto the third and fourth generation." (Ch. 25)

15. Original sin can be defined: the deprivation of required justice, as the result of the disobedience of Adam. It affects an infant as soon as it has a rational soul. The reason for this transmission is that the voluntary forsaking of justice in Adam is a reproach to the human nature he possessed in its entirety, and hence the deprivation of justice and happiness in Adam affects all who have his nature by natural generation. (Ch. 27)

16. Regarding the punishment of unbaptized infants: (1) They are really punished not for the unworthiness of someone else, but their own, for the inherited injustice affects their own souls. (Ch. 26) (2) God bestowed on Adam original justice, and can require in them what he conferred on their nature in Adam. (3) Even human judgment considers that children should be left in slavery if their parents were promoted to undeserved dignity and wealth, and then deliberately lost it by crime. (Ch. 28)

17. Baptized infants are unable to preserve rectitude of will, because they have not the use of reason. Yet their inability is not imputed to them as sinfulness, as it is in the unbaptized. Hence there is no lack of "due justice." Thus, infants who die after Baptism are justified by the justice of Christ and by the faith of Mother Church. (Ch. 29)

C. *Contemporary Background*

The key question of the main treatise, then, is: why, and with what necessity, did God become man, and redeem human beings by His death, although He could have accomplished this by other means? This is not the same as the problem of the "motive" of the incarnation, as later posited by St. Thomas Aquinas: "Whether, if man had not sinned, God would have become incarnate anyway?"[93] Rather, St. Anselm is raising a question that probes into the wisdom and power of God, regarding the reasonableness and fitness of God's becoming man at all, and redeeming the human race from its sin. His answer, in brief, is that satisfaction for human sin can be made only by a God-Man, able by His divinity to give something worthy of God, yet able, by His humanity, to represent mankind.

Because the emphasis is on the God-Man, the title *Cur Deus Homo* is sometimes translated *Why The God-Man?*[94] J. McIntyre proposes: *Why There Should Be A God-Man*, or *The Reason For The God-Man*, or simply, *Why The God-Man?*[95] It is true that Anselm's whole argument "develops around the theme of the God-Man, the unity of His Person, the necessity of His two natures, and the value of His death as atonement for the sins of mankind."[96] But McIntyre's principal argument against the title *Why God Became Man* seems to be that Aulen and others are led by that title to interpret Anselm as saying that "satisfaction is offered to God by a Man who is also God," with the result that redemption would not be fully the work of God.[97] While it is incorrect theologically to consider the redemption as the effect of either God or man *separately*, and unfair to Anselm to ascribe such a view to him, it does not seem to me that the expression "God became man" excludes or obscures the orthodox and traditional Christian conception of redemption as a theandric act, or the act of a God-Man. *Why The God-Man?* seems a very abrupt question to introduce a theological treatise. *The Reason For The God-Man* is smoother, and makes sense, but it is hard to see what that title preserves which is lost by use of *Why God Became Man*, provided one understands, in either case, that the one divine Person has both a divine and a human nature.

Another argument against the title here accepted is that "the sentence *Deus homo factus est* occurs most infrequently in the course of the work."[98] That is true. Yet when Anselm states the central question, he expresses it: "The nub of the question was why God became man, to save man by his death, when it would seem He could do this in some other way." [99] Right in the beginning, too, the question is posed: "for what reason or by what necessity did God become man . . ." [100] Although Anselm does not frequently say that "God became man," he does seem to consider that sentence a fair formulation of what concerns him.[101]

Although, as will appear, St. Anselm made original contributions to theological development, yet there were contemporary factors which were influential in determining his interests, his methods and his statements of doctrines.

One was the challenging claim of Roscelin that Anselm should logically agree with his dangerous view that either the Holy Trinity is to be understood as implying the existence of three Gods, or that, if there is only one God, then all three Persons became incarnate in Christ.[102] In his *Epistola De Incarnatione,* or *De Fide Trinitatis Et De Incarnatione Verbi,* Anselm undertook to show that *if* the incarnation occurred, it must have been only the second Person of the blessed Trinity who became man. Since unbelievers had suggested that the incarnation had not actually occurred, but was imagined by Christians, Anselm felt obliged to show not only that it had really occurred, but that it *had to occur.*[103]

A second factor is that in the monastic and secular schools of his day, and especially in the secular school of Laon, there was already some discussion of the fitness of the redemption of the human race in the manner that has been revealed. The noted scholar J. Rivière discovered an exact and verbal duplication between part of chapter seven of Book One of *Why God Became Man* and a fragment of a script of Radulfus of Laon.[104] It was his opinion that the minor writer borrowed from Anselm, but R. W. Southern seems perfectly justified in concluding that Anselm rather selected the other text and fitted it into his own argument as a concise statement of the "rights of the devil" theory which he was rejecting.[105]

During the eleventh century there were many educated Jews in Normandy and elsewhere, whose traditional criticism of Christianity was becoming vocal and was reaching the ears of the bishops and scholars. Here was a third factor providing occasion for Anselm's theological study of the incarnation and redemption. Certain Jews were saying that the birth of a God-Man, His lowliness, His sufferings and death, as accepted by Christians, were incompatible with God's transcendent dignity, which the Jewish religion held inviolable. Gilbert Crispin, who had been a friend of Anselm's at Bec, and was abbot in Westminster from 1084 to 1117, had met a Jew from Mainz who had taken up residence in London, and who made some very critical remarks about the central Christian doctrines. Crispin wrote and addressed to Anselm a book, *Disputatio Judaei Cum Christiano,* in which he reports the objections and his answers to them.[106] It is not at all certain that this particular book gave a direct stimulus to Anselm's *Why God Became Man,* but at least it bears witness to the prevalence of certain attitudes that Anselm was to consider.

At the end of the book, Boso acknowledges that the arguments of Anselm "would give satisfaction not only to Jews, but even to pagans," [107] at least if a few revealed doctrines, such as the Holy Trinity and the effects of the original sin of Adam, were omitted. He could be referring very generally to people who acknowledge neither the Old nor the New Testament as revelations of God; but it is quite likely that he has Mohammedans specifically in mind.[108]

While it is a work of speculative theology which has value for all time, as an "explanation" of God's plan for the redemption of the human race, this work is also intended to defend that doctrine, to correct false impressions of non-Christians, and to foster the joy and hope of those who have faith in Christ.

D. *Rationalist Theology?*

As soon as Christian revelation was completed, it was natural for Christians who had the intelligence and the education, to try to work out the implications of the revelation. It was also incumbent on them to defend the revealed teaching and their faith in it, against the criticisms and attacks of non-Christians who refused to accept the authority of Christ. Thus was born Christian theology: the systematic study of the meaning and implications of the teachings of Christ and of their relations to the judgments of natural human reason. Above all, the central teaching of Christ, that He Himself is God-Man and the Redeemer of the human race, was a challenge to the intelligence of believers and unbelievers alike. This basic claim became, right from the start, the target of critical objections and the core of doctrinal development.

Some of the early apologists and preachers emphasized the contrast between Christian revelation, which is supernatural, and "human wisdom," especially the philosophical teachings of Greek and Roman thinkers. As St. Paul had spoken of the *wisdom of this world* having been *made foolish* by God,[109] as he avoided the *persuasive words of human wisdom*,[110] so the apologists were not interested in developing Christian doctrine in the terminology and with the concepts of Greek philosophy or Roman law. Their main concern was to obtain from pagan emperors and judges approval of the right of Christians to practice their religion, and to refute accusations of wrong-doing made against them. They did not undertake to expound the whole faith, and even considered the sacred mysteries deserving of secrecy.[111] Some even appear to have disdained Greek rationalizing. Tatian, for example, ridicules Aristotle for the absurdity of setting a limit to God's knowledge and providence, and for making human happiness depend upon wealth and bodily strength and high birth.[112] He thought Christian revelation contained all the truth human beings needed to know, so that Greek philosophers could add nothing to it but erroneous interpretations. The Latin rhetorician Tertullian went so far as to say: "The Son of God died; it is to be believed absolutely, because it is absurd. And He was buried and rose again; the fact is certain because it is impossible." [113] Whether or not he could mean literally that impossibility and absurdity are signs of truth, he at least does not see much fruitfulness in drawing out the implications of revealed truth by application of philosophical principles.

On the other hand, most of the later Fathers of the Church

attempted to explain, defend and develop the teachings of the faith by using the philosophical concepts and dialectical methods of earlier pagan thinkers. Chief among these, certainly, was St. Augustine (354–430), who declared:

No one doubts that we are impelled to learn by a two-fold force: that of authority and that of reason. I am certain that we ought never to depart from the authority of Christ, for I find no stronger one. As to what is to be attained by keenest reasoning, however, my attitude is that I impatiently desire to apprehend the truth not only by belief, but also by understanding. . . .[114]

This attitude, shared by many of the Fathers, led to the development of supernatural theology, expressing in terms derived from philosophers—such as *nature, person, substance, accidents* —the truths revealed by Christ and expressed in the Scriptures in ordinary language. There also developed, among Christians, the consideration, *in the light of natural human reason alone,* of such topics as the existence of God, the spirituality and immortality of the human soul, and the like, which philosophers had traditionally discussed, and on which Christian revelation either gives, or at least implies, definite positions. Thus arose "Christian philosophy," one of the clearest examples of which is *The Consolation of Philosophy* by Boethius (c. 480–c. 524). The author discusses the question: "If God exists, whence comes evil? If God does not exist, whence comes the good?" He answers the question by rational principles alone, without any quotations from Holy Scripture, or any assumption of revealed truths, but with notions of God and providence and divine knowledge that are factually and historically derived from revealed sources and not from Plato or Plotinus, whose concepts and terms he also uses.

In none of his works does St. Anselm indicate the slightest aversion to rational analysis and argument. In fact, "meditating on the rationale of the faith" can be called the principal concern of the author in all his theological quests.[115] In the present work, *Why God Became Man,* also, Anselm has Boso say:

As right order requires that we believe the profound truths of the Christian faith before we presume to analyze them by reason, so it would seem to me a matter of negligence if, after we have been confirmed in the faith, we make no effort to understand what we believe. Therefore, . . . I beg of you to make clear to me . . . by what necessity and for what reason God, although He is almighty, took on the lowliness and weakness of human nature, to restore it.[116]

This certainly gives the impression he is asking his instructor to "meditate on the rationale of the faith," as do many other statements in the course of the book.

The letter to Pope Urban II, submitting one of Anselm's works to the Holy Father's scrutiny,[117] refers to that work as "an explanation of the faith." That letter, however, is given by Gerberon before the *Liber De Fide Trinitatis Et De Incarnatione Verbi*,[118] and it is possible that it does not refer to the *Cur Deus Homo* at all, although Schmitt's arguments are generally accepted by scholars.[119]

What gives rise to special difficulty in regard to *Why God Became Man* is that the arguments seem to be purely rational from start to finish, with faith in Christ and the very existence of Christ being "set aside" as if nothing were known of them.[120] Continually, attention is directed to the "reason" for the incarnation, or proof that the atonement by the God-Man for the sin of the human race is "reasonable." Schmitt points out that the word *ratio* appears one hundred and seven times; *rationabile*, eighteen times.[121] Anselm also insists he is seeking "proof by necessary reasons," as distinct from arguments from mere "fitness." [122] The impression has been taken by some, that the author is trying to establish the existence of a historical fact, the incarnation of God, by purely rational *a priori* arguments, without any reliance upon the revealed word of God. In other words, the work seems to be purely philosophical, and utterly rationalistic.

It is undeniable, nevertheless, that Anselm is concerned to show the reasonableness of the incarnation and redemption, and that these events can be known only by revelation and accepted by faith based on God's truthfulness. By the very nature of his topic, he is in the realm of theology, not philosophy. He certainly does intend, also, to make believers appreciate the beauty of these truths and see their logical consistency with other truths they believe. It is his intention to refute charges of absurdity and impossibility that have been hurled against Christians. But when he constructs his arguments, he lays down certain principles and presuppositions, several of which are revealed truths which require faith, and are accepted by Jews; for example: the consequences of sin, the existence of angels and the fall of some of them, the state of grace or justification as the original state of man. Mohammedans, whom he also seems to have had in mind, at least accept the authority of a supreme being and the existence of a revelation to which faith responds.

He is not excluding all faith as a presupposition, then, but only faith in the actual incarnation of the Divine Word.[123] It is his aim to show the Jews and Mohammedans that if they ponder the implications of what they admit in common with Christians, they must logically admit that God's taking on human nature and dying for the human race is not unreasonable. He is still concerned with "faith seeking understanding."

As far as "a necessary reason" or "the rational necessity of a conclusion" is concerned, it can be said that, leaning on philosophers who preceded him,[124] Anselm meant primarily by "necessary reason," an argument that leads to certainty.[125] He certainly distinguishes "necessary reasons" from "arguments of fitness," which only make the more basic reasons more attractive and persuasive, and which are more like "pictures" than proofs.[126] Then he goes on, however, to insist that if you can show that any attribute or action is *unsuitable to God's nature,* it is impossible to predicate it of Him. Further, he states, what is evidently fitting for God should be attributed to Him unless a stronger reason opposes it.[127]

Of course, there remains the difficulty that, at least sometimes, we cannot show *absolutely* that something is incongruous with God's goodness or wisdom or honor, because we do not know the nature and attributes of God perfectly. St. Anselm does not clarify his position on this "necessity" that is applied to God. No less an authority than Dom Schmitt concludes that the method of argumentation used by Anselm in *Why God Became Man* is, of itself, "rationalistic," and attributes to the human intellect more of an ability to know the designs and actions of

God than is justified.[128] He adds, however, that Anselm saves himself from this extreme by his explicit submission of any of his conclusions to the "higher authority" of Holy Scripture,[129] and his commitment of his writings to the judgment of the pope.

It still remains Anselm's glory to have introduced a method of logical analysis and development which, made more precise by the distinctions between theology and philosophy, the supernatural and natural orders, and absolute and hypothetical necessity, gave birth to Christian theology in its highest reaches and its most exact attainments in the thirteenth century.

E. *Anselm's Doctrine of Atonement*

Why God Became Man is primarily an essay in the theology of atonement [130] or redemption.[131] The basic Christian doctrine on the redemption of man can be summarized in these propositions:

1. The sin of Adam involved all members of the human race in its consequences. *As by one man sin entered into this world, and by sin, death, so death passed upon all men because all have sinned.*[132]

2. God promised a Redeemer,[133] and in *the fullness of time . . . sent His Son . . . that He might redeem them who were under the law, that we might receive the adoption of sons.*[134]

3. This Redeemer is Jesus Christ, *who gave Himself for us, that He might redeem us from all iniquity . . .*[135] His offering of Himself is free and voluntary: *. . . I lay down my life . . . No man taketh it away from me, but I lay it down of myself . . .*[136]

4. The effects of Christ's redeeming acts—including His resurrection—are communicated to Christians by baptism. *Know you not that all we who are baptized in Christ Jesus, are baptized in His death? For we are buried together with Him by baptism into death, that, as Christ is risen from the dead by the glory of the Father, so we also may walk in newness of life.*[137]

It is the function of theologians, and it was the task accepted by Anselm in his chief work, to try to give a reasoned explanation of what is involved in this tremendous event.

Not a small part of his achievement was the discrediting of a view of redemption, which has been called "the ransom theory," or "the rights of the devil theory." [138] Both the statement and the rejection of it are put into the mouth of Boso,[139] but that Anselm shares his view is indicated not only by his not commenting on it, but also by his explicit testimony elsewhere.[140] This view may be summarily stated: by sin, man delivered himself into the hands of the devil as by a contract, and hence the devil justly held man in bondage; when the God-Man redeemed or "bought back" the human race, he was dealing with the devil in a matter of justice, paying up and thus abrogating the contract with the devil.

Although St. Ireneaus was the first to speak of "the devil's rights" over the human race, it was Origen (185–c. 254) who gave the view its currency and seemed to accept all its extreme implications. Beginning with the notion that the Redeemer "ransomed" the human race, he states that by selling ourselves to sin, we became slaves of Satan, so that the God-Man who restored man's right to heaven was "buying back someone else's goods, because through sin we had given ourselves to another master." [141]

Other Fathers, like St. Gregory of Nyssa,[142] repeat the statement that the ransom of Christ was paid to the devil, but most of the theological giants reject this entirely. St. Gregory Nazianzen [143] and later, St. John Damascene,[144] write sharp criticisms of this grotesque theory. St. Ambrose, however, repeats Origen's notion that the human race sold itself into the possession of the devil, and almost outdoes Origen by his elaborate and drawn-out metaphor of buying, selling, debt and credit, with usury worked in.[145]

Some theologians [146] spoke of "the devil's rights" as a power granted by God, but they rejected the notion of a ransom paid to the devil. St. Augustine speaks of the human race being enslaved to the devil and of its being bought back by Christ on the cross; he even refers to the Body of Christ as "bait" set to trap the devil.[147] But nowhere does he speak of a ransom being paid to the devil. He does say that Christ overcame the devil by justice rather than by might, but he makes clear that the payment of a debt in justice is made by Christ to God, not to the devil.[148]

When, in introducing this view, Boso uses the words "we usually say . . ." [149] he indicates that the "devil's rights theory" was still popular in his time, and even after this book was published, it was held by some theologians.[150] The objection to the theory is that since both man and devil are under God's dominion, it would be incongruous and demeaning for God to have to plead a cause with or make a payment to His own creature. There is justice involved, but the payment is made in justice to God, not to the devil.

Even though not all his contemporaries agreed with Anselm, it can be said that his rejection of this view of the redemption deprived it of theological stature for the future.

What Anselm offers, positively, in place of "the devil's ransom" explanation, is called the "satisfaction-theory."

This theory is built on the definition of sin as the refusal to render to God what is due to Him. What is due Him is *honor*, given by subjection of one's will to God's Will. A creature who sins refuses God His due, detracts from His honor and insults Him. There arises an obligation to restore the honor and to undo the insult, and that is *satisfaction*.[151]

If God were to remit the sin without either satisfaction or punishment, Anselm proceeds to say, there would be results incongruous with God's dignity. Disorder would be permitted in God's kingdom,[152] the sinner would be equal before God with one who did not sin,[153] and supreme justice would be violated.[154] Besides, human beings are to replace fallen angels, and they would have to be as the angels orginally were—sinless. Without satisfaction, they could never be sinless again.[155] Furthermore, if man were not restored to justice, God's plans for the human race would be frustrated; and man cannot be restored to his first state without satisfaction.[156]

The only escape from everlasting punishment, then, is satisfaction.[157] Now, neither man nor angel, but only a God-Man can give this satisfaction.[158] Hence, the incarnation and the death of the God-Man were necessary for human redemption. Only the God-Man is able, by His divinity, to offer something worthy of God, yet able, by His humanity, to represent mankind.[159]

His argument for the statement that man is unable to make satisfaction himself is that "satisfaction must be made in proportion to the measure of sin,"[160] and the malice of sin is infinite.[161]

The aspects of this theory which distinguish it from preceding ones, and which have been generally admired and accepted, are that it does not consider Christ punished or in any way degraded, and that it is based on a very definite and exact analysis of sin.[162]

Shortcomings have been found in this view, however, by both Protestant and Catholic theologians. Many of the objections leveled against it can be shown to be based on misunderstanding of the author's purpose or presuppositions. There remain, however, some criticisms that have been proposed by the most loyal and best informed followers and defenders of the saint.

Some have found fault with the theory because it is not Scriptural; no texts are cited for it. Even though it is admittedly not contrary to Scripture, still it is "constructed apart from them and is not based upon their teaching."[163] The fact is, of course, that the book is an attempt to go *beyond* the explicitly revealed truths, to get the fundamental *plan* of God underlying the events whose occurrence is attested by revelation. Besides, in "leaving Christ aside, as if He never existed," Anselm is not, as was stated before,[164] putting the whole of Holy Scripture out of consideration, but only the actual incarnation; he does accept as premises many doctrines that are revealed, especially in the Old Testament.

Perhaps the most common objection that has been made against the "satisfaction-theory" is that it is based on an analogy with Germanic law, and is colored by a feudal notion of "honor" that is not worthy of God.[165]

It was, indeed, a practice in Teutonic law to require and accept a payment of money (*Wergeld*) as a "satisfaction" instead of inflicting a punishment such as incarceration on a malefactor, especially if his offence was to insult or to "impugn the honor" of a member of the nobility. It is also admissible that Anselm's use of the term *satisfactio* was affected by the contemporary legal use of the word. Nevertheless, the word had more ancient origins, and had been applied to the sufferings of Christ by Hilary of Poitiers (c. 315–366): "That passion was freely undertaken precisely to make satisfaction for penal obligation." [166] Whatever the derivation of the word, though, and whatever implications of feudalism it had in Anselm's time, he uses it in a precise theological way. He means that the perfection and supremacy of God ought to be acknowledged by all His creatures, and that a creature who sins refuses that submission and thus violates God's "honor." Divine justice requires satisfaction. But divine justice is identified, in God's self-contained and simple essence, with His mercy and omnipotence. If we say God's nature as justice requires an offering of retribution, the same nature, as mercy or love, makes that offering possible by uniting the Second Person of the Holy Trinity with human nature. The notions of honor and satisfaction are thoroughly Christian, as Anselm uses them.[167]

Perhaps the most basic and most telling criticism of Anselm's account of the redemption is that he does not seem fully to allow for the freedom of God in bringing about human reconciliation in exactly the manner that has been revealed to us.

He does point out that the necessity of God's redeeming the human race is consequent upon the act of His will granting satisfaction and pardon, and is rather God's graciousness. If we can speak of any necessity in regard to God's action, it is rather the unchangeability of His own honor.[168] While Anselm, therefore, admits that God is perfectly free and that any necessity arises out of the divine will, still he does give the impression that it would be repugnant to God's nature to remit sin without reparation or punishment, even though he says only that it is not "fitting." He argues that if God were to remit sin without reparation or punishment, He would be letting a disorder pass in His kingdom, and He would be treating the virtuous and the sinful alike.[169] He is, of course, trying to allow for God's complete liberty, yet show that His choice requiring satisfaction is not arbitrary or impulsive, but based on solid reason. He is definitely right and in harmony with Scripture in asserting that the Divine Word freely accepted human weakness and paid the debt for humanity. He definitely does not proclaim an absolute and antecedent necessity of the incarnation. He does argue, however, to a sort of necessity arising out of God's nature, which tends to blur the generous gratuitousness of the redemption of the human race.

Although his notion of "satisfaction" was accepted and made classical, it had to be developed and clarified by others during the next century and a half, and the commonly accepted Catholic understanding has been synthesized by St. Thomas Aquinas:

1. The death of Christ was not *absolutely* necessary for the salvation of human beings, so that salvation would be simply impossible without the passion.[170]

2. It was not necessary in the sense that God was forced by any extrinsic agent to require that death, or in the sense that Christ was externally forced to endure it.[171]

3. Hence it was still possible, simply or absolutely speaking, for God to free men from sin in some other way, than by the death of Christ.[172]

4. The death of Christ, then, was necessary *on the supposition* that God required satisfaction proportionate to the sin, which only the death of the God-Man could provide.[173]

5. In other words, we can say it was impossible for God to free man in any other way, on the supposition that God had already decided upon proportionate satisfaction.[174]

6. Although we can say that the justice of God required the death of Christ to atone for human sin, even this debt in justice depends upon God's Will to require proportionate satisfaction. If God willed to free man without any satisfaction, He would not be violating any justice, because He has no one superior to Him or independent of Him whose rights would be violated.[175]

7. This method of liberation was the *most fitting*, however, because, besides freeing man from sin, it best manifested God's love for man and stimulated man's love for God. It also gave us an example of obedience, humility, perseverance and justice.

It not only freed us from sin, but merited grace and glory for us. By it, man is better stimulated to persevere in grace. This kind of redemption, involving the death of the God-Man, leads to a greater victory of man over the devil.[176]

St. Thomas also adds other precise aspects to the theory of redemption, such as the description of the evil of original sin not so much as an *infinite* evil as the evil *of nature,* of a group joined in solidarity. It follows that "the reparation of human nature could not be effected either by Adam or by any other purely human being. For no individual man ever occupied a position of pre-eminence over the whole of nature; nor can any mere man be the cause of grace." [177] Only the God-Man, then, could redeem man. St. Thomas brings the notion of "mystical body" and "vine and branches" into the description of the process of redemption in a way Anselm never did.[178] In later centuries, the role of Christ's resurrection in relation to redemption has been more fully described and appreciated. It remains true, however, that all the theological theories in the Catholic tradition, at least, retain the notion of vicarious satisfaction, which Anselm has proposed:

. . . This debt was so great that, although man alone owed the debt, still God alone was able to pay it, so that the same person would have to be both man and God. Hence it was necessary that God assume human nature into the unity of His Person, so that the one who in his nature owed the debt and could not pay it, should be, in His Person, able to pay it. . . . The life of this man was so sublime, so precious, that it can suffice to pay what is owed for the sins of the whole world, and infinitely more . . .[179]

F. *Original Sin And Its Transmission*

Any explanation or defence of the incarnation and redemption, as Christians accept them, necessarily involves an admission of the fact of original sin. Any acknowledgment that the Redeemer is God, and at the same time a member of the human race, involves the problem of safeguarding the utter sinlessness of the one divine Person, and, at the same time, the descent of the human nature He assumed from those who committed the first human sin.

In *Why God Became Man,* St. Anselm treats of the nature of sin.[180] He also treats, there, of one way we can conceive of the God-Man being a descendant of our first parents, yet preserved from original sin.[181]

The same problem provides the entire subject-matter for *The Virgin Conception And Original Sin,* and here he proposes a different answer. Especially in this shorter book, he provides a more complete treatment of "original sin" as such.

On the topic of original sin, as well as on the redemption, Anselm has made an original contribution, and has profoundly influenced the course of theology after his time.

Sin, in general, he defines as the refusal to render to God the honor due to Him,[182] and what is due to Him is, essentially, subjection to His will.[183] To commit a sin, then, is to upset the order and beauty in God's kingdom, the totality of what He has created.[184] He goes on to say that any and every sin is a greater evil than any possible merely human loss.[185]

Going on to "original sin," specifically, he finds it to be the lack of justice or righteousness that affects human individuals because of the personal sin of their first ancestors. "Original justice" is a state of moral goodness [186] and can be defined as "the rectitude of the will preserved for its own sake." [187]

What is particularly noticeable about his description of original sin is that he conceives of it as a deprivation of *justice* or rectitude of will. He thus apparently departs from the view traditionally considered Augustinian, and popular in his own day, that connects original sin mainly with "concupiscence," or a disordered inclination to sense-pleasures, in opposition to reason. While St. Augustine himself does not call concupiscence the essence of original sin, he does so emphasize the former as to give the impression that it is the same as original sin, or at least he exaggerates its role.[188] Anselm, for all his allegiance to Augustine, is careful to avoid such impressions. He clearly defines original sin as "the deprivation, as a result of the disobedience of Adam by which we are all *children of wrath,* of the justice that should be in a human soul." [189] Since Adam's sin was a

wilful abandonment of rectitude of will, original sin primarily
affects the will; and as a consequence there arise actual sins
and miseries and concupiscence.[190]

This unequivocal equation of original sin with the deprivation
of justice or "righteousness" was a landmark in theology. There
remains in St. Anselm's view, however, a certain inadequacy,
since this moral rectitude of will could be something natural.
Although there is no exclusion of sanctifying grace, there is not
explicit description of it, and the beauty, the elevation beyond
the natural order, the comparative "likeness to God" of the soul
in the state of original justice are noticeably missing in Anselm's
treatise.[191] It was left to later theologians, notably St. Thomas
Aquinas, to spell out the points that original justice is a gratuitous gift added to human nature by the generosity of God, that
this justice requires sanctifying grace as its formal and essential
constituent and that it implies, as its material element, subjection
of passions to human will.[192]

The main question of *The Virgin Conception And Original
Sin*, of course, is how the Divine Word could take human nature
from the virgin, without contracting original sin. This involves
an explanation of how original sin is normally transmitted.
Anselm's answer to this latter question is quite characteristic
of him and quite in harmony with the common view of his time.

In Adam, he says, the whole of human nature existed, and it
existed in him totally.[193] Because this human nature could have
and should have resisted temptation, its failure was imputable
first to Adam himself, and also to the nature. ". . . The sin of
Adam has been in man because it is in the nature, and in the
one who was called Adam, because it is in the person." [194] The
person made the nature sinful, and the nature, thus despoiled
of justice, reappears in all the descendants of Adam as sinful
and unjust.[195] All of us were present in Adam "seminally," and
at the moment of his fall, the necessity arose for each of us to
have a nature tainted by sin.[196]

This explanation implies a "realism" that is faithful to the
philosophic tradition stemming from Plato. Especially in the
eleventh and twelfth centuries, many theologians were admitting

the existence of a universal reality—man as such, for example, or justice in itself—to correspond with our universal concepts. Anselm reflects this view in other contexts. To prove the existence of God, for instance, he argues to the existence of a *supremely good being*, from the existence within our experience of various beings that have some goodness.[197] Again, he reproaches Roscelin for saying that one should admit (at least as one alternative), three Gods, by saying: "One who does not yet understand how many men in one species are one man, how will he comprehend, with regard to that least knowable and most exalted of natures, the manner in which three Persons, of which each one is completely God, is one God?"[198] He certainly seems to be attributing real existence to the specific nature of man here. In *The Virgin Conception And Original Sin*, however, it is unequivocally clear that he accepts the extramental existence of human nature as a whole. As this Platonic interpretation of universals lost favor among the Scholastics, especially under the influence of Aristotelians like Thomas Aquinas, this method of accounting for the transmission of original sin naturally lost its vogue.

Anselm goes on to say that within human nature, original sin can be only in the will.[199] In normal conceptions, the soul is affected by original sin because the matter to which it is united is the result of human seed, directed by a human will. But in the case of Christ, the existence of the human soul and the union of the divine Person with a human nature are due to no natural power or human will, but to the will of God alone.[200] Thus, for Anselm, even if Christ were not God, yet because He was born of a virgin, He would not contract original sin, because His existence does not depend upon human generation and human will.[201]

Regarding the spiritual dignity of the virgin mother, Anselm, in the book concerned with Christ's conception, says only that it was most fitting that the virgin be pure and in the state of justice when she conceived. He holds that it is not absolutely necessary that the God-Man be conceived of a spotless virgin.[202] In his greater book, though, he says without hesitation that the virgin mother was "born with original sin, since even she sinned in Adam *in whom all have sinned*." [203] He does not, obviously, admit the Immaculate Conception of Mary.

It is a historical fact, however, that the popular Christian acceptance of this privilege of Mary was due, in large measure, to the influence of Anselm. In 1328, at a provincial council in London, his authority was cited for the institution of the feast of the Conception of Mary, in the province of Canterbury.[204] On September 17, 1438, the Council of Basel made the observance of this feast obligatory, and portions of the *De Conceptione Beatae Mariae Virginis*,[205] ascribed to Anselm, were assigned to be read as lessons at matins.[206]

The explanation of this attribution is that the author of that treatise, although not Anselm, was Eadmer, his friend and biographer. Eadmer had, some time previous to 1125, written a book entitled *The Eminence Of The Virgin Mary*,[207] in which he taught that it was by faith that Mary's soul was cleansed from all sin.[208] This was in agreement with the view of St. Anselm. But in the book *The Conception of the Blessed Virgin Mary*, written about the year 1125, for the express purpose of seeking to restore a feast of Mary's Conception, Eadmer first admits that it is "the Catholic opinion" that Mary was "not altogether exempt from the sin of our first ancestor." [209] Then he goes on to say that, while he does not wish to dissent from the truth of the Catholic Church, nevertheless he wants to raise a question. If, he asks, God can make the chestnut milky white inside, but bristly on its outer surface, could He not make His human mother spotless and sinless of soul, although she was the offspring of sin-stained parents? And he answers his own question: "Clearly, He could and He would want to; and if He wanted to, He did it." [210] This *potuit plane, et voluit; si igitur voluit, fecit* is an emphatic statement of the argument that was to become a common one in the fourteenth and fifteenth centuries. It was not, however, accepted by St. Bernard (1091–1153), Peter Lombard (c. 1100–1160) or St. Thomas Aquinas (1225–1274). The reason why this view continued to attract adherents increasingly during and after the thirteenth century was that the work that proposed it was thought to be St. Anselm's.

It was not, however, without some genuine foundation that Anselm was considered a champion of the Immaculate Conception. Although he explicitly rejected the doctrine in *Why God Became Man,* he nevertheless proclaimed, in the companion piece, a principle that logically led to the acceptance of the Immaculate Conception and to the defence of it by later theologians. "It was fitting, certainly," he wrote, "that this virgin should shine with that purity than which no greater, under God, can be thought of." [211] This "fitness" contains, surely, the fitness of the Immaculate Conception, and is not far removed from the *potuit, decuit, ergo fecit* of later theologians.

G. *General Evaluation*

It may be said that the two books that are presented here have principally an historical value. They illustrate the exercise of a profound and inquisitive mind on problems arising from revealed truths, but the problems have not the currency and relevance in the twentieth century that they had in the eleventh and twelfth. They represent an early medieval effort to synthesize the *reasons* for the acts of God for the benefit of His creatures and the expression of God's revelations in dialectical and philosophical terms. They bear witness to the rise of a scientific theology which remains the glory of the Christian world, and of which St. Anselm was a principal inaugurator. They justify his title of "father of Scholastic theology."

All this is true, but is it all that may be said? Perhaps the *problems* Anselm was trying to solve are not precisely the ones that confront the twentieth century mind with main force, but the *revealed truths* from which those problems grew still demand the attention and acceptance and (to the extent of his ability) the understanding of the Christian thinker. Like the *Monologion* and *Proslogion,*[212] *Why God Became Man* and *The Virgin Conception and Original Sin* are exquisite examples of "meditation

on the rationale of the faith," or of "faith seeking understanding."
The question why God gave us a God-Man to bring us back
when we rejected Him and to take our hardship upon Himself
springs spontaneously to any reflective Christian mind. In pon-
dering the "motives," if we may use that word, for God's acting
in a given way, we become more aware of His Wisdom and
Power and Mercy. Awareness of His love generates love in return, and Anselm's arguments and "proofs" become stimuli for
ardent supernatural love.

In his more devotional reflection on the Redemption, he thus
addresses his soul, and any Christian soul, "redeemed and liberated from miserable slavery by the blood of God":

. . . Consider the source and value of your salvation, ponder it
steadily, take delight in its contemplation . . . taste the goodness
of your Redeemer, enkindle the love of your Savior.[213]

He prayed to be led to savor by love what he tasted by knowledge, and to appreciate with devotion what he experienced by
understanding.[214] These same affective results he would wish to
accrue to his readers as to himself, and from his theological
dialogues and essays as well as from his recorded prayers. Even
in his meditation on the Redemption, he refers to the views
that the Savior chose this kind of atonement "to deceive the
devil who, by deceit, dispossessed man of paradise," or to pay
a ransom, in justice, to the devil, or to satisfy some compulsion
or necessitating influence.[215] Each alternative he summarily un-
dermines, and uses the views as occasions to express his faith
in the contrary truths. Each consideration gives rise to acts of
faith and love. No less in his more speculative treatises, like the
two presented here, does he desire to stimulate devotion as
well as to illuminate the understanding.

It is the hope of the translator that the understanding Anselm
had of the truths of Faith is not obscured but fairly communicated by the present English version, and that not too much
of the fervor of the saint's utterance has been lost by being
relayed through a colder tongue. The only liberty deliberately
and frequently taken was to shorten many sentences in which
St. Anselm not only states a proposition, but works in attesta-

tion from authority, and reference to a related truth, and an ascetical animadversion, all without stopping for breath.

The translation has been made from the critical edition of F. S. Schmitt, O.S.B.,[216] which not only is the best available text, but also copiously provides indications of patristic or Scriptural sources for many of Anselm's theological positions.

I am deeply grateful to my confreres, Fathers Paul V. Bryan, James H. Geiger and John Duffy for critical and helpful suggestions regarding the translation and introduction; and to Fathers Alfred C. Rush, Daniel Hickey and Richard Poetzel, for bibliographical assistance; to Mr. Thomas A. Gallagher, of Magi Books, Inc., for his generous encouragement and most capable guidance and technical assistance; and to Mrs. Mary Rinaldi for her kindness in typing sections of the script.

Joseph M. Colleran
St. Alphonsus College
Suffield, Connecticut

WHY GOD BECAME MAN

SUBMISSION OF THE WORK TO THE SCRUTINY OF POPE URBAN II [1]

Quite a few of our holy Fathers and teachers, following upon the Apostles, make many outstanding statements concerning the explanation of our faith, to confound the folly and break the resistance of unbelievers, and to nourish those who, with hearts already cleansed by faith,[2] find delight in the explanation of that faith,[3] an explanation for which we must have a hunger, after accepting it with certitude. Neither in our times nor in the future, then, may we hope for anyone equal to them in the contemplation of truth. Nevertheless, I do not think anyone ought to be reprehended if, having been confirmed in the faith, he wishes to exercise himself in the investigation of its meaning.[4] For, since *the days of man are short,*[5] even they were not able to say all that they could have said, had they lived longer. Furthermore, the explanation of the truth is so extensive and so deep that it cannot be exhausted by mortals. And the Lord does not cease to impart the gifts of His grace in His Church, for He promised to be with it *even to the consummation of the world.*[6] Further, not to mention other things by which Holy Scripture invites us to inquire into its meaning, the statement *Unless you believe, you will not understand,*[7] openly counsels us to give our attention to understanding, since it shows how we must proceed to that goal. Finally, since I realize that the understanding we achieve in this life is a mean between faith and direct vision, I consider that the more anyone advances toward understanding, the closer he approaches the direct vision we all eagerly desire.

Strengthened, then, by this reflection, I, although I am a person with all too little knowledge, attempt to rise a little closer to the vision of the meaning of what we believe, to the extent

59

that God's favor deigns to grant to me; and when I find something that I did not see before, I gladly make it known to others, so that I may learn by someone else's judgment what I ought to hold without fear.

Therefore, my father and lord, Pope Urban, reverently loved and lovingly revered by all Christians, you whom the providence of God has appointed supreme bishop in His Church, I offer to the scrutiny of Your Holiness, since I can offer it to no one else with greater fitness, the present little work, that the authority of Your Holiness may approve what is acceptable in it and correct what is erroneous.

PREFACE

The present work I have been compelled to complete, as well as I could, with more haste than I found convenient and therefore with greater brevity than I wished. The reason for this is that certain persons had, without my knowledge, copied for themselves the first parts [8] of it, before it had been completed and revised. I should have inserted and added many items that I have not mentioned, if I had been permitted to publish it at leisure and with the right amount of time. It was under great tribulation of heart—the source and the cause of my suffering being known to God—that I began it, by request, in England, and have finished it as an exile in the province of Capua. [9] In accordance with the subject matter of the treatise, I have entitled it *Why God Became Man*, and I have divided it into two short books. The first of these contains the objections of the unbelievers who reject the Christian faith because they consider it opposed to reason, together with the answers of believers. Later on, leaving Christ aside, as if nothing had ever been known of Him, proof is given by necessary reasons that it is impossible for any person to be saved without Him. In the second book, likewise, as if nothing were known about Christ, it is shown with no less evident argument and truth, that human nature was created for the very purpose that finally the whole person, that is, body and soul, should enjoy a blissful immortality. Proof is given, also, that it is necessary that man achieve the purpose of his creation—but that it could occur only through a Man-God; and besides, that all that we believe about Christ must of necessity occur.

I request all who wish to copy this book to put in the beginning this little preface, along with the chapter-titles of the whole work, so that anyone into whose hands it might come may see on its surface, so to speak, whether there is anything in its whole body that is worthy of his consideration.[10]

CHAPTERS OF THE FIRST BOOK

CHAPTERS OF THE SECOND BOOK

9. It is necessary that the Word alone unite with man in one person

10. This man is not obliged to die   In what sense He can and in what sense He cannot, sin   Why He, or an angel, should receive praise for being just, since neither can sin

11. He may die of his own power   Mortality is not a property of the pure nature of man

12. Although He shares our adversities, still He is not unhappy

13. He does not contract ignorance along with our other infirmities

14. How his death overcomes all sins, however numerous and great

15. How the same death blots out even the sins of those who caused His death

16. How God assumed humanity, without sin, from out of the sinful mass   The salvation of Adam and Eve

17. In God there is no necessity, no impossibility   There is a necessity that compels and one that does not compel

18. How the life of Christ is paid to God for the sins of men   In what sense Christ was obliged and in what sense He was not obliged, to suffer

19. The great reason why His death brought about human salvation

20. How great and how just is the mercy of God

21. It is impossible for the devil to be reconciled with God

22. In what has been said, the truth of the Old Testament and the New has been established

BOOK ONE

ONE

The question on which the whole work depends.

Frequently and most earnestly I have been requested by many persons, both by word of mouth and by letter, to commit to writing for posterity, the proofs I usually give as answers to inquirers, regarding a certain special question of our faith.[1] They say that these arguments appeal to them and they think them adequate. They make this request, not to attain to faith by way of reason, but to find delight in the understanding and contemplation of what they already believe; and also to be, so far as possible, *ready always to satisfy everyone that asks* them *a reason of that hope which is in* us.[2] This is a question regularly thrown at us by unbelievers who deride Christian simplicity as absurd, and it preoccupies the minds of many of the faithful. The question is: for what reason or by what necessity did God become man, and by His death, as we believe and acknowledge, restore life to the world, although He could have accomplished this by means of another person, whether angelic or human, or simply by an act of His will? Not only the learned but also many of the unlearned raise this question and want it answered. Many people, therefore, ask to have this matter treated, and although the investigation seems very difficult, the solution is nevertheless intelligible to all, and attractive because of the utility and beauty of the argument. So, although what has been said by the holy Fathers ought still to be enough, nevertheless I shall make an effort to show the inquirers what God will condescend to make clear to me on this subject. And since those matters which are studied in the style of question and answer are more intelligible and therefore more pleasing to many minds, especially to those who are slower to apprehend, I shall take as a disputant with me one of those persons who earnestly make inquiries about this matter—the one who urges me more insistently than the others to discuss it—so that Boso [3] puts a question and Anselm answers, in the following manner.

Boso: As right order requires that we believe the profound truths of the Christian faith before we presume to analyze them by reason, so it would seem to me a matter of negligence if after we have been confirmed in the faith, we make no effort to understand what we believe.[4] Therefore, since I think that by the prevenient grace of God, I have such firm faith in our redemption that even if I could not rationally grasp what I believe, there would still be nothing that could uproot the constancy of my faith, I beg of you to make clear to me what, as you know, many are asking about, as well as myself. That is, of course, by what necessity and for what reason God, although He is almighty, took on the lowliness and weakness of human nature, to restore it?

Anselm: What you ask of me is above me, and I fear to treat things too high for me,[5] for fear that, should anyone think or even see that I do not give him satisfaction, he might judge that I do not have the true doctrine, rather than that my intellect is not capable of understanding it.

Boso: You should not fear that so much. Rather recall that when we talk over some question it often happens that God makes clear what was obscure before. You should expect from the grace of God that if you generously give of what you have freely received,[6] you will merit to receive higher things to which you have not yet attained.

Anselm: There is still another reason why I think it is totally impossible or barely possible for us to treat fully of this subject at the present time. The reason is that we would have to know about power and necessity and will and certain other subjects which are so interrelated that none of them can be considered fully without the others. A discussion of them, then, would require a treatise by itself, and that would be, in my opinion, not very easy, yet not wholly useless. For ignorance of these things makes certain topics difficult, which become easy when these things are understood.

Boso: You could speak briefly of these things, each in its relevant context, so that we may know enough to complete the present treatise, and put off to another time what remains to be said.[7]

Anselm: There is another weighty reason for my holding back from what you ask, and it is this: that the subject matter is not only important but, as it is concerned with Him who is, in appearance, *beautiful above the sons of men,*[8] so it is also imposing in intelligibility beyond human understanding. Hence, as I generally become indignant at debased artists when I see the Lord Himself depicted with an ugly figure, I am equally afraid that the same thing may happen to me, if I dare to write on so beautiful a theme in a rough and vulgar style.[9]

Boso: Even this should not deter you. For, as you let anyone express himself better than you, if he can, so you do not dictate that anyone who is not satisfied with your style should not write more beautifully. Anyway, to put an end to all your excuses—what I am asking for, you will be doing not for the learned, but for me and those with me who are making the same request.[10]

TWO

How the things to be said are to be understood.

Anselm: Seeing your insistence and that of those who join you in this request, out of love and zeal for religion, I shall try to the best of my ability—with the help of God and your prayers, which, while making this request, you have often promised me when I asked for them—not so much to show you what you are looking for, as to look for it with you. I would like you to agree, however, to accept all my statements this way: if I should say anything which a greater authority does not confirm—even though I seem to prove it by reason—it is not to be accepted as any more settled than that I think it probable, until God in some way manifests it to me with greater clarity.[11] But if I am able to answer your question with satisfaction up to some extent, it must be beyond all doubt that someone wiser than I will be able to give more complete satisfaction. Indeed, we must acknowledge that however far human statement can go, the more profound explanation of so great a subject remains still hidden.[12]

THREE

Objections of unbelievers and answers of believers.

Boso: Permit me, then, to use the words of unbelievers.[13] For when we strive to find out the reason for our faith, it is only fair to pose the objections of those who are absolutely unwilling to approach that faith without rational arguments. Although they, of course, seek arguments of reason just because they do not believe, while we seek them because we do believe, what we both are seeking is, nevertheless, one and the same. And if you should make any response which sacred authority seems to oppose, let me bring forth that authority until you show me clearly that there is no opposition.

Anselm: Say what you think.

Boso: Unbelievers, ridiculing our simplicity, accuse us of offending and dishonoring God when we assert that He had descended into the womb of a woman, was born of a female body, that He grew up, nourished by milk and human foods, and— not to mention many other things which do not seem fitting for God—that He endured fatigue, hunger, thirst, scourging and crucifixion and death between thieves.[14]

Anselm: We give no offence or dishonor to God, but, giving wholehearted thanks, we praise and proclaim that inexpressible depth of His mercy. For the more marvelous and unexpected is the manner in which He restored us from such great and such deserved evils that had befallen us, to such great and undeserved favors that we had lost, so much the greater are the love and compassion He has shown toward us. If, then, they would carefully consider how fittingly the restoration of man was procured in this way, they would not ridicule our simplicity, but would join us in praising the wisdom and generosity of God. It was fitting, surely, that just as death had entered into the human race because of the disobedience of man, so by the obedience of man, life should be restored.[15] Further, just as the sin that was the cause of our condemnation had its origin in a woman, it was equally fitting that the author of our justification and salvation should be born of a woman.[16] It was also fitting that the devil, who conquered man by tempting him to taste of the fruit of a tree, should be conquered by a man through suffering he endured on the wood of a tree.[17] There are also many other things which, carefully considered, show a certain indescribable beauty in this manner of accomplishing our redemption.

FOUR

These answers may seem unconvincing to unbelievers, and to be like so many pictures.

Boso: All these statements must be accepted as beautiful and like so many pictures. But if there is no solid foundation for them, unbelievers do not think them adequate to show why we ought to believe that God was willing to suffer what we described. Anyone who wants to produce a picture chooses something solid to paint on, so that his painting will last. No one, surely, paints upon water or air, because no traces of the picture would stay there. Hence, when we present to unbelievers these reasons of fitness which you propose as so many pictures of a real event, since they think that what we believe in is not a historical fact but a fiction, they criticize us, so to speak, for painting upon a cloud. Therefore, we must first show the rational soundness of the truth, that is, the necessity of the inference that God should and could abase Himself to the extent that we proclaim. Then, so that the very body of truth, so to speak, may shine more brightly, those reasons of fitness are to be put on view, like pictures of the body.

Anselm: Do you not think this is a sufficiently necessary reason why God should have done what we described: that the human race, that so precious product of His hand, had been totally lost, and that it was not fitting that all that God had planned for man should come to nothing, and that this plan could not be realized unless the human race were liberated by its Creator Himself?

FIVE

The redemption of man could not be brought about by anyone but a Divine Person.

Boso: If you were to say that, in some way or other, this liberation could have been brought about by someone else than a Divine Person, whether by an angel or by a man, the human mind would have accepted this with far less reluctance. It was possible for God, surely, to create some man free of sin, not out of the sinful mass,[18] nor generated by another human being, but as he made Adam; and by this man, it seems, this task could have been accomplished.

Anselm: Do you not understand that, if any other person had redeemed man from eternal death, man would justly be

considered his servant? But if that were so, man would not at
all have been restored to that dignity he would have had if he
had not sinned. For he who was to be the servant of God alone
and equal in all things to the good angels [19] would be the servant of one who is not God and whom the angels do not serve.[20]

SIX

*How unbelievers criticize our statements that God re-
deemed us by His death and thus showed His love for us
and that He came to conquer the devil for us.*

Boso: What they especially wonder at is that we call this
liberation "redemption." For in what captivity—they say to us
—or in what prison, or in whose power were you held, from
which God could not free you, without redeeming you by such
great efforts and finally, by his own blood? Suppose we say to
them: He redeemed us from sins and from His own wrath and
from hell, and from the power of the devil whom He Himself
came to conquer for us, since we could not conquer him ourselves; and He bought back for us the kingdom of heaven; and
because He has done all these things in this manner, He showed
how much He loved us. Then they will retort: If you say that
God could not accomplish all this by a simple command, yet
say that He created all things by a command, you contradict
yourselves, because you make Him powerless. If, on the other
hand, you admit that He could have saved man in some other
way, but did not wish to, how can you vindicate His wisdom—
since you are asserting that He willed to suffer such unbecoming things without any reason? For all these reasons you adduce
are dependent on His will. The wrath of God, for example, is
nothing but His will to punish. If, then, He does not choose to
punish the sins of men, man is free from sins and also from the
wrath of God, and from hell and from the power of the devil—

all of which he suffers on account of sins—and he regains what he was deprived of because of those very sins. Under whose power is hell, or the devil, or whose is the kingdom of heaven, but His who created everything? Everything you fear or desire, then, is subject to His will, and nothing can resist that will. Hence, if He was unwilling to save the human race except in the way you describe, when He could have done it simply by His will, see—to put it quite mildly—how you depreciate His wisdom. Surely, if a man should, without any reason, do at a cost of greater labor what he could have done easily, no one would consider him wise. As for your statement that God showed in this way how much He loved you,[21] it is rationally indefensible, certainly, unless you prove that He could not have saved man in any other way. Admittedly, if He could not have done it in another way, then perhaps it would have been necessary to show His love in this way. Now, however, since He could have saved man in another way, what reason is there for His doing and undergoing what you describe, to show His love? Does He not show the good angels how much He loves them, without undergoing such things for them? As for your assertion that He came to conquer the devil for you, in what sense do you dare to propose that? Does not the omnipotence of God have sway everywhere? How, then, did God need to descend from heaven, to conquer the devil?—These are the objections unbelievers seem to be able to make against us.[22]

SEVEN

The devil had no justice on his side in opposing man. Why he seems to have had it. Why God should free man in this way.

Boso: We usually say, moreover, that to set man free, God must have acted against the devil more through justice than through fortitude. It would follow that when the devil slew Him who was God, and in whom there was no reason for death, it was through justice that he lost the power he had over sinners. Otherwise God would have inflicted unjust violence on him, since the devil was rightfully in possession of man, for the devil had not dragged man by violence, but man had willingly delivered himself to him. Now, I do not see what value this argument has. Of course, if the devil, or man, belonged to himself or to any other being but God, or remained under any other power than God's, perhaps it would be right to say that. Since the devil, however, or man, belongs to no one but God, and neither one is exempt from the power of God, what case did God have to plead with someone who belonged to Him, regarding another who belonged to Him, in a matter which concerned Himself, except to punish His servant, who, with what he had stolen from his master, had persuaded his fellow servant to desert their common master and go over to his own side, and being a traitor, had received him as a fugitive, and being a thief had received him as a thief? Each one, surely, was a thief, since one persuaded the other to steal himself from his master. What, indeed, would be more just than for God to do this? Or if God, the judge of all, had liberated man, thus possessed, from the power of the one who so unjustly possessed him—either to punish him in another way than by the devil, or to spare him—what injustice would there have been? For although it was just that man be tormented by the devil, yet the devil was unjust in tormenting him. Man, indeed, had deserved punishment, and by no one more fittingly than by the one to whom he gave his consent to commit sin. The devil, though, had deserved no right to inflict the punishment; on the contrary, his action was all the more unjust in that he was not motivated by love of justice, but was driven by an impulse of malice. For he did not do this at the command of God, but by permission of God's incomprehensible wisdom, by which He disposes even evil things toward good.

I believe, moreover, that those who think the devil has some right in justice to hold man in possession, come to this conclusion because they see that it is just for man to be subjected to abuse by the devil, and that it is just for God to permit this, and consequently they think it is just for the devil to inflict it. Sometimes, you know, one and the same thing is just and unjust, when considered from different points of view, and for this reason it is judged entirely just or entirely unjust by those who do not view the matter carefully. It may happen, for example, that someone unjustly strikes an innocent person, so that he justly deserves to be struck himself. If, however, the one who has been struck ought not to avenge himself, yet strikes the person who has struck him, he acts unjustly. This assault, therefore, is unjust for the one who strikes the blow, because he should not avenge himself; but from the standpoint of the one who receives the blow, it is just, because, for unfairly striking someone, he has deserved in justice to be struck back. The same action, then, is just and unjust, from different points of view, and it can happen that one person will judge the action simply right and another will judge it simply wrong. In this sense, therefore, we say it is just for the devil to molest man, because it is just for God to permit this, and it is just that man suffers it. But when we say it is just that man suffers, we mean that he suffers justly, not by reason of any justice proper to himself, but because he is punished by the just verdict of God.[23]

Suppose, now, someone cites that *handwriting of the decree* which the Apostle says *was against us* and was blotted out by the death of Christ.[24] Someone may think this means that the devil, as if under some sort of signed contract, justly exacted sin of man, before the passion of Christ, as a sort of interest on the first sin which he persuaded man to commit and as a penalty for sin, so that thereby he would seem to prove his just rights over man. I cannot at all agree with this interpretation.[25] That handwriting, surely, is not the devil's, for it is called *the handwriting of the decree*. Now, that decree was not the devil's, but God's. For it was decreed by a just judgment of God and confirmed as it were, by a signed document, that man who had freely sinned could not, by himself, avoid either sin or the punishment for sin. For he is a *wind that goeth and returneth not*.[26]

Besides, *whosoever committeth sin is the servant of sin*[27] and whoever sins should not be let go without punishment, unless mercy spares the sinner and liberates and restores him. Therefore, we should not think that this *handwriting* indicates any possible justice on the devil's part, when he harms man.

Finally, just as there is no injustice at all in a good angel, so in an evil angel there is absolutely no justice. Hence there was nothing in the devil to prevent God from using His power against him to liberate man.

EIGHT

Although the humiliations we attribute to Christ do not affect His divinity, nevertheless unbelievers think it unfitting that they be attributed to Him as man. The reasons why they think this man did not die voluntarily.

Anselm: The will of God must be enough of a reason for us, when He does something, even though we do not see why He wills it. For the will of God is never unreasonable.

Boso: That is true, if it is evident that God wills the thing in question. But many people refuse to admit that God wills something, if it seems to be opposed to reason.[28]

Anselm: What do you think is opposed to reason, when we say that God has willed whatever we believe about His incarnation?

Boso: To put it briefly: that the Most High is brought down to such an abyss; that the Almighty does something with such great effort.[29]

Anselm: Those who talk like that do not understand our beliefs. We do, beyond doubt, assert that the divine nature is incapable of suffering and absolutely incapable of being brought down from its eminence, and it does not expend effort in doing what it wills to do. But we say that the Lord Jesus Christ is true God and true man, one person in two natures and two natures in one person. Therefore, when we say God is subjected to some abasement or weakness, we do not understand this with regard to the sublimity of His impassible nature, but with regard to the weakness of the human substance He bore. So it is evident there is no rational objection to our faith. For we are not attributing any abasement to the divine substance, but we are showing that the God-Man is one person. Hence in the incarnation of God there is no thought of any abasement of God, but we believe in the exaltation of the nature of man.

Boso: All right; let us not attribute to the divine nature anything said of Christ that implies human weakness. But how will you ever prove that it is just and reasonable for God to treat, or allow to be treated in such a way, that man whom the Father called His *beloved Son,* in whom He was *well-pleased,*[30] and with whom the Son identified Himself? What sort of justice is it to hand over to death the most virtuous man of all, in place of a sinner? What man would not be judged deserving of condemnation if he condemned the innocent to free the guilty? It looks, then, as if the whole thing leads to the same incongruity that we spoke of before.[31] I mean: if He could not save sinners any other way than by condemning the just, where is His omnipotence? If He could, but would not, how shall we defend His wisdom and His justice? [32]

Anselm: God the Father [33] did not treat that man in the way you seem to think, nor did He hand over the innocent to death in place of the guilty. For God did not compel Him to die, or allow Him to be slain, against His will; rather, He Himself, by his own free choice, underwent death, to save men.

Boso: Even if He was not unwilling, since He consented to the Father's will, still it does seem, in a way, that the Father did compel Him by giving Him a command. For it is recorded that Christ *humbled Himself, becoming obedient* to the Father, *unto death, even to the death of the cross, for which cause God also hath exalted Him,*[34] and that *He learned obedience by the things which He suffered* [35] and that *the Father spared not even His own Son, but delivered Him up for us all.*[36] And the Son Himself says: *I came down, not to do mine own will, but the will of Him that sent me.*[37] And when about to go to His passion, He says: *As the Father hath given me commandments, so do I.*[38] Likewise: *The chalice which my Father hath given me, shall I not drink it?*[39] And in another place: *Father, if it be possible, let this chalice pass from me. Nevertheless, not as I will, but as Thou wilt.*[40] Again: *Father, if this chalice may not pass away but I must drink it, Thy will be done.*[41] In all these texts, the impression is given that Christ bore death by the compulsion of obedience rather than by the choice of His own free will.

NINE

He died voluntarily. The meaning of: "He became obedient unto death" and "for which cause God also hath exalted Him," and "I came . . . not to do my own will," as well as: "God spared not His own Son," and "Not as I will but as thou wilt."

Anselm: As I see it, you fail to distinguish between His doing something under the requirement of obedience, and His enduring what happened to Him, without obedience requiring it, because He persevered in obedience.

Boso: I need a clearer explanation of that.

Anselm: Why did the Jews persecute Him to the point of death?

Boso: Simply because He was unswervingly devoted to truth and justice in His life and in His speech.

Anselm: This, I believe, is what God requires of every rational creature, and what this creature owes to God under obedience.

Boso: We have to admit that.

Anselm: Therefore that man owed this obedience to God the Father and His humanity owed it to His divinity, and the Father required it of Him.

Boso: No doubt about that.

Anselm: Here you have something He did under the requirement of obedience.

Boso: Right! And now I am beginning to see what he endured as imposed upon Him, because he persevered in obedience. Death, surely, was imposed upon Him, because he stood firm in obedience, and He endured death. But how obedience did not require this, I do not understand.

Anselm: If man had never sinned, would he have had to suffer death, or should God have required this of him?

Boso: According to our faith, man would not have died, and this would not have been exacted of him. But I would like you to tell me the reason for this.

Anselm: You do not deny that the rational creature was created in a state of justice, and for the purpose of being happy in the enjoyment of God.

Boso: No.

Anselm: Now you will never think it fitting for God to compel a creature to be wretched, through no fault of his own, after He created him just and destined for happiness. And surely, it would be wretched for man to have to die, contrary to his desire.

Boso: It is obvious that if man had not sinned, God should not have required him to die.

Anselm: Therefore, God did not compel Christ to die, there being no sin in Him. But Christ freely endured death, not by giving up His life out of obedience, but by obeying a command to preserve justice, in which He persevered so unwaveringly that He incurred death as a result.

It can even be said that the Father commanded Him to die, when He commanded that on account of which He met His death. In this sense, then, He did just as the Father commanded Him [42] and He drank the chalice which the Father gave,[43] *and He became obedient* to the Father *unto death,*[44] and thus *He learned obedience by the things which He suffered,*[45] that is, to what extent obedience must be observed. Now, the expression "He learned" that is used here can be interpreted in two ways. "He learned" means either that "He made others learn," or that He learned by experience what He was not unaware of through infused knowledge.[46] When the Apostle said *He humbled Himself, becoming obedient unto death, even to the death of the cross,*[47] he added: *for which cause God also hath exalted Him, and hath given Him a name which is above all names.*[48] Similar to this is what David said: *He drinks of the torrent in the way, therefore He lifts up his head.*[49] These expressions do not mean that He absolutely could not arrive at this exaltation but by this obedience unto death, and that this exaltation was given only in reward for this obedience. For before He suffered He said that *all things* were *delivered* to Him by the Father [50] and that everything belonging to the Father was His.[51] The meaning rather is that the Son, together with the Father and the Holy Spirit, had determined that He would manifest to the world the height of His omnipotence, in no other way than by death. Surely, since it was determined that this occur only by that death, and since it actually occurred by that death, it is not incorrect to say that it occurs "on account of" it.

For if we intend to do something, but decide to do something else first, by means of which our intended goal may be achieved, then, if our goal is achieved after we have done what we wished to do first, it is correct to say that the intended action occurred precisely *because* that other action occurred which caused a delay in achieving our goal; and the reason is that it was decided that the intended action occur only by means of the other. Suppose, for example, I can cross a river either by horseback or by boat, and I decide to cross it only by boat, and then I defer making the crossing because there is no boat handy. Then, when a boat is available, and I make the crossing, it is correct to say of me: the boat was ready, therefore he went across. Further, we speak in this way when we have decided to do something else not only *by means of* that which we wish to precede, but also when it is not *by means of* it, but only *after* it. If, for instance, someone postpones eating because he has not yet been present at the celebration of Mass on that day, then when he has finished what he wanted to do first, it is not inexact to say to him: "Now take some food, because you have already done that *on account of which* you put off eating." Much less strange, then, is our expression, when we say Christ was exalted *because* He underwent death, since He determined to achieve that exaltation both *by means of* His death and *after* it. This can be understood also, in the same way as the text stating that the Lord *advanced in wisdom and . . . grace with God*,[52] not meaning that He really advanced, but that He acted as if He did so.[53] For He was exalted after death, just as if this occurred *on account of* His death.

Now, His statement: *I came not to do my own will, but the will of Him who sent me*,[54] is of the same sort as: *My doctrine is not mine.*[55] For what a person possesses, not of himself, but from God, he ought not to call his own, so much as God's. And no man has from himself the truth he teaches or rightness of will—but from God. Hence Christ came not to do His own will, but the Father's, because the justness of will which He had was not from His humanity, but from His divinity. The statement that God *spared not His own Son, but delivered Him up for us* [56] means, in fact, only that God did not free Him. Many similar statements are found in Sacred Scripture. Where He says, for example, *Father, if it be possible, let this chalice pass from me; nevertheless, not my will, but thine be done*,[57] and *If this chalice may not pass from me, but that I drink it, thy will be done*,[58] He means by "His own will," the natural desire for well-being by which His human flesh shunned the pain of death. He did, it is true, speak of the will "of the Father," not however, because the Father preferred His Son's death to His life, but because the Father was unwilling that the human race be restored unless man performed some deed as outstanding as that death was to be. Since reason did not require something another could not do, the Son says the Father wills His death, and He would rather endure His own death than the loss of the human race. It is as if He said: "Because You do not will the world to be reconciled in any other way, I declare that in this way You are willing my death. May this will of yours, then, be done

—that is, let my death occur, that the world may be reconciled to You." For we often say a person wills something, for the reason that he does not will something else, when, if he did will the other thing, what he is said to will would not occur. We say, for example, that a person wills the lamp to be blown out, if he does not wish to close a window through which a wind enters and blows out the light. In this way, then, the Father willed the death of His Son, because He did not will the world to be saved except by a man performing some outstanding deed, as I have said. Since no one else could perform such a deed, this was equivalent to the Father's commanding the Son to die, since the Son willed the salvation of men. Hence He did *as the Father gave* Him *commandment*,[59] and He drank the chalice which the Father gave Him,[60] being *obedient unto death*.[61]

TEN

It is possible that a different interpretation of the same texts is correct.

Anselm: It can also be correct to interpret these texts to mean that, through that holy will by which the Son was willing to die for the salvation of the world, the Father, without compelling the Son, gave Him a command,[62] and gave Him the chalice of suffering,[63] and did not spare Him, but *delivered Him up for us* [64] and willed His death; and that the Son Himself was *obedient unto death* [65] and *learned obedience by the things which He suffered.*[66] For just as, from the standpoint of His humanity, He had the will to live in the state of justice, not from Himself but from the Father, so also He could have had that willingness to die to bring about so much good, only from *the Father of lights* from whom is *every best gift and every perfect gift.*[67] And as the Father is said to "draw" a person when He confers a willingness on him, it is equally proper to assert that He "moves" him. Just as, for example, the Son says to the Father, *No man comes to me, except the Father . . . draw him,*[68] He could just as well have said: "unless the Father move him." He could also have continued in a similar way: "No one hastens toward death for my name's sake, unless the Father move or draw him." For since it is through the will that a person is drawn or moved to what he unwaveringly chooses, it is not unfitting to assert that God draws or moves him, when He confers this willingness. We are to understand this drawing or moving as implying not any compulsion of violence, but a spontaneous and loving tenacity of the good will that has been received. If in this sense, then, we cannot deny that the Father, in imparting that willingness, drew or moved the Son to death, who would not see that, in the same sense, He gave Him a "commandment" willingly to endure death, and a "chalice" which He would drink without reluctance.[69] And if it is correct to say that the Son did not spare Himself, but delivered Himself up for us with unforced willingness,[70] who can deny it is correct to say that the Father, from whom He had such a willingness, *spared* Him *not, but delivered Him up for us* [71] and willed His death? In this sense, too, by unswervingly and freely persevering in the willingness He received from the Father, the Son became *obedient* to Him *unto death* [72] and *learned obedience by the things which He suffered,*[73] that is to say, He learned how great a result is achieved through obedience. For that is simple and genuine obedience when a rational nature maintains, not by necessity but freely, the willingness it has received from God.

We can interpret the statement that the Father willed the death of the Son in other ways, too, but these can suffice. For as we say that he wills something who influences another to will it, so we also say that he wills something who approves of another person's choice, even though he does not influence the choice. For example, when we see someone resigned to endure hardship bravely, to accomplish something good he intends, although we admit we want him to undergo that pain, it is nevertheless not his pain that we desire and approve, but his willingness. We commonly say, also, that a person who can prevent something and does not prevent it, is willing what he does not prevent.[74] Since, therefore, the Son's desire was acceptable to the Father, and He did not prevent Him either from willing as He did or from fulfilling what He willed, it is right to say that He willed that the Son suffer death so loyally and so fruitfully, even though He did not love the Son's suffering. He said it was not possible for the chalice to pass without His drinking it,[75] not because He could not avoid death if He chose, but because—as has been said—it was impossible to save the world in any other way, and He unwaveringly willed rather to suffer death than let the world be lost. He used that expression, therefore, to point out that the human race could not be saved in any other way than by His death, not to show that He had no power to avoid death. Whatever statements are made of Him, similar to those which have been made, are, of course, to be interpreted as meaning that He died not of necessity, but by free choice. For He was almighty, and we read of Him that *He was offered, because it was His own will.*[76] He Himself also says: *I lay down my life, that I may take it up again. No man taketh it away from me, but I lay it down of myself. And I have power to lay it down and I have power to take it up again.*[77] It is not at all right, then, to say that He is compelled to do what He does by His own power and by His own choice.[78]

Boso: The single fact that God permits Him to be so treated does not seem to be fitting for such a Father [79] with regard to such a Son, even though He is willing.

Anselm: On the contrary, it is eminently fitting for such a Father to give consent to such a Son if He wills something for the glory and honor of God and conducive to the salvation of man, which could not be achieved in any other way.

Boso: We are still concerned with the problem of showing how that death was reasonable and necessary. If it is not such, indeed, it seems that neither the Son ought to have willed it, nor the Father ought to have required or permitted it. For the question is: why God could not have saved man in another way, [80] or, if He could, why He chose to save him in this way? It really seems unfitting for God to have saved man in this way, and further, it is not apparent what that death can accomplish for the salvation of man. It is surely to be wondered at if God so derives delight from, or has need of, the blood of the innocent, that He neither wishes nor is able to spare the guilty without the death of the innocent.[81]

Anselm: Since, in this inquiry, you are playing the role of those who wish to believe nothing unless it is previously proved by reason,[82] I would like to make an agreement with you not to attribute to God anything even slightly unsuitable, and not to reject any explanation, however weak, unless there is a stronger argument contradicting it. For in regard to God, just as whatever is unsuitable, however slightly, is consequently impossible,[83] so a rational argument, however weak, induces certainty unless there is a stronger argument to refute it.

Boso: There is nothing I would rather have than our mutual agreement on this matter.

Anselm: Our inquiry is concerned only with the incarnation of God, and with what we believe regarding that humanity assumed by God.

Boso: That's right.

Anselm: Then let us suppose that the incarnation of God and what we say of that man never occurred. Let us agree that man was made for happiness, which cannot be possessed in this life, also that no one can arrive at happiness unless his sins are forgiven, and that no person passes through this life without sin, and anything else, the belief of which is necessary for eternal salvation.[84]

Boso: Fine! There is nothing in these matters that appears impossible or unsuitable to God.

Anselm: It is necessary, then, that man's sins be forgiven, so he may arrive at happiness.

Boso: That we all hold.

ELEVEN

What "to sin" and "to satisfy for sin" mean.

Anselm: We must inquire, now, into the reason why God forgives the sins of men. And to do this more clearly, let us first see what "to sin" and "to satisfy for sin" mean.

Boso: It is your function to explain, and mine to listen.

Anselm: If an angel or a human being always rendered to God what he should, he would never sin.

Boso: I can only agree.

Anselm: "To sin," then, is nothing else than not to render to God His due.

Boso: What is the debt we owe God?

Anselm: The will of every rational creature must be subject to the will of God.

Boso: Perfectly true.

Anselm: This is the debt which angel and man owe to God, so that no one sins if he pays it and anyone who does not pay it, sins. This is justice or rectitude of will, which makes persons upright or *right in heart*,[85] that is, in will.[86] This is the only and the total honor which we owe to God and which God exacts of us. For only such a will produces works pleasing to God, when it is able to act; and when it is unable to act, it gives satisfaction by itself alone, because no effect of activity gives satisfaction without it. A person who does not render God this honor due Him, takes from God what is His and dishonors God, and this is to commit sin. Now, as long as he does not repay what he has plundered, he remains at fault. Neither is it enough merely to return what was taken away, but on account of the insult committed, he must give back more than he took away. For example, one who harms the health of another does not do enough if he restores his health, unless he makes some compensation for the injury of pain he has inflicted.

Similarly, for one who violates the honor of some person, it does not suffice to render honor, if he does not make restitution of something pleasing to the person dishonored, in proportion to the injury of dishonor that has been inflicted. This also must be given attention: when someone pays back what he unjustly pilfered, he must give what could not be demanded of him if he had not defrauded the other person. Thus, therefore, everyone who sins must pay to God the honor he has taken away, and this is satisfaction, which every sinner must make to God.

Boso: Since we have set out to follow reason, I have no objection I can make on any of these points, although you frighten me a bit.

TWELVE

Is it fitting for God to remit sin out of mercy alone, without any payment of the debt?

Anselm: Let us go back and see whether it is fitting for God to remit sin out of mercy alone, without any payment for honor taken away from Him.

Boso: I do not see why it is not fitting.

Anselm: To remit sin in such a way is the same as not to punish it. And since to deal justly with sin, without satisfaction, is the same as to punish it, then, if it is not punished, something inordinate is allowed to pass.

Boso: What you say is reasonable.

Anselm: It is, however, not seemly for God to let pass something inordinate in His kingdom.[87]

Boso: If I wanted to say otherwise, I would be afraid of sinning.

Anselm: Hence it is not fitting for God to remit sin without punishing it.

Boso: That follows.

Anselm: There is another consequence, if an unpunished sin is remitted: one who sins and one who does not sin will be in the same position before God. And that would be unseemly for God.

Boso: I cannot deny that.

Anselm: Look at this, also. Everyone knows that the justice of human beings is subject to the law that the measure of recompense is weighed out by God in proportion to the degree of justice.

Boso: So we believe.

Anselm: But if sin were neither atoned nor punished, it would not fall under any law.

Boso: I cannot disagree.

Anselm: If pardon is given out of mercy alone, injustice is less encumbered than justice. And this appears extremely incongruous. This incongruity even goes so far as to make injustice resemble God, for as God is subject to no law, neither would injustice be.

Boso: I cannot refute your argument. But since God commands us absolutely to forgive those who offend us,[88] it seems to be inconsistent for Him to command us to do what is not fitting for Him to do.

Anselm: There is no inconsistency here, because God gives us this command precisely that we may not usurp what belongs to God alone. For it belongs to no one to carry out vengeance, except to Him who is the Lord of all.[89] Even when earthly rulers exercise vengeance justifiably, the one who is really exercising it is the One who established them in authority for this very purpose.[90]

Boso: You have gotten rid of the inconsistency which I thought was there. But there is another problem for which I would like to have your answer. For since God is so free that He is subject to no law, to no one's judgment, and so kind that nothing kinder can be imagined, and since nothing is right or becoming but what He wills, it does seem extraordinary to say that He absolutely does not will, or has not the freedom, to pardon an injury to Himself, although it is from Him that we are accustomed to ask remission even of the wrongs we do to others.

Anselm: What you say about His freedom and will and kindness is true. But we must understand these things by reason in such a way as not to seem to compromise His dignity. For freedom extends only to what is advantageous or to what is becoming, and a kindness which would bring about something unworthy of God ought not to be called kindness at all. But when we say that what God wills is just and what He does not will is not just, this is not to be understood in the sense that if God should will something unbecoming, it would become right by His willing it. It is not, for example, logical to say: "If God wants to lie, it is right to lie"; rather, one who wants to lie is not God. For a will can never choose to lie unless it be a will in which the truth is impaired, in fact, a will which is itself impaired by deserting the truth. When, then, someone says: "If God wants to lie" all he means is: "If God were of such a nature that He could wish to lie"; and so it does not follow that a lie is right. Perhaps, though, it may be interpreted in the same sense as when we say of two impossible things: "If this is, that is," although neither the one or the other is so. Should a person say, for instance: "If water is dry, then fire is wet," neither statement is true. Therefore, it is true to say: "If God wills this, it is right," only regarding those things which it is not unfitting for God to will. If, for example, God wills that it rain, it is right that it rain, and if He wills that some man be killed, it is right that he be killed. Hence, if it is not fitting for God to do anything unjustly or inordinately, it does not pertain to His freedom or kindness or will to pardon without punishment a sinner who does not make recompense to God for what he took away.

Boso: You are making irrelevant every objection I thought I could make against you.

Anselm: Consider, further, why it is not fitting for God to do this.

Boso: I am gladly listening to whatever you say.

THIRTEEN

Nothing is less tolerable in the order of things than for a creature to take away honor due to the Creator and not make recompense for what he takes away.

Anselm: Nothing is less tolerable in the order of things than for a creature to take away the honor due to the Creator and not make recompense for what he takes away.

Boso: That is perfectly clear.

Anselm: Now, nothing would be less justifiably tolerated than what is least tolerable.

Boso: This is clear, too.

Anselm: Then I think you will not say that God ought to tolerate that than which nothing would be less justifiably tolerated, such as that a creature not restore to God what he takes from Him.

Boso: On the contrary, I see that that is to be denied, absolutely.

Anselm: Likewise, if there is nothing greater or better than God, there is nothing more just than for the supreme justice which is the same as God Himself,[91] to preserve His honor in the order of the universe.

Boso: Nothing is clearer to me than that.

Anselm: Therefore, God preserves nothing with greater justice than the honor of His dignity.

Boso: I have to agree.

Anselm: Do you think He would be preserving it entirely, if He permitted it to be taken away from Him in such a way that there would be no reparation and no punishment for the offender?

Boso: I dare not say yes.

Anselm: Then it is necessary either that the honor taken away be restored, or that punishment follow. Otherwise, either God will not be just to Himself or He will be unable to attain either. And it would be monstrous even to entertain that thought.

FOURTEEN

What kind of honor does the punishment of a sinner give to God?

Boso: I understand that nothing more reasonable can be said. But I want you to tell me if the punishment of a sinner gives honor to God, or rather, what kind of honor it is. For if the punishment of a sinner is not for the honor of God, when the sinner does not repay what he took away, but is punished, then God loses His honor in such a way as not to regain it. But this seems to contradict what we have said.

Anselm: It is impossible for God to be deprived of His honor. For either the sinner freely pays what he owes, or God takes it from him against his will. It may be that a person by free choice shows due subjection to God—either by not sinning or by making reparation for sin—or it may be that God subjects him to Himself, against the person's will, and thus He shows Himself his Lord, which is what the person himself refuses to acknowledge voluntarily. And in this matter, we must observe that just as man, by sinning, plunders what belongs to God, so God, by punishing, takes away what belongs to man. Surely, not only that which he already possesses is said to belong to a person, but also what is in his power to possess. Since, then, man is so made that he could have possessed happiness if he had not sinned, it follows that when, because of sin, he is deprived of happiness and every good, he is paying back what he plundered, out of what belongs to himself, although he is paying unwillingly. For although God does not transfer to His own use, for His own advantage, what He takes away—as a man directs to his own use, money he takes away from another—nevertheless, what He takes away He uses for His own honor, by the very fact that He takes it away. For by taking it away, He shows that the sinner and the things that belong to him are subject to Himself.

FIFTEEN

May God permit His honor to be violated, even in the least degree?

Boso: I like your explanation. But there is still another question I would like you to answer. If God must preserve His own honor, as you are establishing, then why does He allow it to be violated, even in the slightest degree? For what is allowed to be damaged in any measure is not entirely and perfectly protected.

Anselm: Considered in itself, God's honor cannot be increased or diminished. It is itself, by itself, honor incorruptible and absolutely unchangeable. But when each single creature, either by natural impulse or by the use of reason, fulfills its direction toward a goal proper to itself, and, so to speak, prescribed for it, it is said to obey God and to honor Him. This is especially true of rational nature, which has the gift of knowing what it ought to do. When it wills what it should, it honors God—not that it confers anything on Him, but that it freely subjects itself to His will and plans and keeps its place in the order of the universe, and to the best of its power, it preserves the beauty of that universe. But when it does not will what it should, it dishonors God so far as it can, since it does not subject itself freely to His plan, and, to the extent of its power, it disturbs the order and the beauty of the universe, although it does not injure or degrade the power and dignity of God, at all.

If, for example, those things that are contained within the sphere of the sky should wish not to be under the sky or to be released from the sky, they could not at all exist except under it, nor can they flee from the sky except by drawing nearer to it. For no matter where they were to come from or where they were to go, or what direction they took, they would be under the sky, and the greater the distance they would get away from any part of the sky, the closer they would approach to the opposite part. Similarly, even though a man or a fallen angel is unwilling to submit to the divine will and plan, still he cannot escape it; for if he wants to escape the dominion of the will that commands, he rushes under the dominion of the will that punishes. And if you ask how he passes from one state to another, it is only under a permissive will; and supreme wisdom directs his perversity of will or action toward the order and beauty of the universe I have been talking about. For a willing satisfaction for wickedness, or at least the exaction of a penalty from one who refuses satisfaction—granting that God draws good out of evils in many ways—takes its proper place in this same universe, and contributes to the beauty of its order. If divine wisdom did not impose these sanctions where wickedness tries to disturb right order, there would arise in the very universe which God has to keep in order, a certain deformity from the violation of the beauty of order, and God would seem to be deficient in His providence.[92] As these two consequences are unfitting, they are therefore impossible, with the result that it is necessary that satisfaction or punishment follow every sin.[93]

Boso: You have answered my objection satisfactorily.

Anselm: It is evident, then, that no one can honor or dishonor God, as God is in Himself; but to the extent of his own nature, a person appears to do one or the other, when he subjects his own will to God's, or withdraws it from God's.

Boso: I know nothing to say against that.

SIXTEEN

The reason why the number of the angels who fell is to be made up from among human beings.

Anselm: Let me add still more.

Boso: Keep on talking until I am tired of listening.

Anselm: It is certain that God intended to make up the number of angels who had fallen, out of human nature, which He made sinless.[94]

Boso: This we believe, but I would like to have some reason for it.

Anselm: You are tricking me. We intended to treat only of the incarnation of God, and nothing else, and here you are interspersing other questions for me.[95]

Boso: Do not be angry. *God loveth a cheerful giver.*[96] Now, no one gives greater proof that he is cheerfully giving what he promises, than one who gives more than he promises. So tell me with good grace, what I am looking for.

Anselm: It is not to be doubted that rational nature which either is, or is going to be, made happy by the contemplation of God, was known by God before its existence, as having a definite, calculable and perfect number, which cannot fittingly be greater or less. For either God does not know what number of rational creatures would be more appropriate—and that is false—or, if He knows it, He will create it in the number He knows to be more appropriate for His purpose. Therefore, either those angels who fell were created to be within that number, or else, their fall was necessary, since, being excluded from that number, they could not persevere—and it is absurd to think that.

Boso: What you say is evident truth.

Anselm: Therefore, since they must have been included in

that number, either their number was necessarily to be substituted, or else the rational nature, which was foreseen to exist in a perfect number, will remain numerically incomplete; and that cannot be.

Boso: Without doubt, there had to be substitutions for them.

Anselm: Then the substitutions had to be made from human nature, since there is no other nature from which they could be made.[97]

SEVENTEEN

Other angels cannot replace the fallen ones.

Boso: Why cannot they themselves be restored, or other angels replace them?

Anselm: After you see the difficulty of our restoration, you will understand that their reconciliation is impossible.[98] As for other angels supplanting them—not to mention how incompatible this seems to be with the perfection of the first creation—it is impossible for the reason that they ought not to replace them unless they could be the same as the fallen angels would have been if they had not sinned. Had the latter persevered, it would have been without their having witnessed any punishment for sin, and after their fall, that would have been impossible for the others who would have been substituted for them. For one who has no knowledge of any punishment for sin, and one who always has in view eternal punishment, are not equally praiseworthy for standing firm in the truth.[99] We ought never to think, surely, that the good angels were confirmed in goodness by the fall of the evil ones; it was rather by their own merit. If the good ones had sinned with the evil ones, they would have been condemned together with them; it is equally true that if the unfaithful ones had stood firm with the virtuous ones, they would likewise have been confirmed. Indeed, if some of the angels were not to be confirmed except by the fall of others, either no one would ever have been confirmed, or it would have been necessary for someone to fall, so that he might be punished for the strengthening of others—and both of these alternatives are absurd. Therefore, those who were steadfast were confirmed in exactly the same way in which all would have been confirmed if they had persevered. What that way is, I have shown, to the best of my ability, when I treated the question why God did not grant perseverance to the devil.[100]

Boso: You have proven that the evil angels were to be replaced from human nature; and it is evident from this reasoning that the elect among human beings will not be less numerous than the reprobate angels. But show, if you can, whether they are to be more numerous.

EIGHTEEN

Are there to be more human saints than evil angels?

Anselm: If the number of angels, before any of them fell, was that perfect one of which we have spoken,[101] human beings were created solely to replace the lost angels, and it is evident that they will not outnumber those angels. But if all the angels did not constitute a perfect number, then human beings were to replace both what was lost and what was lacking from the beginning, and the human beings destined for glory will exceed the reprobate angels in number. And thus we shall say that human beings were created not only to replace the diminished number, but also to make perfect a number that was not yet perfect.

Boso: Which is the better view to hold? Were the angels from the beginning, created in a perfect number, or not?

Anselm: I shall tell you my opinion.

Boso: I cannot ask more of you.

Anselm: If man was created after the fall of the evil angels, as some interpret *Genesis*,[102] I do not see how I can, on that basis, prove either of these alternatives decisively. In my opinion, it is possible that the angels first existed in a perfect number, and afterwards man was created to complete their diminished number. It is also possible they did not exist in a perfect number, because God deferred—as He is still deferring —to complete that number, since He was to create human nature in its own time. It would follow either that He might only make perfect a number that was not yet total, or even that He might restore it if it had been diminished. But if the whole of creation was produced all together[103] and those "days" which Moses mentions, seeming to imply that this world was not created all at once, are to be understood as different from these days of our life,[104] I cannot understand how the angels were created in that complete number. Indeed, if it had been so, it seems to me that of necessity, either some angels or some men were to fall, or else that there were to be more inhabitants in that heavenly city than that suitability of a perfect number would require. Therefore, if all things were created at once, it would seem that angels and the first two human beings were in an imperfect number, so that, if no angel were to fall, only the number that was lacking would be completed from human beings, and if anyone should be lost, the part that fell would also be replaced. Then the nature of man, which was the weaker one, would, as it were, vindicate God and confound the devil if he should impute his own fall to his weakness, since a weaker than he remained constant. Should that human nature itself fall, moreover, much more would it show God to be just, against the devil and against itself, since, although it had been made much weaker and mortal, it was to have advanced among the elect from such extreme weakness to an eminence so much more exalted than that from which the devil had fallen—as exalted as that the good angels, with whom it ought to be on the same level, attained after the ruin of the evil ones, because they persevered.

For these reasons, it seems to me more likely that the angels did not constitute that perfect number by which that celestial

city will be brought to completion. This view is possible, if man
was not created together with the angels. And it seems to be
a necessary assumption if they were created together—which
many think more likely, since we read: *He that liveth forever
created all things together.*[105] But even if the perfection of a
created world is to be understood not so much with regard to
the number of individuals as with regard to the number of
natures, it is necessary that human nature was created either
to complete that same perfection or else that it is superfluous
to it—which we dare not say regarding the nature of the low-
est little worm. Hence, it was created on the earth for its own
sake and not merely to replace the individuals of another nature.
From this it is evident that even if no angel had been lost,
human beings would still have had their own place in the heavenly city. It follows, then, that the number of the angels, before any of them fell, was not that perfect one. Otherwise it
would have been necessary that either human beings or certain
angels fall, since no one could remain in that city in excess of
the perfect number.[106]

Boso: You have accomplished something.

Anselm: There is another reason, also, I think, which gives
more than a little support to that opinion that angels were not
created in a perfect number.

Boso: Tell me what it is.

Anselm: If angels were created in that perfect number, and
human beings were created for no other reason than to replace
the lost angels, it is evident that unless some angels had fallen
from that blessedness, human beings would not have ascended
to it.

Boso: That is clear.

Anselm: If anyone should say, then, that the human beings
chosen for blessedness will rejoice in the loss of the angels as
much as in their own elevation—since, without doubt, the latter
would not occur unless the former occurred—how will it be
possible to defend them from this perverse gratification? Or how
shall we say that the angels who fell have been replaced by
human beings, if the angels, in case they had not fallen, were
to have remained free from this vice—that is, free from gratifi-

cation over the fall of others—although human beings cannot be free from it? What sort of blessedness will they deserve, in fact, having this defect? How rash, then, we would be to say that God is not willing or is not able to bring about this replacement without this defect!

Boso: Is it not similar to the case of the Gentiles [107] who were called to the faith because the Jews rejected it?

Anselm: No. For even if all Jews had accepted the faith, the Gentiles would still have been called, because *in every nation, he that feareth God and worketh justice, is acceptable to Him.*[108] But the fact that the Jews despised the apostles was the occasion for the latter to turn to the Gentiles.

Boso: I cannot see the slightest objection to make to this.

Anselm: What do you think is the origin of that joy in individuals over another's fall?

Boso: What, but that every individual will be convinced that he would not possibly be where he is unless another fell from there?

Anselm: Then, if no one had this conviction, there would be no reason for anyone to rejoice over another's loss?

Boso: So it seems.

Anselm: Do you think any one of them will have this conviction if there are many more of them than of those who fell?

Boso: It is simply impossible for me to think that anyone would have it or should have it. For how could anyone know whether he was created to replace what was lost, or to complete what is still lacking to the number required to constitute the city? But all will be certain that they were created to complete that city.

Anselm: Therefore, if they are more numerous than the reprobate angels, none of them will be able to know or ought to know he has been brought up there only because of someone else's fall.

Boso: That is right.

Anselm: Hence no one will have reason for rejoicing over someone else's loss.

Boso: That follows.

Anselm: Since, therefore, we see that if there will be more chosen human beings than reprobate angels, there will not be that unseemly result that would have to follow if there were not more. And since it is impossible that there will be anything unseemly in that city, it appears to be an inescapable conclusion that the number of angels created was not that perfect number, and there were to have been more human beings in blessedness than there were wicked angels.

Boso: I do not see any reason for denying that.

Anselm: I think that still another argument can be given for that same opinion.

Boso: You ought to give that one, too.

Anselm: We believe that this bodily mass of the universe is to be renewed in a better state,[109] and that this will neither occur until the number of human beings destined for eternal life is completed and that blessed city is perfected, nor will it be deferred beyond its perfection.[110] From this we can conclude that God intended from the beginning to bring both to perfection together. Thus the inferior nature which did not see God, would not be brought to perfection before the superior one which ought to enjoy God. Having been changed for the better, it, in its own way, would share in the joy, as it were, of the perfection of the superior nature. Indeed, every creature would derive delight from so glorious and so wonderful an achievement of its own perfection, each one, in its own way, eternally finding joy in its Creator and itself and one another. By God's ordering, even a creature not having sensation would manifest, in accordance with its nature, what the will does freely in a rational nature. For we are accustomed to share the joy of the exaltation of our ancestors, as when we celebrate the birthdays [111] of the saints with festive exultation, taking delight in their glory. It seems that this opinion is bolstered by the fact that, if Adam had not sinned, God would nevertheless have deferred completing that city, until the number He desired was fulfilled from among human beings, and these human beings themselves would also be—so to say—transmuted into the immortal immortality of their bodies. For in paradise they had immortality of a sort, that is, the power of not dying; but this power was not immortal, because it was able to die, with the result that the human beings themselves would be unable not to die.[112]

If all this is true, that is, if God from the beginning determined to bring to perfection together, that intelligent and blessed city and this earthly and irrational nature, it seems that the following alternatives are possible. It may be that the number of angels before the fall of the wicked ones did not fill up that city, but God was waiting to complete it from among human beings, when He would change the bodily nature of the universe into something better. Or it is possible that, although it was numerically complete, it was not complete in having full confirmation, and its confirmation was to be deferred, even if no one in it should sin, until that renewal of the universe which we are awaiting. Another possibility is that if that confirmation was not to be deferred any longer, the renewal of the earth was to be accelerated, so as to take place together with this confirmation. But that God determined to renew the universe right after it was created, and in the very beginning, before the reason for their creation was evident, to destroy those things which will not exist after that renewal— that does not make sense at all. Hence it follows that the number of the angels was not perfect in such a way that their confirmation was not to be long deferred, since it would be necessary for the renewal of the new universe to have taken place at once—and this is not fitting. On the other hand, that God should will to defer that confirmation until some future renewal of the universe also seems unfitting, especially since He had brought about that confirmation so soon in certain creatures, and since we can assume that He would have confirmed the first human beings at the time of their sin, if they had not sinned, as He did the angels who persevered. For, although they would not yet be advanced to that equality with the angels at which human beings were to arrive, when the number to be taken from them was completed, nevertheless, it seems that if they had triumphed by not sinning when they were tempted, they, with all their posterity, would have been so confirmed in that state of justice in which they were, that they would be unable to sin again—just as, for the reason that they were vanquished and have sinned, they were so weakened that, of themselves, they cannot be without sin. Who, indeed, would dare to say that lack of justice has more power to bind man in slavery when he gives consent to its first suggestion, than justice has to confirm in freedom the person who is faithful to it in the same first temptation? Since the whole of human nature was in our first parents, the whole of it was conquered for sin in them—with the single exception of that Man [113] whom God knew how to exempt from Adam's sin, just as He knew how to fashion Him from the Virgin without the seed of a male. In the same way, the whole of human nature would have triumphed in the same parents, if they had not sinned. We are left to conclude, then, that the heavenly city was not completed by that original number of angels, but was to have been completed from among men. If all this is valid, there will be more human beings chosen for salvation than there are reprobate angels.

Boso: What you are saying seems extremely reasonable to me. But how shall we interpret the statement that God *appointed the bounds of people according to the number of the children of Israel?* [114] Some, reading "angels of God" for "children of Israel," expound it to mean that the number of human beings chosen for eternal life corresponds to the number of good angels. [115]

Anselm: This does not contradict the opinion given before, if it is not certain that just as many angels fell as persevered. For if the angels chosen for eternal life are more numerous than the reprobate, it is both necessary that the human beings chosen for eternal life replace the reprobate, and also possible that they be equal in number to the blessed; and thus there will be more human beings in the state of justice than angels in the state of injustice. But remember on what condition I undertook to respond to your questioning, that is, that if I should say anything which higher authority does not confirm—even though I seem to prove it by reason—it is not to be accepted as settled except that it is my present opinion, until God in some way makes known to me something better. For I am certain that if I say anything that is certainly in opposition to

Holy Scripture, it is false; and if I knew it was opposed to Scripture, I would not want to hold it. But suppose we are dealing with matters on which different opinions can be held without danger, such as the one we are now discussing. If we do not know, for example, whether or not a greater number of human beings is to be chosen for eternal life than angels were lost, and we consider one of the alternatives more probable than the other, I do not think there is any danger for the soul. If, in matters of this kind, we expound the words of God in such a way that they seem to favor different opinions and no texts are discovered anywhere which indisputably determine what should be held, I do not think we should be censured.[116]

Now for the text you cited: *He appointed the bounds of people* or nations *according to the number of the angels of God,* which, in another translation, reads: *according to the number of the children of Israel.* Since both translations either have the same meaning, or have different but compatible meanings, there are various interpretations possible. Both *angels of God* and *children of Israel* could signify good angels alone, or the chosen human beings alone, or both angels and the chosen human beings together, that is, that whole heavenly city. Again, *angels of God* could mean holy angels alone, and *children of Israel,* virtuous human beings alone. Or *children of Israel* could designate angels alone, and *angels of God* could mean virtuous human beings. If only good angels are designated by both phrases, it is the same as if only the expression *the angels of God* were used. If, however, the whole heavenly city is referred to by both phrases, the meaning here is that people, that is, multitudes of the chosen human beings, will be taken up or that there will be peoples in this world until the predetermined but not yet completed number of residents of that city is brought to completion from among human beings.

But right now, I do not see how *children of Israel* can mean angels alone, or angels and holy human beings taken together. It is not strange, however, to call holy human beings *children of Israel,* as well as *children of Abraham.*[117] They can also be correctly called "angels of God" for the reason that they imitate angelic life, and likeness to the angels and equality with the angels are promised to them in heaven;[118] and because all who live in the state of justice are angels of God. That is the reason why they are called "confessors" or "martyrs." For anyone who acknowledges the truth of God or bears witness to it, is His messenger, that is, His angel. And if a sinful man is called a devil, as Judas was, by the Lord,[119] because of a likeness in malice, why should not a good man be called an angel, because of imitation of justice? Hence we can say, I think, that God established *the bounds of people according to the number* of His chosen human beings, because there will be peoples and procreation of human beings in this world until the number of those chosen ones is completed; and when it is completed, generation of human beings which occurs in this life, will cease.

But if by *angels of God* we understand holy angels alone, and by *children of Israel,* virtuous human beings alone, there are two other ways in which we can interpret the text: *God appointed the bounds of people according to the number of the angels of God.*[120] We may interpret it either in the sense that as great a people, that is, as many human beings, as there are holy angels of God, will be elevated; or else in the sense that the peoples will continue to exist until the number of angels of God is to be completed from among human beings. And I see only one possible way of explaining *he appointed the bounds of people according to the number of the children of Israel,*[121] and that is, as I said before, in the sense that the peoples in this world will exist up to the point when the number of saintly human beings is elevated; and we may infer from both translations that as many human beings will be elevated as there are angels who remained steadfast. From this, nevertheless, it will not follow that as many angels fell as persevered, even though the lost angels are to be replaced from among human beings. If anyone says that it does follow, however, he will have to find the flaws in the arguments just proposed,[122] since they seem to show that the angels, before some of them fell, did not constitute that perfect number I spoke of before,[123] and that the number of human beings chosen for future eternal life is greater than the number of angels who sinned.

Boso: I am not sorry that I made you discuss these questions about the angels. It certainly has not been useless. Return, now, to the subject from which we have digressed.

NINETEEN

Man cannot be saved without satisfaction for sin.

Anselm: We agree that God has intended to replace with human beings the angels who fell.[124]

Boso: That is certain.

Anselm: Then the human beings in that heavenly city who will be taken up into it in place of angels ought to be in the same condition as those whom they replace, that is, the same condition in which the good angels are now. Otherwise those who have fallen would not be replaced, and it will follow that God is not able to complete the good that He began, or that He will regret having begun such a blessing. And both of these alternatives are absurd.

Boso: Surely, it is necessary that the human beings be equal to the good angels.

Anselm: Did the good angels ever sin?

Boso: No.

Anselm: Can you imagine that man who once sinned and never made satisfaction to God for sin, but was only pardoned without punishment, would be equal to an angel who never sinned?

Boso: I can imagine and speak those words, but I cannot commit myself to their meaning, any more than I can understand falsity to be truth.

Anselm: Then it is not fitting for God to elevate a sinful human being who has made no satisfaction, to replace the lost angels, since truth does not allow him to be raised to equality with the blessed.

Boso: Reason proves it.

Anselm: With regard to man alone, regardless of his having to be the equal of angels, consider also whether God must elevate him in such a way to any happiness, even such as he had before he sinned.

Boso: Say what *you* think, and I shall consider it to the best of my ability.

Anselm: Let us suppose that some rich man is holding in his hand a precious pearl, totally unspotted by the slightest stain. No one else can take it from his hand without his permission. Suppose he decides to store it in his treasury, where his dearest and most precious possessions are.

Boso: I am imagining this as if it were present before us.

Anselm: What if he himself permits some envious person to knock the same pearl out of his hand into the mud, although he could prevent it, and afterwards, picking it up from the mud, puts it away, soiled and unwashed, in some clean and costly receptacle, to preserve it as it is. Would you think him wise?

Boso: How can I? Would it not be much better for him to hold on to his pearl and preserve it while it is clean, rather than when it is soiled?

Anselm: Would not God be doing something similar, if He, so to speak, held in His hand, in Paradise, the human being who was to be in the company of the angels, free from sin, and then allowed the devil, inflamed with envy, to throw him down in the mire of sin, although man gave his consent (for if God chose to prevent him, the devil could not have tempted man)? Would not God, I say, be doing something similar, if He had brought back at least to Paradise from which he had been cast out, the human being now stained with the filth of sin and uncleansed, that is, without making any satisfaction, and always to remain in that condition?

Boso: I dare not deny the similarity, if God were to do this, and for that reason I do not admit He can do it. For it would seem either that He could not bring about what He had planned, or that He regretted His good intention—and these things cannot happen to God.

Anselm: Hold it as most certain, then, that without satisfaction, that is, without voluntary payment of the debt, God cannot remit sin without punishment, nor can the sinner arrive at happiness, even such as he had before he sinned. For man would not have been rehabilitated in this way, not even to the state he had before his sin.

Boso: I am absolutely unable to contradict your arguments. But how is it that we say to God: *Forgive us our debts,*[125] and that every people prays to the God it believes in, to forgive it its sins? For if we have paid what we owe, why do we pray Him to pardon us? Is God unjust, that He demands, a second time, what has already been paid? But if we have not paid our debt, why do we uselessly beseech Him to do what He cannot do because it is unfitting?

Anselm: One who has not paid the debt is uselessly saying "Pardon!" One who has paid, is praying because this very act of praying is part of the payment. For God owes nothing to anyone, but every creature has a debt to Him; and therefore it is not proper for a human being to act toward God as one equal with another. But on this point it is not necessary to answer you now. For when you come to know why Christ has died, perhaps you will see the answer to this question by yourself.

Boso: For the present, then, I am satisfied with your answer to this question. But that no human being in the state of sin can attain happiness or be released from sin unless he repays what he appropriated to himself by sinning, you have so clearly proved that I could not doubt it if I wanted to.

TWENTY

*Satisfaction must be made in accordance with the measure
of the sin. And man cannot do this by himself.*

Anselm: You do not doubt this, either, I suppose: that satisfaction must be made in accordance with the measure of the sin.

Boso: If it were otherwise, sin would remain to some extent outside the rule of order; and this cannot be, if God leaves no disorder in His kingdom.[126] But we have already established the principle that the slightest incongruity in God is impossible.[127]

Anselm: Tell me, then: what will you pay to God for your sin?

Boso: Repentance, a contrite and humbled heart, fasting, and all sorts of bodily work, mercy in giving and forgiving, and obedience.

Anselm: In all these things, what are you giving to God?

Boso: Do I not honor God, when, because of fear and love of Him, in sorrow of heart I give up temporal joy; when by self-denials and labors I trample underfoot the delights and repose of this life; when, in giving and forgiving, I give liberally of what is mine; when, in obedience, I subject myself to Him?

Anselm: When you render to God what you owe to Him, even without having sinned, you ought not to count it as payment for a debt you owe because of sin. Now all those things you mention, you owe to God. In this mortal life, so great must be your love and so great your desire to arrive at the goal for which you were created (this is the purpose of prayer), and so great your sorrow at not being there yet, and your fear that you may not arrive there, that you ought not to experience any joy except from those things which give you either the help or the hope to arrive at your goal. For you do not deserve to have what you do not love and desire in proportion to its nature, and regarding which you are not in sorrow when you do not yet possess it and you are still running such a great risk of never possessing it. This risk also involves fleeing the repose and earthly pleasures which distract the mind from that genuine repose and delight, except to the extent that you know they foster your intention to persevere. But you must regard your giving as a paying of a debt, just as you recognize that what you are giving you have, not from yourself, but from Him whose servant you are—both you and the one to whom you are giving.[128] Nature also teaches you to do for your fellow-servant, that is, as one human being to another, what you want him to do for you; [129] and it makes clear that whoever is not willing to give what he has, ought not to receive what he does not possess. With regard to forgiveness, I say briefly that vengeance does not at all belong to you, as we said before.[130] The reason is that you do not belong to yourself, nor does he who did you any injury belong to you or to himself, but you are servants of one Lord, created by Him out of nothing; and if you have revenge on your fellow-servant, you are proudly arrogating to yourself a right of judgment over him which belongs exclusively to the Lord and Judge of all. As for obedience, now, what do you give to God that you do not owe Him, to whose command you owe all that you are and have and are able to do?

Boso: I do not dare to say now, that in all these cases I give anything to God which I do not owe Him.

Anselm: What payment, then, will you make to God for your sin?

Boso: If, even when I am not in the state of sin, I owe Him myself and whatever I can do, in order to avoid sinning, I have nothing to offer Him in compensation for sin.

Anselm: What, then, will become of you? How can you be saved?

Boso: If I take your arguments into consideration, I do not see how. But if I have recourse to my faith—I hope that in Christian faith *that worketh by love,*[131] I can be saved. Besides, we read: *If the unjust be converted from his injustice and do justice,*[132] all his injustices are forgotten.

Anselm: This is said only to those who either awaited Christ before He came, or who believe in Him after His coming. But we excluded Christ and the Christian faith as if they never existed, when we proposed to seek by reason alone, whether His coming was necessary for the salvation of men.[133]

Boso: So we did.

Anselm: Let us, then, proceed by reason alone.

Boso: Although you lead me into some tight corners, still I greatly desire you to continue as you began.

TWENTY-ONE

How great a burden sin is.

Anselm: Let us suppose that you are not obliged to give all those things you just claimed you are able to give in compensation for sin, and let us see whether they can suffice for the satisfaction of even one slight sin, such as a single glance opposed to the will of God.

Boso: Except for hearing you question it, I should think that I would wipe out such a sin with a single act of remorse.

Anselm: You have not yet considered what a great burden sin is.

Boso: Show me now.

Anselm: Suppose you recognize that God sees you. Suppose someone should say to you: "Look there!" and God, on the contrary, should say: "I absolutely do not want you to look." Now ask yourself in your own heart what there is among all the things that exist, for which you ought to cast that glance, in opposition to the will of God.

Boso: I find nothing for the sake of which I ought to do this, unless perhaps I were placed in the necessity of having to commit either this sin or a more grievous one.

Anselm: Disregard this necessity, and regarding this sin alone, consider whether you can commit it to save yourself.

Boso: I clearly see that I cannot.

Anselm: Not to delay you too long—what if the whole world and whatever is not God had to perish and be annihilated, unless you did such a slight thing against the will of God?

Boso: When I consider the action itself, I see it is something very slight. But when I give attention to what "against the will of God" means, I understand that it is something very serious and beyond comparison with any loss. Still, we are accustomed, at times, to act against someone's will, without blame, to preserve his interests, and he against whose will we have acted is afterwards pleased.

Anselm: This occurs in the case of a human being who sometimes does not understand what is useful to himself, or who cannot replace what he loses, but God is in need of nothing, and if all things should perish, He could replace them, just as He has created them.

Boso: I must acknowledge that I should do nothing against the will of God, to preserve the whole of creation.

Anselm: What if there were more worlds like this one, full of creatures?

Boso: If the number of them were multiplied indefinitely, and they were spread out before me in a similar way, my answer would be the same.

Anselm: You could not be more right. But consider also what compensation you could make for that sin, if it should happen that you cast that glance, against the will of God.

Boso: I have nothing more to say than I said before.

Anselm: So we sin seriously, whenever we knowingly do anything, however slight, against the will of God, because we are always within His sight and He is always commanding us not to sin.

Boso: As I understand you, we live in a very dangerous condition.

Anselm: It is evident that God demands satisfaction in proportion to the gravity of the sin.[134]

Boso: I cannot deny that.

Anselm: Therefore, you do not make satisfaction if you do not return something greater than that for whose sake you were bound not to commit the sin.

Boso: I see that reason requires that, and yet I see that it is absolutely impossible.

Anselm: And God cannot admit into happiness anyone who is bound in any way by the debt of sin, because it would not be right for Him.

Boso: This thought is a very crushing one.

TWENTY-TWO

What an affront man gave to God, when he let himself be overcome by the devil, and for this he cannot make satisfaction.

Anselm: Listen to still another reason why it is not less difficult for man to be reconciled with God.

Boso: Unless faith gave me comfort, this one alone would drive me to despair.

Anselm: Listen, anyway.

Boso: Go ahead.

Anselm: Man, created in paradise without sin, was placed, as it were, on God's side, between God and the devil, to overcome the devil by not consenting to his temptations to sin. He was intended, in this way, to vindicate and honor God and confound the devil, since man, although the weaker one, would not sin on the earth when tempted by that very devil, who, despite his greater strength, sinned in heaven, although no one tempted him. And although man could have done this easily, and was not compelled by any force, he freely permitted himself to be overcome, by urging alone, in accordance with the will of the devil and against the will and honor of God.

Boso: What is your drift?

Anselm: Judge for yourself if it is not contrary to the honor of God for man to be reconciled to Him while man still bore the shame of this outrage inflicted on God, without first honoring God by overcoming the devil, just as he had dishonored Him by being overcome by the devil. But the victory must be of this sort. Man, while strong and potentially immortal, easily gave in to the devil, so as to sin, for which reason he justly incurred the penalty of having to die. Now, when he is weak and mortal by his own doing, he should overcome the devil by the hardship of death, so as to be without sin entirely. This he can not do, as long as, due to the wound of the first sin, he is conceived and born in sin.[135]

Boso: I repeat that what you say is proven true by reason —and yet that it is impossible.

TWENTY-THREE

What man, when he sinned, took away from God, which he cannot repay.

Anselm: Take one thing more, without which man is not reconciled in justice, and which is equally impossible.

Boso: You have already proposed to us so many obligations we have to fulfill that nothing else you add can make me more fearful.

Anselm: Listen, anyway.

Boso: I am listening.

Anselm: What did man take away from God, when he allowed himself to be overcome by the devil?

Boso: You give the answer, as you have begun to do, because I do not know what he could add to these evils you have indicated.

Anselm: Did he not take from God whatever He had intended to make out of human nature?

Boso: That cannot be denied.

Anselm: Take strict justice into account, and judge, in accordance with that, whether man gives God satisfaction equivalent to his sin, unless, by overcoming the devil, he restores exactly what he took away from God by allowing himself to be conquered by the devil. Thus, just as by the very fact that man was conquered, the devil stole what belonged to God and God lost it, so by the very fact that man triumphs the devil loses what belonged to God and God regains it.

Boso: I cannot think of anything more strict or more just.

Anselm: Do you think supreme Justice can violate this justice?

Boso: I dare not think so.

Anselm: Hence it is absolutely wrong and even impossible for man to receive from God what God intended to give him, if he does not render back to God all that he took from Him; so that as God has lost it through him, so He was to regain it through him. This cannot occur in any other way than that, as through him who was vanquished, the whole human nature was corrupted and, as it were, leavened, by sin—and God takes no one afflicted by sin to complete that heavenly city—so by his triumph, as many men were justified as were required to total that number which man was created to complete. But it is absolutely impossible for sinful man to do this, because a sinner cannot justify a sinner.

Boso: Nothing is more just, yet nothing is more impossible. But out of all this, the mercy of God and the hope of man seem to vanish, so far as the happiness for which man was created is concerned.

TWENTY-FOUR

As long as man does not render to God what he ought, he cannot be happy, and he is not excused by inability.

Anselm: Wait a little longer.

Boso: What more do you have to say?

Anselm: If a man is called unjust for not repaying what he owes to a man, he is much more unjust who does not render to God what he ought.

Boso: If he is able to render it, and does not, he is indeed unjust. But if he is unable to do it, how is he unjust?

Anselm: If the reason for the inability is not something within himself, perhaps he can be to some extent excused. But if the source of his inability is a fault, then, as it does not mitigate his sin, so it does not excuse him from paying his debt. Suppose someone, for example, assigns some task to his servant and directs him not to throw himself into a pit which he points out to him, and from which he simply cannot escape. Suppose that servant, having no regard for the command and the warning of his master, voluntarily throws himself into the pit that has been pointed out to him, so that he cannot perform the task assigned. Do you think this inability can in any way excuse him from not performing the assigned task?

Boso: Not at all. Rather, it would increase his guilt, since he brought that inability on himself. For he sinned in two ways: in not doing what he was commanded to do, and in doing what he was commanded not to do.

Anselm: Thus, man is inexcusable, for he voluntarily incurred that debt which he could not pay, and by his own fault lapsed into the inability, so that he could neither fulfill the obligation he had before sin—that is, to avoid sin—nor pay the debt he owes because he sinned. For his very inability is a fault because he ought not have it; indeed, he was obliged not to have

it. Just as it is a fault, of course, not to have what one should
have, so it is a fault to have what one should not have. Therefore, as it is a fault for man not to have that ability to avoid
sin which he was given, so it is a fault for him to have that
inability either to preserve justice and guard against sin, or to
give due compensation for sin. For he voluntarily did that on
account of which he lost that ability and lapsed into that inability. Not to have an ability one ought to have is the same,
surely, as to have an inability one ought not have. Hence, the
inability to render to God what is His due, which prevents
man from rendering it, does not excuse him if he does not render
it, since the effect of sin does not excuse the sin he commits.

Boso: This is extremely hard to accept, and yet it must be
so.

Anselm: Man, then, is unjust if he does not render to God
what he owes Him.

Boso: That is all too true. For he is at fault for not rendering it and at fault for not being able to render it.

Anselm: No one, however, who is unjust will be admitted
into happiness, since happiness is a state of sufficiency in which
there is nothing lacking,[136] and it is not suitable for anyone, unless his justice is so pure that there is not a speck of injustice
in him.

Boso: I dare not believe otherwise.

Anselm: But if you wish to say: "The merciful God remits
the debt of one who supplicates Him, for the very reason that
he cannot repay it"—well, God cannot be said to remit a debt
except in two senses. Either He remits what a human being
ought voluntarily to return to Him, but cannot, that is, some
compensation for the sin he should not have committed even
to preserve everything which is not God;[137] or else He remits
the punishment which, as I said before,[138] is the deprivation of
happiness, against the person's will. If, however, He remits what
man is obliged to render voluntarily for the reason that he cannot render it, what else would that mean but that God is re-
mitting what He cannot obtain? But to attribute such "mercy"
to God would be to deride Him. And if He remits what He
was to take away from man against his will, on account of man's

inability to repay what he should voluntarily repay, then God is relaxing the penalty and making a man happy on account of his sin, because he would be possessing what he should not possess. For he ought not have that inability and so, as long as he has it without making satisfaction, it is a sin for him. But divine "mercy" of this sort is quite opposed to God's justice which allows nothing but punishment to be the return for sin. Therefore, just as it is impossible for God to contradict Himself, so is it impossible for Him to be merciful in this way.

Boso: I see we are to look for a different kind of divine mercy than this one.

Anselm: Let us suppose it were true that God pardons him who does not pay his debt for the reason that he cannot.

Boso: That is the way I would like it to be.

Anselm: But as long as he will not make restoration, he is either willing or unwilling to make it. Now, if he is willing but unable to make it, he will be in a state of insatiable desire. If, however, he is unwilling, he will be unjust.

Boso: Nothing is clearer than that.

Anselm: Now, if he is in a state of insatiable desire, or if on the other hand, he is unjust, he will not be happy.

Boso: This is also evident.

Anselm: Therefore, so long as he does not make restoration, he cannot be happy.

Boso: If God follows the rule of justice, there is no way for miserable little man [139] to escape, and the mercy of God seems to come to an end.

Anselm: You have asked for a reason; accept the reason. I do not deny that God is merciful, since He saves *men and beasts* as He has *multiplied* His mercy.[140] But we are speaking of that ultimate mercy by which He makes man happy after this life. That this happiness must not be granted to anyone except to one whose sins are totally forgiven, and that this forgiveness must not be granted except after payment of the debt which is due for sin in proportion to the magnitude of the sin, I think I have adequately shown by the arguments given before.[141] If you think any objection can be brought against these arguments, you ought to say so.

Boso: Indeed, I do not see that any of your arguments can be weakened in the least degree.

Anselm: Neither do I, if they are carefully examined. Nevertheless, if only one of all that I have proposed is confirmed as indisputably true, that must satisfy us. For whether truth is proven indisputably by one or many arguments, it is equally well defended against every doubt.

Boso: Quite so.

TWENTY-FIVE

It is necessarily through Christ that man is saved.

Boso: How, then, will man be saved, if he does not pay what he owes, and if he should not be saved without paying? Moreover, how shall we dare to assert that God, who is rich in mercy [142] beyond human understanding, is not able to exercise this mercy?

Anselm: You ought, at this point, to demand of those in whose place you are speaking, who believe Christ is not necessary for that salvation of man, that they tell you how man can be saved without Christ. But if they absolutely cannot do this, let them stop deriding us and let them approach and join us who do not doubt that man can be saved by Christ, or else let them despair of man's being saved at all. But if they dread this alternative, let them believe in Christ as we do, that they may be saved. [143]

Boso: I shall ask you, as I did in the beginning, to show me in what way man is saved through Christ.

Anselm: Is there not adequate proof that man can be saved through Christ, since even unbelievers do not deny that man can in some way attain happiness, and it has been sufficiently shown that if we suppose Christ does not exist, it is absolutely impossible to find a means of human salvation? For man can be saved either through Christ or by someone else or not at all. Consequently, if it is false that salvation is impossible, or that it can be due to another, it is necessary that it be accomplished through Christ.

Boso: If someone, seeing the reason why man cannot be saved in another way, yet not understanding just how we can be saved through Christ, wants to assert that human salvation is impossible, either through Christ or in any way at all—what answer shall we give him?

Anselm: What answer is to be given to him who maintains that something which has to be is impossible, for the simple reason that he does not know how it occurs?

Boso: That he is out of his mind.[144]

Anselm: Therefore, what he says is to be met with disdain.

Boso: Yes. But we ought to show him precisely how what he thinks impossible really exists.

Anselm: Do you not understand from what we said before,[145] that it is necessary that some human beings attain to happiness? For if it is unfitting for God to bring a human being with some stain upon him to that for which He created him free from stain, lest He seem either to regret having undertaken something good or to be unable to fulfill His plan, much more is it impossible, because of the same unsuitableness, that no man at all attain to the goal for which he was created.[146] Therefore, the satisfaction for sin such as we showed before [147] to be necessary, is either to be found outside the Christian faith—which cannot be proved by any argument—or we are to believe without the slightest doubt that it exists within that faith. For what is proved to be true on the basis of a necessary reason cannot at all be called into doubt, even if we do not see the reason why it is so.[148]

Boso: You are right.

Anselm: Then what more do you ask for?

Boso: I have come to you, not to have you remove doubts about the faith from me, but to have you show me the reason for my certitude.[149] Hence, now that you have led me along the way of reason to the point of seeing that a human sinner owes to God, for sin, a debt which he cannot repay, and cannot

be saved without repaying, I would like you to lead me further.
Help me to understand by rational necessity how all those things
which the Catholic faith requires us to believe regarding Christ,
if we wish to be saved, must be true,[150] and what value they
have for the salvation of man,[151] and how it is that God saves
man by mercy when He does not forgive his sin unless man
pays back what he owes on account of it.[152] And to make your
arguments more certain, begin from far enough back to establish them upon a firm foundation.

Anselm: May God help me now, since you are not sparing
me at all, and are not taking into consideration the weakness of
my knowledge, in imposing such a great task upon me. I shall
make the effort, however, now that I have started, trusting not
in myself but in God, and by His help I shall do what I can.
But for fear of causing repugnance in anyone who wants to
read this, by too long and uninterrupted a discourse, let us separate what remains to be said from what has already been said,
by a new introduction.

BOOK TWO

ONE

Man was created in the state of justice, that he might be happy.

Anselm: We should not doubt that God created rational nature in the state of justice so that it might be happy by enjoying Him. For it is rational precisely in order to distinguish between right and wrong, between good and evil, and between the greater good and the lesser good. Otherwise it would have been made rational without a purpose. There is no doubt, then, that it was made rational for this reason. By a similar argument we prove that it received the power of discernment that it might hate and avoid evil, and love and choose good, and love and choose the greater good above other things. For otherwise God would have given it that power of discernment without any purpose, because it would exercise discrimination fruitlessly if it did not love and avoid in accordance with that discrimination. But it is not fitting that God give so great a power uselessly. So it is certain that rational nature was created for the purpose of loving and choosing the supreme good above all things, not as a means toward something else but as a goal in itself. For if it loved a good as a means toward something else, it would really be loving not that good but the other thing.[1] Now, it cannot love the supreme good unless it is in the state of justice. In order, therefore, that it be not rational without purpose, it was created simultaneously rational and just, for this purpose. Now, if it was created in the state of justice, to choose and love the supreme good, it either was or

119

was not created such for the purpose of eventually obtaining what it loved and chose. If, however, it was not created in the state of justice for the purpose of attaining the object of its love and choice, it was in vain that it was created to love and desire it in such a way, and there will be no reason why it should ever attain its object. Therefore, as long as it will exercise justice by loving and choosing the supreme good for which it was created, it will be miserable because it will be in need against its will, not having what it desires. But that is all too absurd.[2] Hence rational nature was created in the state of justice, in order to be happy by enjoying the supreme good, that is, God. Man, therefore, who has a rational nature, was created in the state of justice precisely for the purpose of being happy in the enjoyment of God.[3]

TWO

Man would not have died if he had not sinned.

Anselm: Now, it is easy to prove that man was created in such a state that he would, of necessity, not be subject to death. The reason is that, as we already said,[4] it is contrary to the wisdom and justice of God to compel him to suffer death without having committed a fault, whom He created in a state of justice, for the attainment of eternal happiness. It follows, therefore, that if man had never sinned, he would never have died.

THREE

Man will arise with the body in which he lives in this life.

Anselm: From this, we clearly prove the eventual future resurrection of the dead. Surely, if man is to be perfectly restored, he must be restored to the same state he was to have had if he had not sinned.[5]

Boso: It cannot be otherwise.

Anselm: Therefore, just as, if man had not sinned, he was to be transformed into a state of incorruptibility with the same body that he bore,[6] so it is necessary that when he will be restored, he is to be restored with his own body in which he lives in this life.

Boso: What answer shall we give, if anyone should say that this must occur with regard to those in whom the human race will be restored, but is not necessary with regard to the reprobate?

Anselm: We can conceive nothing more just and fitting than that, as man if he had persevered in justice, would be eternally happy in his entire being—that is, in soul and body—so also, if he perseveres in lack of justice, his whole person, likewise, is to be eternally miserable.

Boso: Your brief answers have satisfied me on these questions.

FOUR

God will complete what He began with regard to human nature.

Anselm: From all this it is easy to draw a conclusion. Either God will bring to completion what He began in regard to human nature, or it was pointless for Him to create such a sublime nature for so great a good. But if God, so far as we know, has created nothing more precious than a rational nature to find enjoyment in Himself, it would be extremely adverse to Him to allow any rational nature to perish entirely.[7]

Boso: A rational mind can be of no other opinion.

Anselm: Therefore it is necessary that He bring to perfection what He began concerning human nature.[8] This, however, cannot occur, as we said,[9] except through a complete satisfaction for sin, which no sinner can accomplish.[10]

Boso: I now understand that it is necessary for God to accomplish what He has begun, so as not to appear to fail in His undertakings, for this would not be fitting.[11]

FIVE

Although this must take place, nevertheless God will not bring it about under the necessity of compulsion. There is a necessity that eliminates gratitude or diminishes it, and there is a necessity which increases it.

Boso: But if this is so, it seems that God is compelled, so to say, to bring about the salvation of the human race by the necessity of avoiding what is unsuitable. How, then, shall we be able to deny that He does this more for His own sake than for ours? Or, if this is so, what gratitude do we owe Him for what He does for His own sake? How shall we ever ascribe our salvation to His favor if He saves us out of necessity?

Anselm: There is a necessity which eliminates or diminishes gratitude to a benefactor, and there is a necessity which entails a greater gratitude for the benefit. When anyone does a favor unwillingly, because he is subject to necessity, he deserves little or no gratitude. But when he voluntarily subjects himself to the necessity of doing good and does not merely endure it unwillingly, then, surely, he deserves greater gratitude for his favor. For this is not to be called necessity, but graciousness because, without being compelled by anyone, he accepts or observes this necessity, but he does it spontaneously. Suppose, for example, you freely promise today to give something tomorrow, and tomorrow you give that thing with the same willingness. Then, although it is necessary for you, if you are able, to fulfill that promise on the following day, or else be guilty of a lie, nevertheless he to whom you make the gift is no less indebted to you for the favor imparted, than if you had not promised it, since you were not reluctant to make yourself a debtor to him before the time of presenting the gift. The case is similar when someone freely obliges himself by vow to enter religious life.[12] After making the vow, of course, he is under obligation to keep it, so as not to incur condemnation as an apostate, and he can be compelled to keep it if he does not want to do so. Although all this is true, nevertheless, if he willingly keeps his vow, he is not less but more pleasing to God than if he had not made the vow, since he has renounced, for love of God, not only an ordinary life, but even his freedom to lead such a life, and he should be said to live a holy life not by necessity but with the same freedom by which he made the vow.

Much more, then, if God performs for man the good He began, even though it is not fitting for Him to discontinue the good He has commenced, we must ascribe the whole work to His graciousness, because He began this for our sakes, not for His own, since He is not in need of anything. He was not unaware, surely, of what the future conduct of man was to be, when He made him, and yet in creating man out of His own goodness, He freely obligated Himself, as it were, to complete the good work that had been begun. Lastly, God does nothing by necessity, because absolutely nothing compels Him to do anything or prevents Him from doing anything. And when we say that God does something as if out of the necessity of avoiding dishonor, which, surely, He has no reason to fear, it is rather to be understood that He does this by the necessity of preserving His honor. This sort of necessity is nothing but the unchangeability of His honor, and this He has of Himself and not from another, so it is improperly called necessity. Let us say, nevertheless, that it is necessary for the goodness of God, on account of His own unchangeableness, to complete in man what He began, although the whole of the good work He performs is a gratuitous favor.

Boso: I agree.

SIX

Only a God-Man can make the satisfaction by which man is saved.

Anselm: This, however, cannot be done unless there is some-one to render to God, for the sin of man, something greater than everything that exists outside of God.

Boso: So it is agreed.[13]

Anselm: For anyone to be able to give something of his own to God which surpasses everything that is less than God, it is also necessary for him to be greater than everything that is not God.

Boso: I cannot deny that.

Anselm: But there is nothing that surpasses everything that is not God but God Himself.

Boso: That is true.

Anselm: Therefore no one but God can make this satisfaction.

Boso: That follows.

Anselm: But no one ought to make it but man. Otherwise it would not be man making the satisfaction.

Boso: Nothing would seem more just.

Anselm: If, then, as we agree,[14] it is necessary that that heavenly city be completed from among men, and this cannot occur unless the satisfaction we have spoken of before is made, and if no one but God can make that satisfaction and no one but man is obliged to make it, then it is necessary that a God-Man make it.

Boso: *Blessed be God!*[15] Now we have discovered an im-portant conclusion about the subject of our inquiry. Go on, then, as you have begun. I hope God will help us.

SEVEN

It is necessary that the same person be perfect God and perfect man.

Anselm: We must inquire now, how there can be a God-Man. For divine nature and human nature cannot be changed into each other, so that the divine nature would become human or the human divine. Neither can they be so mingled that the two would constitute some third sort of nature which is neither entirely divine nor entirely human. In brief, if it were possible that one were changed into the other, it would be only God and not man, or only man and not God. Or if they were mingled in such a way that some sort of third nature would arise out of the two corrupted ones in the way that, of two individual animals, a male and a female of different species, there is born a third individual which does not preserve the entire nature of its father nor the entire nature of its mother, but has a third nature composed of both—that third thing would be neither man nor God. Therefore, the Man-God we are looking for cannot arise out of divine and human nature either by change of one into the other, or by a corruptive mingling of both into a third, because these things are impossible; or if they are possible, they are totally unable to explain our problem.[16]

Now, if we say these two complete natures are joined in some way or other, yet in such a way that the human nature is one being and the divine nature is another, and it is not the same person who is both God and man, it is impossible for the two natures to accomplish what must be accomplished. God, surely, will not accomplish it because it is not His obligation; and man will not accomplish it because he has not the ability. In order that a God-Man accomplish it, therefore, it is necessary

that one and the same person be perfect God and perfect man
to make this satisfaction. For no one can make the satisfaction
unless he is truly God, and no one has the obligation unless he
is truly man. While therefore, it is necessary to find a God-Man,
with the integrity of both natures preserved, it is no less necessary that these two complete natures be united in one person
—just as the body and rational soul are united in one man [17]—
because otherwise it is impossible for the same person to be
perfect God and perfect man.

Boso: Everything you are saying is perfectly satisfactory to
me.[18]

EIGHT

*God ought to assume human nature from the race of
Adam, and from a virgin.*[19]

Anselm: It remains, now, to inquire from what source and
in what manner God will assume human nature. For either He
will assume it from Adam, or He will create a new man, as He
made Adam, without fashioning him from any other man.[20]
But if He creates a new man who is not of the race of Adam,
this man will not belong to the human race which is descended
from Adam. Hence he will not be obliged to make satisfaction
for it, because he will not be its offspring. For as it is right
that man make satisfaction for the fault of man, so it is necessary that the one who makes satisfaction be the one who committed the fault, or a member of the same race. Otherwise,
neither Adam nor his race will be making satisfaction for themselves. Therefore, as sin was transmitted to all men from Adam
and Eve, so no one but themselves or someone descended from
them is obliged to make satisfaction for human sin. Hence, since
they themselves are unable to make it, the one who will make
it must be descended from them.

That is not all. As Adam and his whole race would have stood firm by themselves, without the support of any other creature, if he had not sinned, so, if that race rises again after its fall, it is proper that it rise and be lifted up by itself. For whoever the person is who restores it to its own state, it will surely stand in dependence on him through whom it will recover its state. Besides, when God, in the beginning, created human nature in the person of Adam alone, and did not choose to create even the woman—so that human beings might be multiplied from both sexes—except from Adam, He showed clearly that whatever He intended to accomplish regarding human nature, He desired to bring forth from Adam alone. Therefore, if the race of Adam is raised up through some human person who is not of the same race, it will not be restored to that dignity which it was to have if Adam had not sinned. In that case, it would not be fully restored; and God's design will appear to fail. And these two things are unfitting. So the man through whom the race of Adam is to be restored must be taken from the descendants of Adam.[21]

Boso: If we follow reason, as we decided, the necessity is inevitable.

Anselm: Let us now inquire whether God should assume a human nature from a father and mother, like other human beings, or from a man without a woman, or from a woman without a man. For in whichever of these three ways it may be assumed, it will be descended from Adam and Eve, from whom all human beings of both sexes originate; and no one of these three ways is easier for God than the others, so that He would have to choose one way rather than the others.

Boso: You are proceeding methodically.

Anselm: Now, it does not require great effort to show that it is more beautiful and more distinguished for that man to be brought forth from a man alone or a woman alone, than from a union of the two, like all other children of men.

Boso: Clear enough.

Anselm: Hence he must originate either from a man alone or a woman alone.

Boso: No other origin is possible.

Anselm: God can make a human being in four ways. They
are: from a man and woman, and that is the usual way; or
neither from a man nor a woman, as He created Adam; or from
a man without a woman, as He fashioned Eve; or from a woman
without a man, a way He had not yet used. To show, then, that
even this way was within His power, and that it was reserved
for this very purpose, nothing was more fitting than that He
assume that human nature which is the subject of our inquiry,
from a woman without a man. Whether it was more worthy
that it come from a virgin or a non-virgin, however, there is
no need to discuss; but without any doubt we must assert that
the God-Man ought to be born of a virgin.[22]

Boso: I heartily approve what you are saying.

Anselm: Is what we have said solid, or is it something
empty like a cloud, as you said the unbelievers object to us.[23]

Boso: There is nothing more solid.

Anselm: Exercise your pictorial art, then, not on an empty
fiction, but upon a solid truth, and say that it is extremely fitting that, as the sin of man and the cause of our condemnation
took their origin from a woman,[24] so the cure for sin and the
cause of our salvation must be born of a woman. And so that
women may not despair of attaining to the lot of the blessed,
because such great evil has issued from a woman, it was fitting
that such a great good should issue from a woman, to revitalize
their hope. Add this to your painting: If it was a virgin who
was the cause of all evil to the human race, it is far more fitting
that it be a virgin who will be the cause of all good. Depict
this also: If the woman whom God made from a man without
a woman was made from a virgin, it is also extremely fitting
that the man who will originate from a woman without a man
be born of a virgin. But for the present let these examples suffice of the pictures that can be depicted on the fact that the
God-Man must be born of a virgin woman.[25]

Boso: These pictures are extremely beautiful and reasonable.

NINE

It is necessary that the Word alone unite with man in one person.

Anselm: Now, since in God there are three Persons, we ought also to inquire in which person God assumed human nature. For more than one Person cannot assume one and the same human nature in the unity of a Person. So it is necessary that this take place in only one Person. But I have spoken of this unity of Person of God and man, and what Person of God it was specially fitting for this to occur in, in a letter *On The Incarnation Of The Word* addressed to the lord Pope Urban, and I think this suffices for our present investigation.

Boso: Anyway, touch briefly here on the question why the Person of the Son, rather than that of the Father or the Holy Spirit ought to become incarnate.

Anselm: If any other Person were to become incarnate, there will be two Sons in the Trinity, namely: the Son of God who is Son even before the Incarnation, and the One who through incarnation will be the Son of the Virgin, and there will be among the Persons, who must always be equal, an inequality in accordance with the dignity of their births. Surely, the One born of God will have a more noble birth than the One born of the Virgin. Likewise, if the Father were to be incarnate, there would be two grandsons in the Trinity, because the Father, by assuming human nature, would be the grandson of the parents of the Virgin, and the Word, although He has nothing human in Him, would nevertheless be the grandson of the Virgin, because He would be the Son of her Son. All these things are incongruous, and they are excluded if it is the Word who becomes incarnate. There is still another reason why it is more fitting for the Son to become incarnate than the other Persons: it sounds more fitting for the Son to pray in petition to the Father than for one of the other Persons to pray to either of the remaining two.[26] Besides, man, for whom He was to plead, and the devil whom He was to conquer, had both, by their own will, dared to claim an unwarranted likeness to God. Hence they had sinned more specially against the Person of the Son who, according to our faith, is the true likeness of the Father.[27] It is more fitting, then, to attribute the punishment or the pardon of the crime to the Person to whom the insult was more specially directed. Therefore, since reason has inevitably led us to the conclusion that it was necessary for divine nature and human nature to be united in one Person, that this could not occur in more than one Divine Person, and that it is evident it should occur more fittingly in the Person of the Word than in the others, it is necessary that God the Word and human nature be united in one Person.[28]

Boso: The route along which you are leading me is so fortified by reason on both sides that I cannot see any possibility of swerving from it either to the right or the left.

Anselm: It is not I who am leading you; rather, He of whom we are speaking, without whom we can do nothing, is leading us, so long as we stay on the road of truth.

TEN

This man is not obliged to die. In what sense He can and in what sense He cannot, sin. Why He, or an angel, should receive praise for being just, although neither can sin.

Anselm: We must now inquire whether that man is to die by reason of an obligation, as all other men die because of an obligation. If Adam was not to die if he had not sinned,[29] much more ought He not to suffer death, in whom there could be no sin, because He is God.

Boso: I would like you to linger over this awhile. For whether we say He can or cannot sin, in either case no slight problem arises for me. If we say He cannot sin, that must seem difficult to believe. To speak for a little while not of someone who never existed, as we have done up to now, but of Him whom we know and whose deeds we know—who will deny that He could do many things which we call sins? For example—not to mention other things—how shall we say He could not tell a lie, which is always a sin? When, for instance, He said to the Jews, regarding the Father: *If I shall say that I know Him not, I shall be like to you, a liar,*[30] and in that sentence He speaks the clause "I know Him not," who will say He could not utter those four words, without the others, so as to say merely: "I know Him not"? But if He did this, as He Himself says, He would be a liar, which is the same as being a sinner. So because He could say this, He could sin.

Anselm: He could say this, and yet He could not sin.

Boso: Explain that.

Anselm: All power is subordinated to the will. When I say, for instance, that I am able to speak or walk, "if I will" is understood. For if the will is not implied, there is not power but necessity. When I say that I can be dragged off or defeated against my will, surely, what is indicated is not my power, but a necessity for me, and the power of someone else. Indeed, "I can be dragged off or defeated" means nothing other than "someone else is able to drag or defeat me." We can say of Christ, therefore, that He could tell a lie, provided "if He willed" is understood. And since He could not tell a lie without willing it, and He could not will to lie, it is not too much to say that He was unable to lie. In this way, then, He could, and yet could not, tell a lie.[31]

Boso: Let us now go back to making inquiry about Him as if He did not yet exist, as we began to do. I say, then: if He cannot sin because, as you say, He could not will anything sinful, then He will preserve justice out of necessity. Hence He will not be in a state of justice by freedom of choice. What credit will be due to Him, then, for His virtuousness? We are accustomed to say that God made angelic and human nature able to sin, precisely for this purpose that, although they could abandon justice and yet preserved it by freedom of choice, they deserve credit and praise which would not be due to them if they were in the state of justice by necessity.

Anselm: Are not the angels who cannot sin now, worthy of praise?

Boso: They certainly are, because they deserved their present inability to sin by having been unwilling to sin when they were able.

Anselm: What do you say about God, who is unable to sin without having merited this by not exercising the power of sinning? Is He not worthly of praise for His holiness?

Boso: I wish you would give the answer to this one for me. For if I say He is not to be praised, I know I shall be lying. But if I say He is to be praised, I am afraid of weakening the argument I gave regarding the angels.

Anselm: The angels are to be praised for their justice not for the reason that they could have sinned, but for the reason that because of having been able to sin, they themselves are, in a certain way, the cause of their being unable to sin.[32] In this they are somewhat like to God, who is Himself the reason for any perfection He possesses. A person is said to give something, in fact, if he does not deprive someone of it when he is able to; and he is said to make something exist, when he could make something cease to exist, but does not do so. In that way, then, since an angel could have divested himself of his state of justice and did not do so, and could have made himself wicked and did not so do, it is correct to assert that he gave himself justice and that he made himself virtuous. In this way, therefore, he is the source of his own justice because a creature cannot be the source of it in any other way; and for this reason he is to be praised for his justice. Moreover, he is just, not by necessity but by exercise of freedom, because it is not exact to speak of necessity where there is neither compulsion nor restriction. Therefore, since God is Himself completely the source of whatever He possesses, He is above all to be praised for the perfections He has and preserves, not by any necessity but, as I said before,[33] by His own eternal unchangeableness. Hence that man who will be at the same time God, since He Himself will be the source of all the good He will possess, will be of himself in the state of justice not by necessity but by freedom, and for that reason will deserve to be praised. For although His human nature receives from the divine nature what it will possess, it will be one and the same subject who will possess it of Himself, since the two natures will be in one Person.

Boso: You have satisfied me with this explanation, and I clearly see that He will not be able to sin, and yet will be worthy of praise for His justice. But now I think we ought to raise the question why God, since He can make such a man, has not created angels and the first two human beings in such a state that, like Him, they would not be able to sin and yet would be worthy of praise for their justice.

Anselm: Do you realize what you are saying?

Boso: I think I do, and for that reason I am asking why He did not create them in that state.

Anselm: Because it was neither fitting nor possible that any one of them be the very same as God, which is what we say this man is. And if you want to know why He did not do this for as many creatures as there are Divine Persons, or at least for one creature, my answer is that reason did not at all require this to be done at that time, but was entirely opposed to it, because God does nothing without a reason.

Boso: I am ashamed that I raised that question. Let me know what you were going to say.

Anselm: Let us say, then, that He will not be obliged to die, since He will not be a sinner.

Boso: I must concede this.

ELEVEN

*He may die of His own power. Mortality is not a property
of the pure nature of man.*

Anselm: Right now, it remains for us to investigate whether
He can die in His human nature; for from the standpoint of
His divine nature, He will always be incorruptible.

Boso: Why should we have any doubt about this, since He
is to be a real human being, and every human being is naturally
mortal?

Anselm: It is my opinion that mortality is a property not
of pure human nature, but of corrupted human nature.[34] In
fact, if man had never sinned, and his immortality had remained permanently confirmed, he would, all the same, have
been no less a genuine human being, and when mortals rise
to incorruptibility [35] they will be no less truly human. For if
mortality pertained to the essence of human nature, there could
never be a human being who was immortal.[36] Neither corrupti-
bility nor incorruptibility pertains to the integrity of human
nature, since neither constitutes man and neither one is incompatible with him, but one contributes to his misery and one to
his happiness. Precisely because there is no human being who
is not to die, however, philosophers include "mortal" in their
definition of man, because they did not believe that the whole
man ever could have been or ever can be immortal.[37] Hence,
the fact that He is truly human is not enough to prove that
that man must be mortal.

Boso: Look, then, for another argument to prove He is able
to die; because I do not know of any, if you do not.

Anselm: There is no doubt that as He will be God He will
likewise be almighty.

Boso: That is true.

Anselm: If He wills it, then, He will be able to lay down His life and take it up again.[38]

Boso: If He cannot do this, it seems He is not almighty.

Anselm: He will be able, therefore, never to die if He wills that, and He will be able to die and rise again. But whether He lays down His life without any other person intervening, or whether another person makes Him lay it down, while He Himself permits that influence, makes no difference so far as His power is concerned.

Boso: There is no doubt about that.

Anselm: If, therefore, He should will to permit it, He could be slain; and if He did not will it, He could not be slain.

Boso: Reason leads us straight to that conclusion.

Anselm: Reason also has shown us that He must have something greater than anything inferior to God, which He gives to God voluntarily, and not as something He owes.[39]

Boso: That is right.

Anselm: But we cannot discover such a thing either below Him or outside Him.

Boso: That is so.

Anselm: It must be found within Himself, then.

Boso: That follows.

Anselm: Therefore He will give either Himself or something belonging to Himself.

Boso: I cannot think of any other alternative.

Anselm: Let us inquire, now, what sort of gift this will have to be. For He will not be able to give to God Himself or something belonging to Himself, to become God's possession, as if God did not possess Him, because every creature belongs to God.

Boso: This is so.

Anselm: This "giving," then, must be understood in the sense that in some way this man will offer Himself or something belonging to Himself, to the honor of God, without being in debt to God.

Boso: That follows from what we said before.[40]

Anselm: If we say that He will give Himself to obey God in such a way that He will submit to God's will by constantly preserving justice, this will not be giving what God does not exact of Him out of indebtedness. For every rational creature owes this obedience to God.

Boso: This cannot be denied.

Anselm: It must, therefore, be in some other way that He gives to God either Himself or something belonging to Himself.

Boso: Reason forces us to admit this.

Anselm: Let us see whether this way consists of giving His life, or laying down His life, or delivering Himself up to death for the honor of God. God will not require this of Him as an obligation, for, as we have said,[41] He will not be obliged to die, because there will be no sin in Him.

Boso: I cannot disagree.

Anselm: Let us consider, further, whether this conforms to reason.

Boso: You go on talking and I shall be listening gladly.

Anselm: If man sinned through pleasure, would it not be fitting for him to make satisfaction through hardship? And if the devil has overpowered him into dishonoring God by sinning, so easily that his victory could not be easier, is it not right that man, in making satisfaction for sin, should have such great difficulty in overcoming the devil, for the honor of God, that the difficulty could not be greater? Is it not fair that he who has so alienated himself from God by sinning, that he could not alienate himself any further, should, by making satisfaction, give himself to God in such a way that he cannot give himself any more completely?[42]

Boso: Nothing is more reasonable.

Anselm: But there is nothing more bitter or more difficult for man to suffer for the honor of God voluntarily and without obligation, than death, and man absolutely cannot give himself more fully to God than when he commits himself to death for God's honor.

Boso: All this is true.

Anselm: He who wants to make satisfaction for the sin of man, therefore, must be such as to be able to die if he wills.

Boso: I see plainly that that man whom we are looking for ought to be such that he would not die out of necessity, because

He will be almighty, nor out of obligation, because He will never be a sinner, but also that He be able to die by free choice, because this ability will be necessary.

Anselm: There are many other reasons why it is extremely fitting for Him to be like human beings and to dwell among them, yet to be *without sin*,[43] but it is easier and clearer to see those reasons directly in His life and actions than to be able to prove them by reason alone, prior to experience. For who will explain with what necessity, with what wisdom, it has been brought about that He who was to redeem men and by His teaching to bring them back from the way of death and perdition to the way of life and eternal happiness, should associate with men,[44] and in this association, should present Himself as a model, while He taught them, by word, how they ought to live? How, though, would He present Himself to those who are weak and mortal, as a pattern of not abandoning justice on account of injuries or insults or sufferings or death, if they did not know that He Himself experienced all these things?

TWELVE

Although He shares our adversities, still He is not unhappy.

Boso: All these arguments prove plainly that He ought to be mortal and to share our adversities. But all these adversities are to us sources of unhappiness. Will He, then, be unhappy?

Anselm: Not at all. For as an advantage which someone possesses against His will does not constitute happiness, so it is not a source of unhappiness voluntarily to bear some adversity, with some knowledge of purpose and without any compulsion.

Boso: I must agree.

THIRTEEN

He does not contract ignorance along with our other infirmities.

Boso: But tell me whether, in this likeness which He must bear to men, He will also have ignorance, along with our other infirmities.

Anselm: Why do you doubt that God knows everything?

Boso: Because, although this Person is to be immortal by His divine nature, He will nevertheless be mortal by His human nature. Why, then, can He not be truly subject to ignorance, just as He will be truly subject to death?

Anselm: That assumption of human nature into the unity of a Divine Person cannot be effected by supreme wisdom except in the way of wisdom. Therefore, He will not assume in human nature what is not at all a help, but very much a hindrance, to the task which that man is to accomplish. Ignorance, surely, would be of no utility to Him at all, but would be harmful in many respects. How will He achieve so many and such great deeds as He is to accomplish, without immense wisdom? Or how will men have faith in Him, if they know He is ignorant? If, on the other hand, they do not know it, of what use will this ignorance be to Him? Furthermore, if nothing is loved but what is known, then, just as there will be nothing good which He will not love, so there will be nothing good which He will not know. But no one knows the good perfectly unless he knows how to distinguish it from evil. No one, in turn, knows how to make this distinction if he is ignorant of evil. Hence, the one of whom we are speaking will not be ignorant of any evil, just as he will know every good thing perfectly. Thus He will have all knowledge, even though He does not show it publicly in His dealings with men.[45]

Boso: What you say seems to apply to Him in His adult age, but in infancy there would be no need, and thus no suitability, for His possession of wisdom, since this would not be an apt period for its manifestation.

Anselm: Did I not say that that incarnation will take place in a wise manner? Surely, God will assume mortality in conformity with wisdom, to use it in conformity with wisdom, since He will employ it in a very useful way. But it could not be in conformity with wisdom to assume ignorance, because that is never useful but always harmful, except, perhaps, when it prevents a perverse will from doing evil—and there will never be any perversity in Him. For although on occasion, it may not produce any further harm, ignorance is still harmful by depriving man of the benefit of knowledge. And to dispose of your question briefly, from the instant this man begins to exist, He will always be replete with Divinity, as constituting His very self. Hence He will never be without Divine power and might and wisdom.

Boso: Although I would not doubt that this was always true of Christ, still I raised this question precisely to hear the reason for this, too. For we often have certainty about something, and yet are not able to prove it by reason.

FOURTEEN

How His death prevails over all sins, however numerous and great.

Boso: Now I ask you to show me how His death prevails over all sins, however numerous and great. You showed that a single sin which we consider very slight is so infinite that if the number of worlds were stretched out indefinitely, and each of them were as full of creatures as this one is, and if they could not be preserved from being totally annihilated unless someone took one glance against the will of God, that should not be done.[46]

Anselm: If that man were present, and you knew who He was, and someone said to you: "Unless you kill this man, this whole world and everything other than God will perish," would you do that to preserve every other creature?

Boso: I would not do it, even if an indefinite number of worlds were stretched out before me.

Anselm: What if someone were to say to you again: "Either you will slay Him, or all the sins of the world will come upon you?"

Boso: I would answer that I would rather bear the blame of all other sins, not only the past and future ones of this world, but also all the additional ones that can be imagined, than commit that single sin. And I think I ought to give this answer not only with regard to slaying that person, but also with regard to any slight harm that might befall Him.

Anselm: You are right in thinking so. But tell me why you judge in your heart that the one sin of harming this man is more horrible than all others imaginable, since each and every sin committed is committed against Him.

Boso: Because a sin which is committed against His person is incomparably more serious than all imaginable ones which are not directed against His person.

Anselm: What will you say to the objection that frequently someone is willing to suffer injuries in his own person, to avoid suffering greater ones in what belongs to him?

Boso: That God does not need to suffer this latter injury, since all things are subject to His power—which is the answer you gave before, to some one of my questions.[47]

Anselm: Good answer! We see, then, that no sins, however grievous or however numerous, that are not directed against the Person of God can be compared to a violation of the bodily life of this man.

Boso: That is perfectly evident.

Anselm: How great, do you think, is the goodness of that person, whose murder would be so evil?

Boso: If the measure of goodness of every good thing is

the evil of its destruction, this man represents a good incomparably greater than the evil of all sins which His murder immeasurably surpasses.

Anselm: You are right. Take into consideration also, that sins are to be detested exactly in proportion to their malice, and that this life is deserving of love exactly to the extent that it is good. It follows from this that this life is more worthy of love than sins are deserving of hate.

Boso: I cannot but agree.

Anselm: Do you think that such a great good, so worthy of love, can suffice to make recompense for what is owed for the sins of the whole world?

Boso: Indeed, it can do infinitely more than suffice.

Anselm: You see, therefore, how this life overcomes all sins, if it is given for their remission.

Boso: Evidently.

Anselm: If, then, to give one's life is to accept death, then just as the giving of this life outweighs all the sins of men, so also does the acceptance of death.

Boso: That is certainly true with regard to all the sins that do not affect the Person of God.

FIFTEEN

How the same death blots out even the sins of those who caused His death.

Boso: But now I see another problem to solve. If the evil of putting Him to death is proportioned to the goodness of His life, how can His death overcome and blot out the sins of those who killed Him? Or if it blots out the sin of any one of them, how can it undo any sin of other human beings, also? For we believe that many of these, too, have been saved, and that countless others are saved now.

Anselm: The Apostle solved this problem when he said that *if they had known it, they would never have crucified the Lord of glory.*[48] For a sin knowingly committed and something resulting from ignorance differ so much from each other, that an evil which they could never have committed because of its enormity, if they recognize it, becomes venial because it was done in ignorance. No human person, surely, could ever desire, at least consciously, to put God to death; and so those who did put Him to death without knowing what they were doing have not fallen headlong into the infinite sin, to which no other sins can be compared. In order to see how good that life was, however, we have been considering the magnitude of that sin, not from the point of view of its having been committed in ignorance, but as if it had been committed knowingly, which is what no one ever has done or could have done.

Boso: You have shown by solid argument that the slayers of Christ were able to obtain pardon for their sin.[49]

Anselm: What more are you looking for now? You already see how we show with irrefutable reasons that the celestial city is to be completed from among human beings, and that this cannot occur except by remission of sins, which no man can obtain except through the man who is himself God, and who by His death will reconcile sinful human beings with God. It is evident, then, that we have discovered Christ, whom we acknowledge as God and man, and as one who has died for us. How, once we know this with certitude, we must admit without hesitation that everything He says is true, because God cannot deceive us, and that everything He has done has been done wisely, even though we do not understand the reasons.[50]

Boso: What you say is right, and I have not the slightest doubt that what He has said is true, or that what He has done was done with good reason. But the thing I would like you to explain to me is the reason for the necessity or possibility of the tenets in the Christian faith which unbelievers think are not necessary or even impossible—not to confirm me in the faith, but to give me, already confirmed in the faith as I am, the joy of understanding the truth itself.

SIXTEEN

How God assumed humanity, without sin, from out of the
sinful mass. The salvation of Adam and Eve.

Boso: Just as you have explained the reasons for your previous statements, I ask you also to make clear the basis of
those truths I am still to ask about. First, for example, how
did God take for Himself a human nature without sin, from
the sinful mass,[51] that is, from the human race which was wholly
infected by sin, as if He were taking unleavened bread from
fermented dough?[52] For although the very conception of this
individual human nature is pure and free from the sin of bodily
pleasure, the Virgin herself from whom it was taken was nevertheless conceived *in iniquities* and her *mother had conceived*
her in sins[53] and she was born with original sin,[54] since even
she sinned in Adam *in whom all have sinned.*[55]

Anselm: Once it is established that that man is God, and
the one who reconciled sinners, there is no doubt that He is
entirely without sin. But this cannot be, unless He was taken
from the sinful mass, free from sin. If we cannot understand
in exactly what way the wisdom of God has accomplished this,
however, we should not be surprised, but we must reverently
admit that there is something in the hidden depths of so exalted
a reality which surpasses our knowledge.[56] Surely, God has restored human nature in a more marvelous way than He created
it.[57] Both achievements are equally easy for God, of course. But
before he existed, man did not commit sin, and thus disqualify
himself for existence. After he was created, however, he deserved, by his sin, to lose his existence and the goal for which
he was created. Still, he did not simply lose his very existence;
rather, he exists either to be punished or to receive the mercy
of God. Neither of these would be possible if he were annihi-

lated. So much the more wonderful, then, was God's restoration
of man than His creation of man, since He redeemed him from
the state of sin against man's deserts, whereas his creation did
not follow upon the state of sin and was not contrary to what
he deserved. Besides, how great a thing it is to unite God and
man in such a way that the same one is God and man, without
losing the integrity of each nature! Who, then, would dare even
to imagine that the human intellect could perceive how wisely,
how marvelously, such an unfathomable deed was done?

Boso: I agree that no human person in this life can perfectly penetrate so great a mystery, and I am asking you, not
to do what no man can do, but only as much as you can.
Surely, you will more readily persuade me that deeper reasons
lie hidden in this matter [58] if you show that you see one or
other of them, than if you give evidence by saying nothing,
that you do not understand any meaning in it at all.

Anselm: I see that I cannot escape from your insistence. But
if I can succeed in some small way in showing you what you
are looking for, let us give thanks to God. If I cannot, however,
let what has already been established suffice. For once it is
acknowledged that God should become man,[59] it is beyond
doubt that He will not lack wisdom and power to bring this
about without sin.[60]

Boso: I admit this willingly.

Anselm: It was necessary, certainly, that that redemption
which Christ effected should be beneficial not only to those
who lived at that time, but to others also. Suppose, for instance,
that there is some king and suppose the whole population of
one of his cities, with the exception of a single person, who is
nevertheless a member of their race, committed such offences
against the king that none of them would be able to escape
condemnation to death. Suppose, too, that the one innocent
person has such favor with the king that he has the ability,
and such love for the guilty ones that he has the desire, to
reconcile with the king all those who have confidence in his
plan, by means of some service which is most agreeable to the
king, and which he will perform on a day set by the decision
of the king. And since not all who need to be reconciled are

able to assemble on that day, the king, having regard for the great value of that service, grants forgiveness from every past fault to all who, before or after that day, acknowledge their desire to seek pardon through that action performed on that day, and to give consent to the agreement that was made there. And should it happen that they again give offence after this pardon, they may obtain pardon anew through the efficacy of the same agreement, on condition that they are willing to make adequate satisfaction and to correct their conduct. No one, however, may enter his palace until the condition of the remission of his faults is fulfilled. Parallel with this illustration, since not all men who were to be saved could have been present when Christ effected that redemption, so great was the efficacy in His death that its effect reaches even to those who live in other places and times. That it must be of benefit not only to those who were present, moreover, is easily known from the fact that not so many could be present at his death as are required to build up the heavenly city, even if all who lived all over the world at the time of His death were allowed to share in that redemption. For the demons whose number must be restored were more numerous than the human beings who were living at that time.

Nor is it to be believed that there has been any time since the creation of man, in which this world with the creatures made for the use of men, was so empty that not one member of the human race existed in it, heading for the goal for which man was created. It surely seems incongruous that God should, even for one moment, permit the human race, from whom the heavenly city is to be completed, and what he has made for their use, to have existed without a purpose. For they would more or less seem to exist without a purpose, so long as they seemed not to exist for the principal purpose for which they were created.

Boso: That is an apt argument and one that nothing seems to contradict, that you are using to show there never has been a time since the creation of man when there was not someone who should have a share in that reconciliation without which the creation of the whole human race would have been deprived of a purpose. We can form this conclusion for reasons not only of fitness but even of necessity.[61] For if this is more fitting and more reasonable than the opinion that at some time there existed no person in whose favor there would be fulfilled the intention God had in mind in making man, it is necessary that there was always someone who had a share in the reconciliation we have been talking about. Hence it is beyond doubt that Adam and Eve had a share in that redemption, although divine authority does not state this explicitly.

Anselm: It also seems incredible that God would exclude this couple from this purpose, since He created them and had the unalterable intention to bring into existence from them, all human beings whom He was to take up to the heavenly city.

Boso: In fact, we must believe that He created them especially to be included with those for whose sake they were made.

Anselm: You are right. Nevertheless, no soul could enter the heavenly paradise before the death of Christ, as I said before, in speaking of the palace of a king.

Boso: That is what we hold.

Anselm: But that virgin from whom this man of whom we are speaking was born, was among those who before His birth, were cleansed from sin through Him and He was taken from the virgin in this state of purity.

Boso: Your statement would be quite satisfactory to me, except that it would then seem that He has exemption from sin through His mother, and is sinless because of her, not because of Himself, although He ought Himself to be the reason for His own sinlessness.

Anselm: Not so! Rather, since His mother's purity, through which He is pure, came from no one but Himself, He also is pure through Himself and by Himself.

Boso: All right, on that point. But it seems to me there is still another question to be asked. We have previously said [62] that it was not of necessity that He was going to die, and now we see that His mother was pure by virtue of His future death, and that unless she were so purified He could not have been born of her. How, then, was it not necessary for Him to die, since He could not have existed unless He was going to die?

For if He were not going to die, the virgin of whom He was formed would not have been pure, since this could never occur except by belief in the reality of His death; and He could not have been born of her if she had not been pure. Therefore, if He did not die by necessity after He was taken from the virgin, He could have been *not* taken from the virgin after He *was* taken from her—but that is impossible.

Anselm: If you pondered carefully what was said before, you would understand, I think, that your problem has already been solved.

Boso: I do not see how.

Anselm: When we raised the question whether He was able to lie, did we not show that there are two powers involved in lying, namely: first, the power of intending to lie, and secondly, that of telling a lie; and that although He had the power of telling a lie, He was, of His own being, unable to intend to lie; and hence that He deserves praise precisely for His own state of justice which made Him preserve the truth? [63]

Boso: That is so.

Anselm: With regard to preserving life, there is a similar distinction between the power of willing to preserve it and the power of actually preserving it. When, therefore, the question is raised whether this God-Man could have preserved His life, so as never to die, there is no doubt that He always had the power to preserve it, although He was unable to will to preserve it so as never to die. And since it was due to Himself that He was unable to will to preserve His life, it was not by necessity but by the power of His freedom that He laid it down.

Boso: Those two powers of His—that is, of lying and of preserving life—are not entirely alike. In the first case, it follows that He was able to lie if He chose to lie; in this case, however, it seems that if He willed not to die, He could no more do this than He could be other than He was. For the precise purpose of His being human was to die, and it was because of her faith in His future death that He was able to be born of the virgin, as you said before.

Anselm: Just as you think that He was unable to avoid death, or that He died out of necessity, because He was unable not to be what He was, so you can assert that He was unable to will not to die, or that He willed to die out of necessity, since He was unable not to be what He was. The fact is that the purpose of His becoming man was no more to die than to be willing to die. Hence, as you should not say that He was unable to will not to die, or that it was necessary for Him to will to die, so you should not say that He was unable not to die or that it was necessary for Him to die.

Boso: Rather, because both dying and being willing to die fall under the same principle, it seems that He was subject to both by necessity.

Anselm: Who was it who freely chose to become man, so that, with the same unchangeable willingness, He might die, and so that the Virgin from whom that man was born might be made pure by faith in the certainty of His death?

Boso: God, the Son of God.

Anselm: Did we not prove before, that the will of God is not compelled by any necessity, but that when it is described as doing something "by necessity," it is freely keeping itself on its own unchangeable course? [64]

Boso: We did prove that, surely. But we see, on the other hand, that what God unchangeably wills cannot fail to occur, but occurs necessarily. Therefore, if God willed this man to die, He is unable not to die.

Anselm: From the fact that the Son of Man assumed human nature for the very purpose of dying, you conclude that the same man was unable not to die.

Boso: That is how I understand it.

Anselm: Was it not equally apparent from what we said,[65] that the Son of God and the humanity He assumed are one person, so that the same being is God and man, the Son of God and the Son of the Virgin?

Boso: Yes.

Anselm: Then it was by His own will that this man was unable not to die, and did die.

Boso: I cannot deny that.

Anselm: Then, since it is not out of any necessity, but out of its own power, that the will of God does anything, and since that man's will was the will of God, it was not out of any necessity, but only by His own power, that He died.

Boso: I cannot escape from your arguments. For I am unable to find any weakness at all in either the premises you begin with, or in the conclusions you draw from them. Yet what I said keeps coming back to me: that if He should will not to die, He could no more avoid death than He could cease to be what He is. Surely, He was really to die, since if He were not to undergo a real death, the faith in His future death, by which both that Virgin of whom He was born, and many others were cleansed from sin, would not have been real. And if it were not real, it would not have been of any value. Hence if He were able not to die, He could bring it about that something which was real would be unreal.

Anselm: Why was it really true, before His death, that He was going to die?

Boso: Because He chose this freely and with an unchangeable decision.

Anselm: If, then, as you say, He was unable to avoid death for the reason that He was really going to die, and if He was really going to die for the reason that He Himself freely and irrevocably decided this, it follows that He was unable to avoid dying for the single reason that He willed to die by His irrevocable choice.

Boso: That is right. But whatever the reason was, it is still true that He was unable to avoid death, and that it was necessary for Him to die.

Anselm: You are finding a difficulty where there is none, and as the saying goes, you are looking for a knot on a bulrush.[66]

Boso: Have you forgotten how I countered your excuses in the beginning of this discussion of ours? I asked you to give answers not to the learned, but to me and to those who joined in my request.[67] Bear with me, then, when I put questions in proportion to the slowness and dullness of our minds, so as to give satisfaction to me and to them, even in puerile questions, as you did in the beginning.

SEVENTEEN

*In God there is no necessity, no impossibility. There is a
necessity that compels and one that does not compel.*

Anselm: We have already stated [68] that it is only in a less
proper sense that we say God cannot do anything, or that He
does it necessarily. In fact, all necessity and all impossibility
are subject to His will, but His will is not subject to any necessity or impossibility. For nothing is necessary or impossible
except for the reason that He wills it so; on the other hand,
it is absolutely untrue that He wills or does not will anything
because of necessity or impossibility. Therefore, since He does
whatever He wills, and does nothing but what He wills, then,
just as no necessity or impossibility leads up to His willing or
not willing, so no necessity or impossibility comes before His acting or not acting, although He might choose and do many things
in an inalterable way. And when God does something, then, after
it has been done, it is no longer possible for it not to have been
done, but it is always true that it has occurred. Still, it is not
right to say that it is impossible for God to make what is past
not to be past. For it is not the necessity of not acting or the
impossibility of acting that has effect in this case but only the
will of God, who, being Himself the Truth, wills the truth, as
it is, to be always unchangeable. In a similar way, if He intends inalterably to do something, although what He intends,
before it occurs, cannot but occur in the future, yet He is subject to no necessity of doing it or to no impossibility of not
doing it, because in Him it is only will which acts. So whenever someone says that God is unable to do something, there
is no denial of any power in Him, but there is reference to God's
unconquerable power and strength. All that is meant is that
nothing can make Him do what is said to be impossible.

Expressions of this sort are quite common, indeed, as when we say that something has an ability, not because it can do anything, but because something else can do something to it; and when we say something is incapable, not because there is a lack of power in that thing, but in something else. We say, for example: "that man is able to be overcome," meaning "someone is able to overcome him," and "that man is unable to be overcome," meaning "no one is able to overcome him." For the ability to be overcome is not a power, but a lack of power; and the inability to be overcome is a power, not a lack of power. Likewise, we do not say God does anything by necessity, in the sense that there is any necessity in Him, but because it is in something else, as I explained with regard to inability when we say "He cannot do something." Every necessity, you see, is either compelling or preventing, and these two types of necessity are related to each other as contraries, like necessity and impossibility. For whatever is compelled to exist is prevented from not existing, and what is compelled not to exist is prevented from existing; just as it is impossible for something which necessarily exists, not to exist and for that whose non-existence is necessary actually to exist, and vice versa. Now, when we say that something is or is not necessary in God, that is not to be interpreted to mean that there is in Him either compelling or preventing necessity, but it means that in all other things there is a necessity preventing them from acting and compelling them not to act, in a way opposed to what we say about God. For example, when we say that it is necessary for God always to tell the truth, and that it is necessary for Him never to lie, we are saying simply that there is in Him such great constancy in preserving the truth that, necessarily, nothing can influence Him not to tell the truth, or to lie.

Hence, when we say that that man, who, in accordance with the unity of His Person, as we said before,[69] is the same as the Son of God, and Himself God, was unable not to die, or to will not to die, after He was born of the Virgin, we do not mean that He is at all unable to preserve or to wish to preserve His immortal life. What we are referring to is the unchangeability of His will, by which He has freely become human precisely to die, persevering in the same intention, and we mean that nothing can change that decision. Surely, it would be more an inability than an ability if He could choose to lie or make a mistake or change His intention, which from the beginning He willed to be unchangeable. As I said before,[70] when someone freely commits himself to accomplish something good and, persevering in the same intention, afterwards accomplishes what he undertook to do—although he could be compelled, if he were unwilling, to keep his promise—we should nevertheless not say that he performs his action by necessity, but that he performs it by that free decision by which he committed himself to it. Surely, nothing should be said to occur or not occur by necessity or inability, where neither necessity nor inability achieves anything, but only the will. If, let me add, it is this way with regard to man, much less should we ever speak of necessity or inability in God, since He does nothing but what He wills, and no force can compel or restrict His will. Now, the diversity of natures and the singleness of person in Christ had this effect, that if His human nature could not do what was required for the restoration of human beings, the divine nature would accomplish it, and if it were incongruous with the divine nature, the human nature performed it. Yet it would not be two different persons. Rather, one and the same person, existing in perfection in two natures, would make indemnity through his human nature for what that owed, and would be able to do by His divine nature what was appropriate to that.[71] Finally, the Virgin, who was purified by faith, so that He could be born of her, believed that He was going to die for the sole reason that He willed it, as she had learned from the prophet who said of Him: *He was offered because it was His own will.*[72] Therefore, since her faith was well founded, it was necessary that it should come about just as she believed it would. But if you are again disturbed because I say "it was necessary," remember that the truth of the Virgin's faith was not the cause of His dying freely; rather, her faith was true because His death was going to occur. Hence, if we say "it was necessary for Him to die, merely because of His willingness, because the faith and the prophecy which concerned and preceded this event are true," that is the same as saying: "It was necessary for it to occur this way, because it was going to occur this way." Necessity of this sort does not compel the reality to exist, but the existence of the reality brings about the necessity.

There is, of course, an antecedent necessity which is the cause of a thing's existence; and there is a consequent necessity which the thing brings about. When we say the sky turns around because it is necessary for it to turn around, we are referring to an antecedent and efficacious necessity. But when I say that you are necessarily speaking because you are speaking now, the necessity is consequent, and is not a cause of anything, but a result of your speaking. For in saying this, I mean that nothing can make it a fact that you are not speaking while you are speaking. I do not mean that anything compels you to speak. The impetus of its physical state, indeed, compels the sky to turn, but no necessity makes you speak. Wherever there is an antecedent necessity, however, there is a subsequent one; but there is not an antecedent necessity just because there is a subsequent necessity. We can say, for example: "It is necessary that the sky turns around," because it *is* turning around; but it is not equally true that you are speaking because it is necessary for you to speak.

This consequent necessity runs through all periods of time, in this way: Whatever has been, necessarily has been. Whatever is, necessarily is, and will necessarily have been. Whatever is going to occur, necessarily will occur. This is that necessity which, in Aristotle's exposition of singular and future propositions, seems to do away with choice of alternatives, and to establish that everything exists of necessity.[73] It was by this consequent necessity, which is not the cause of anything, that it was necessary that the past happened as it did, since the faith and prophecy regarding Christ were true because He was going to die by choice, not by necessity. By this necessity, He became man; by this, He accomplished and suffered all that He did accomplish and suffer; by this He willed whatever He did will. It is, therefore, by necessity that these events occurred, because they were going to be; and it is by necessity they were going to be, because they did occur; and it is by necessity that they did occur, because they did occur. And if you want to know the true necessity of all He did and all He suffered, know that all these things occurred by necessity because He willed them. But there was no necessity antecedent to His choice. Hence if they occurred only because He willed them, then if He had not willed them, they would not have occurred. Thus, therefore, no one took his life from Him, but He laid it down, and again He took it up, because He had 'power' to lay down His life and to take it up again, as He Himself says.[74]

Boso: You have shown me satisfactorily that no one can prove that He underwent death under any necessity. And I do not regret that I was so insistent on your doing this.

Anselm: We have presented, in my opinion, a trustworthy explanation of how God assumed human nature without sin, from the sinful mass. But I think we should never deny that there is some other explanation than the one we mentioned, due to the fact that God is able to do what the reason of man cannot understand.[75] But I believe this explanation is able to satisfy us. Besides, if I wanted to look for a different one now, it would be necessary to investigate the essence of original sin, and how it is communicated from our first parents to the whole human race, with the exception of that Man of whom we are speaking. It would be necessary, too, to touch on some other questions which require a treatise of their own. So let us be content with that explanation we have discussed, and go on with what remains of the task we have begun.

Boso: As you wish—but on condition that some day you will, so to speak, pay your debt by giving me, with God's help, that other explanation you do not want to look into now.

Anselm: Since I know I have this intention, I am not refusing your request; yet because I have no certainty about the future, I dare not make any promise, but I leave it in God's hands.[76]

EIGHTEEN

How the life of Christ is paid to God for the sins of men.
In what sense Christ was obliged and in what sense He
was not obliged, to suffer.

Anselm: But tell me now, what you think ought still to be
explained, of that problem which you proposed in the beginning,
on account of which many other problems forced themselves
upon us.

Boso: The nub of the question was why God became man,
to save man by His death, when it would seem He could do
this in some other way.[77] In answering this question, you
showed, by many conclusive arguments, that the restoration of
human nature ought not to be neglected, and that it could not
be accomplished unless man paid to God what he owed for
sin. But this debt was so great that, although man alone owed
the debt, still God alone was able to pay it, so that the same
person would have to be both man and God. Hence it was
necessary that God assume human nature into the unity of His
person, so that the one who in his nature owed the debt and
could not pay it, should be, in His Person, able to pay it. Then
you showed that that man who was God had to be taken from
a virgin, and by the person of the Son of God, and you showed
how He could be taken from the sinful mass without sin. Besides, you very clearly established that the life of this man was
so sublime, so precious, that it can suffice to pay what is owed
for the sins of the whole world, and infinitely more. It now remains, therefore, to show how that life is paid to God for the
sins of men.

Anselm: If He permitted Himself to be slain for the sake
of justice, did He not give up His life for the honor of God?

Boso: If I can understand what I do not doubt, although I

do not see how He did this with good reason, since He could have both preserved justice firmly and kept His life eternally, I shall admit that He freely gave to God for His honor, a gift of such a kind that anything that is not God cannot be compared to it, and which can make compensation for all the debts of all human beings.

Anselm: Do you not understand that when He bore with generous patience the injuries and outrages and death on the cross in the company of brigands, all inflicted upon Him, as we said before,[78] on account of justice which He obediently preserved, He gave to men the example of never turning away from the justice they owe to God, no matter what disadvantages they can experience? And do you not understand that He would absolutely not have given this example, if, by using His power, He had escaped the death inflicted on Him for such a cause?

Boso: It seems that there was no need for Him to give this example, since we know that many people, before His coming, and John the Baptist, after His coming but before His death, have adequately given that example by bravely enduring death for the sake of truth.

Anselm: No person other than Himself ever gave to God by dying, anything he was not at some time necessarily to lose, or paid what he did not owe. He, however, freely offered to the Father what He would never have necessarily lost, and He paid for sinners a debt He never owed Himself. So He gave us a far greater example to influence every person not to hesitate to give back to God, in his own name, when reason requires it, what he is sometime suddenly going to lose. For He, without having any need to do it for Himself, or without being compelled to do it for others to whom He owed nothing but punishment, has given up a life so precious, yes, His very self, that is to say, so exalted a person, with such tremendous willingness.

Boso: You are coming very close to what I am looking for. But permit me to ask a question which I could not readily answer if it were put to me, although you probably think it is a foolish question. You say that when He died, He gave what

He did not owe. But no one will deny that when He gave this example in such a way, He did something better and something that gives greater pleasure to God than if He had not done it. No one will say, either, that He had no obligation to do what He understood to be better and more pleasing to God. How, then, can we assert that He did not owe to God what He did —that is, what He knew to be better and more pleasing to God —especially since a creature owes to God all that he is and all that he knows and all that he is able to do?

Anselm: Although a creature possesses nothing entirely as his own, yet when God grants him the right to do or not to do something, He puts both alternatives in the creature's control, so that, even though one may be better than the other, neither one is definitely stipulated. Whether the person does what is better, however, or does the alternative, he may be said to have to do what he does; and if he does what is better, he should have a reward, because he freely gives what is his own. Although virginity is better than marriage, for example, still neither one is definitely required of a person, but whether the person prefers to use marriage or prefers to preserve virginity, we may say that he ought to do what he does. No one says, certainly, that it is not necessary to choose either virginity or marriage, but we do say that a man ought to do what he prefers, before he decides on one of these alternatives, and if he preserves virginity, he expects a reward for the voluntary gift which he offers to God. When you say, therefore, that a creature owes to God what he knows to be better, and is able to give, this is not always true, if you mean "by reason of debt," and do not understand "if God commands it." Indeed, as I have said, a human being is not obliged to embrace virginity as something due, but if he prefers, he ought to make use of marriage.

But if the word "ought" disturbs you, and you cannot understand it apart from some obligation, bring to mind that the words "can" and "cannot" and "necessity" may sometimes be used, not as applying to the subjects to which they are attributed, but as referring to other beings. It is just the same with the word "ought." Surely, when we say that the poor *ought* to receive alms from the rich, we mean precisely that the rich ought to give alms to the poor. This debt, obviously, is not to be exacted of the poor, but of the rich.[79] We also say that God ought to be above all other beings, not in the sense that He is in any way obliged, but with the meaning that all things ought to be subject to Him. Again, we say that He ought to do what He wills, because what He wills ought to exist. Similarly, when some creature wills to do what is within his power to do or not to do, we say he ought to do it, because what he wills ought to occur. Hence when the Lord Jesus, as we said,[80] willed to undergo death, since it was within His power either to suffer or not to suffer, he ought to have done what He did, because what He willed ought to occur. Yet He was not obliged to do it, because He had incurred no indebtedness. In accordance with His human nature, once He became man, since He is Himself God and man, He received from His divine nature, which is different from the human nature, the right to claim as His own whatever He possessed, with the result that He was not obliged to give anything but what He chose to give. But in accordance with His *Person,* He was so fully the reason for possessing what He possessed, and He was so perfectly self-sufficient, that He neither owed any recompense to anyone else nor did He need to give anything to have recompense made to Him.

Boso: Now I clearly see that He gave Himself up to death for the honor of God, not at all out of obligation, as my reasoning seemed to indicate, yet that He ought to have done what He did.

Anselm: That honor, surely, belongs to the whole Trinity. Hence, since He Himself is God, the Son of God, He offered Himself to the Father and the Holy Spirit; that is, He offered His humanity to His divinity, which is one and the same for the three Persons. To say what we want to say more clearly, however, without departing from exactly the same truth, let us say, in the usual manner, that the Son freely offered Himself to the Father. This is the most apt way of expressing it, both because, even in one Person, we understand the whole of Divinity, to whom He offered Himself in His human nature, and because when we say the Son intercedes with the Father for us in this way, a certain immense devotion is felt in the hearts of our hearers because of the names of the Father and the Son.

Boso: This I accept most willingly.

NINETEEN

The great reason why His death brought about human salvation.

Anselm: Let us consider, now, so far as we can, the important reason why His death brought about our salvation.

Boso: This is what my heart is longing for. For although I think I understand it, still I would like you to give me a connected outline of the reasoning.

Anselm: How grand a thing the Son's free gift is, scarcely needs explanation.

Boso: That is clear enough.

Anselm: You will not entertain the thought that He who freely gives to God such a great gift ought to go without a reward.

Boso: Rather, I see that it is necessary for the Father to reward the Son. Otherwise, He would seem unjust if He were unwilling, or limited in power if He were unable, to reward Him. And both of these are foreign to God.

Anselm: Whoever rewards someone either gives him what he does not possess, or he remits what he could demand of him. Now, before the Son performed such a wonderful task, all that belonged to the Father belonged to Him; [81] and He never owed anything that could be remitted. What recompense, then, will be given to one who is in need of nothing, and to whom there is nothing that can be given or remitted?

Boso: I see, on the one hand, that it is necessary to give

Him a reward, and on the other, that it is impossible; for it is necessary that God render what is due another, and yet there is nothing to give.

Anselm: If so grand and so deserved a reward is not granted either to Him or to someone else, it will seem that the Son has done such a wonderful thing uselessly.

Boso: It would be wrong to think that.

Anselm: Then it is necessary that the reward be given to someone else, because it cannot be given to Him.

Boso: That follows inevitably.

Anselm: If the Son willed to give to another what is due to Himself, could the Father legitimately prevent Him, or refuse it to the one to whom the Son transfers His right?

Boso: On the contrary, I understand that it is both just and necessary that the Father make recompense to the one to whom the Son willed to give it; both because it is permissible for the Son to give away what belongs to Him, and because the Father can give what is due to the Son only to someone else.

Anselm: To whom will it be more appropriate for Him to transfer the fruit and recompense of His death than to those for whose salvation, as we have learned from reliable arguments, He made Himself man and to whom, as we said,[82] He gave by His death an example of dying for the sake of justice. It is useless, surely, for them to imitate Him if they will not share in His merit. Or whom will He more justly make heirs of what is due Him, and which He does not need, and of the superabundance of His own fullness, than His kinsmen and brethren, whom He sees bound by so many and such great debts, perishing in penury, in an abyss of miseries, so that what they owe for their sins may be pardoned, and what they have need of because of their sins, may be granted them?

Boso: Nothing more reasonable, nothing more agreeable, nothing more desirable can be proclaimed to the world. In fact, I derive such great confidence from this that even now I cannot describe the tremendous joy with which my heart exults. For it seems to me that surely God rejects no person who draws near to Him under this name.

Anselm: That is right, if he approaches the way he should.

And just how we should draw near to share in such tremendous grace, and how it should guide our lives, is taught to us on every page of Holy Scripture, which is based, as on a firm foundation, upon solid truth, which, with God's help, we have examined to some extent.

Boso: Certainly, whatever is built upon this foundation is based on a solid rock.[83]

Anselm: I think I have already answered your question satisfactorily, at least in part, although someone better than I could do it more fully; and there are more and greater explanations of this topic than my talent or any mortal talent is able to comprehend.[84] It is clear, also, that God had absolutely no need to do what we have been describing, but the inalterable truth required it. For although we may say that God accomplished what that Man accomplished, on account of the unity of person, nevertheless God did not need to descend from heaven to conquer the devil, nor to contend against him by justice, to liberate man. But God did require man to conquer the devil and to make satisfaction by justice, because he had offended God by sin. Certainly, God owed the devil nothing but punishment, and man owed him nothing but revindication, conquering the one by whom he had been conquered. But whatever was exacted of man was due to God, not to the devil.[85]

TWENTY

How great and how just is the mercy of God.

Anselm: When we were considering the justice of God and the sin of man, you thought the mercy of God disappeared.[86] But we have found it to be so great and so in accord with His justice, that it could not be conceived to be either greater or more just. What greater mercy could be imagined, for example, than for God the Father to say to the sinner condemned to eternal torments and having no way to redeem himself: "Receive my only begotten Son and present Him instead of yourself"; and for the Son Himself to say: "Take me and redeem yourself"? This is what they say, in effect, when they call us and draw us to the Christian faith. What could be more just, furthermore, than for Him to whom is given a price that surpasses all that is owed Him, provided the offering is made with proper dispositions, to remit the whole debt?

TWENTY-ONE

It is impossible for the devil to be reconciled.

Anselm: You asked about the reconciliation of the devil.[87] You will understand this is impossible, if you reflect carefully on the human reconciliation. For just as man could not be reconciled except by a Man-God who could die, by whose justice there would be restored to God what He was deprived of by the sin of man, so the condemned angels could not be saved except by an angel-God who could die and who by His justice would make reparation to God for what the sins of other angels took away. And as it would not have been proper for man to be raised up by another man who was not of the same race, even though he would be of the same nature, so no angel ought to be saved by another angel, since, even though they are all of a single nature, they are not of a common species, as men are. It is not a fact that all angels are descended from one angel, as all men are descended from one man.[88] There is another obstacle to their restoration: as they fell without anyone else injuring them and bringing about their fall, so they ought to rise up again without anyone's assistance. And for them this is impossible. They are unable to be restored in any other way to the dignity which they should have had, since, had they not sinned, they would have stood firm in the truth [89] by their own power, which was a gift to them, and without anyone else's help. Hence, if anyone thinks that the redemption by our Savior ought eventually to be extended to them, he is convicted by reason of being irrationally deceived. And I am saying this, not as if the price of His death would not, by its magnitude, have efficacy for all the sins of men and angels, but because inalterable reason is opposed to the resurgence of the lost angels.

TWENTY-TWO

In what has been said, the truth of the Old Testament and the New has been established.

Boso: It seems to me that everything you say is reasonable, and nothing can contradict it; and I am convinced that by the solution of the single problem we have posed, whatever is contained in the New and the Old Testaments is established.[90] For you prove it was necessary for God to become man, in such a way that, at least if the few things which you have quoted from our books—such as what you said when you touched on the three Persons of God[91] and on Adam[92]—were left out, you would give satisfaction not only to Jews but even to pagans, by reason alone. Furthermore, it is the same God-Man Himself who established the New Testament and gave approbation to the Old. As it is necessary to acknowledge Him as truthful, then, so no one can deny the truth of anything which is contained in those Testaments.[93]

Anselm: If we have said anything that ought to be corrected, I do not refuse correction, if it is given with reasons. But if what we think we have discovered by the use of reason is corroborated by the testamony of the Truth, we must attribute this, not to ourselves, but to God, who is blessed for ever. Amen.

THE VIRGIN CONCEPTION
AND ORIGINAL SIN

CHAPTERS

THE VIRGIN CONCEPTION AND ORIGINAL SIN

Although it is my wish, most beloved brother and son, Boso, to conform with your devout desire in every instance, if I can, I surely consider myself most especially bound to satisfy you whenever I realize I myself have awakened that desire in you. And when you read in the book *Why God Became Man*—which you, together with others, but more insistently than they, induced me to publish, and in which I associated you as a disputant with me [1]—that there appears to be another possible explanation than the one I set down there, of the way God took human nature, without sin, from the sinful mass of the human race,[2] I am certain that your assiduous mind will be more than slightly challenged to ask what that explanation is. Hence I am afraid I should seem unfair to you if I were to conceal from you, my friend, my subsequent opinion on the matter. I shall, therefore, speak briefly about my opinion, in such a way as not to condemn anyone's view on this subject that is in accord with the faith, nor to be stubborn in defending my own opinion, if anyone can reasonably show that it is opposed to the truth. But I do think that explanation of the matter which I set forth in the same little work is absolutely valid and adequate if it is carefully considered. There is, of course, nothing against having many explanations of the same thing, of which each one by itself may be adequate.

ONE

What "original justice or injustice" and "personal justice or injustice" mean.

To see how God took human nature without sin, from the sinful mass of the human race, then, it is first necessary to make an inquiry about original sin, because this problem arises only out of the fact of original sin. For if we see how Christ could not be subject to the latter, it will be evident how the assumption or the conception of that humanity was free from all sin.

There is no doubt that the word "original" is derived from "origin." If, then, original sin exists only in a human being, it seems that it derives its name either from the origin of human nature—that is, "original" comes from the beginning of nature, in the sense that the sin is contracted from the very origin of human nature—or else from "origin" in the sense of the beginning of each and every person, because it is contracted in the very origin of the individual. The sin does not seem to pass down from the beginning of human nature, however, since the origin of that was just, our first parents having been created just, not having any sin.[3] So it seems it is called "original" from the origin of each single human person. If anyone should say, though, that the sin is called "original" because it passes down to individuals from those from whom their nature originated, I shall not oppose him so long as he does not deny that original sin is contracted with the very origin of each single person. There are in each human being at the same time, of course, both a nature making him human, like all the others, and a personality distinguishing him from others, as when he is called "this one" or "that one," or by his proper name, such as Adam or Abel. Besides, each one's sin is in his nature and his person, for the sin of Adam has been in man because it is in the nature, and in the one who was called Adam, because it is in the person. Although all this is so, still, there is a sin which each one contracts with the nature in the very origin of the self, and there is a sin which one does not contract with nature itself, but which he himself commits after he has become a person distinct from other persons. What is contracted in his very origin is called "original," and it can also be called "natural," not in the sense that it arises from the essence of the nature, but because, due to the nature's corruptness, it is received with the nature. On the other hand, the sin which anyone commits after he is a person can be called "personal," because it occurs by the fault of a person.[4] In a similar sense, we can speak of "original" and "personal" justice.[5] For example, Adam and Eve were in a state of justice "originally," that is, right in the very beginning of their existence as human beings, without any lapse of time. Justice can be called "personal," however, when a person without justice receives the justice he did not possess from the beginning.

TWO

How human nature was corrupted.

If Adam and Eve had preserved their original justice, then, those who were to be born of them would have been originally in the state of justice, as they were. Since they committed personal sin, however, despite the fact that, being originally strong and uncorrupted, they had the power of preserving justice forever, without difficulty, their whole being was weakened and corrupted. The body, indeed, was weakened, because after sin it was just like the bodies of brute animals, subject to corruption and carnal desires. The soul, likewise, was weakened, because it was tainted by passions of the flesh, due to the corruption of the body and to carnal desires, as well as to the lack of the benefits it had lost. And because the whole of human nature was in them and there was nothing pertaining to it that was not in them, it was weakened and corrupted in its entirety.[6]

There remained in it, therefore, the obligation of being in the state of undiminished justice which it had received, free from any injustice, and the obligation of making satisfaction for having abandoned justice, along with the state of corruption which it incurred on account of sin. Hence, just as, if it had not sinned, it would have been propagated in the same condition in which it had been created by God, so, after sin, it is propagated in the condition in which it put itself by sinning. By itself, then, it is unable either to make satisfaction for sin or to recover the justice it has forsaken,[7] and *the corruptible body is a load upon the soul* [8]—and most especially when it is in a weaker condition, as in infancy and in the mother's womb —so that it cannot even understand the state of justice. This being so, it seems necessary for human nature to be born in infants with the obligation of making satisfaction for the first sin, which it was always able to avoid, and with the obligation of having original justice, which it was ever capable of preserving. Nor does lack of power excuse it even in the case of infants, when in them it does not fulfill its obligations, since it was itself the cause of its own lack of power, by abandoning the state of jusice in our first parents. For in them it wholly existed, and it is always under the obligation to have the power which it received for the purpose of preserving the state of justice always. This, it appears, is what original sin is in infants.

Let us also add the sins of closer ancestors, which are paid for *unto the third and fourth generation.*[9] It is debatable, of course, whether or not all these are to be understood as being included in original sin. Still, for fear of seeming to minimize the seriousness of that sin for the sake of solving my problem, I shall present it as being such that no one could describe it as more grave.

THREE

Sin exists only in the rational will.

But whether original sin is all this, or something less, I think it is absolutely impossible to say that it exists in an infant before he has a rational soul, just as we cannot say there was any justice in Adam before he became a rational human being. For if Adam and Eve had brought forth offspring before they committed sin, there would nevertheless have been no justice, nor could there have been any, in the seed before it was fashioned into a living human being. If, then, the seed of man is not capable of receiving justice before it becomes a human being, it cannot receive original sin before it is a human being.

We should have no hesitation in admitting, certainly, that original sin is injustice. For if every sin is injustice, and original sin is a sin, surely it is injustice also. But should someone say: "Not every sin is injustice," he might as well say there can be some sin in a person and no injustice in him—and that seems incredible. If it be said, however, that original sin is not to be called "sin" unrestrictedly, but "sin" only with the qualifier "original," just as a painted man is not really a man but a painting of a man, it would surely follow that an infant who has no sin but original sin is free of sin; and the Son of the Virgin would not be the only one among human beings who was sinless while in the womb of His mother and when He was born of her. Besides, an infant who dies without baptism, having no sin but original sin, either would not be condemned or would be condemned without sin. But we do not accept any of these consequences. Hence every sin is injustice, and original sin is sin in an unrestricted sense. It follows, then, that it is also injustice. Besides, if God does not condemn a human being except for injustice, but does condemn someone because of original sin, then original sin is not excluded from injustice. But if this is so, and if injustice is nothing but the lack of due justice [10]—for it is obvious there is no injustice except in a nature which does not possess justice when it should have it— then, certainly, original sin is included under the very definition of injustice.

Now, if justice is "the rectitude of the will preserved for its own sake," [11] and if that rectitude cannot exist except in rational nature, then there is no nature obligated to possess justice except the rational one, just as there is no nature capable of being endowed with justice except the rational one. Since injustice cannot exist, then, except where justice ought to be, original sin, which is injustice, is not found except in the rational nature. Now, the only rational natures are God and the angel and the human soul, by which a man is said to be rational and without which he is not human. Since, then, original sin is not in God nor in an angel, it is only in the rational human soul.

It must be acknowledged, also, that if justice is rectitude of will preserved for its own sake, justice cannot exist except in the will. The same is true, then, of injustice. For the absence

of justice is not called injustice except in a being that should
have justice. Other than justice or injustice themselves, then,
nothing is called just or unjust but the will, or something done
on account of a just or unjust will. Because of this, we say a
man or an angel, a soul or an action, is either just or unjust.

FOUR

*Nothing is, by itself, just or unjust, except justice or in-
justice itself. Nothing is punished but the will.*

Nothing, indeed, be it substance or action or anything else, is
just, considered by itself, with the exception of justice; and
nothing is unjust or sinful by itself but injustice—not even the
will itself, in which justice or injustice is found. For that power
of the soul by which the soul itself desires something, the
power which can be called the instrument of willing, as sight
is the instrument of seeing, and which we call the will, is one
thing; and justice, by the possession of which the will is called
"just" and for lack of which it is called "unjust," is something
else. (The dispositions and acts of this same instrument are
also called "wills," but it would take too long to introduce this
here.) [12]

Even the very appetites which the Apostle calls *the flesh*
which *lusteth against the spirit,*[13] and the *law of sin* which is
in the *members fighting against the law of the mind,*[14] are not
just or unjust, considered by themselves. For they do not make
a person just or unjust simply because he experiences them,
but they make him unjust only if he consents to them voluntarily, when he should not. The same Apostle says: *There is
. . . no condemnation to them that are in Christ Jesus, who
walk not according to the flesh,*[15] that is, who do not give
consent of the will to the flesh. Now, if they made unjust any-

one who experienced them without consent, condemnation would follow. Hence it is not experiencing them but consenting to them that is a sin. For if they were of themselves unjust, they would cause injustice whenever consent is given to them. But when brute animals consent to them, they are not called unjust. Similarly, if they were sins, they would be removed in Baptism, when every sin is washed away, and it is evident that they are not. Therefore there is no injustice in their essence, but in the rational will acceding to them inordinately. For when the will, being *delighted with the law of God according to the inward man,*[16] resists them, then the will has justice. The Apostle, you see, calls the justice which the law prescribes both the *law of God,*[17] because it comes from God, and *the law of* the *mind,*[18] because it is understood by the mind; just as the Old Law is called the *law of God* [19] because it comes from God, and the *law of Moses* [20] because it was transmitted by Moses.

What I have said about no action being unjust by itself, but by reason of injustice of will, is illustrated in those actions which can sometimes be done without injustice, such as killing a person, as Phinees [21] did, and having sexual intercourse, as in marriage or among brute animals. But those actions which can never be performed without injustice, such as committing perjury, and certain others which should not be so much as mentioned,[22] are not so easy to understand in the same way. Suppose, however, these things were sins: some action which brings something into existence and which does not endure except while the effect is being produced, and after the effect is completed, passes away so as not to exist any more; or a product which is brought into existence and remains—for example, when we write something that should not be written, the act of writing ceases, but the letters produced by it remain. Then, when the action ceased, so as not to exist any more, the sin likewise would cease and not exist any more; or, so long as what was produced remained, the sin would never be wiped out. But we see that sins are frequently not blotted out when the action has ceased, and also that they frequently are blotted out when their effect has not been destroyed. Hence neither the action which passes away nor the effect which remains is now a sin.

Finally, if they are accused of voluntary actions which occur without justice, the limbs and senses performing them can answer: "God has subjected us and the power that is in us to the will, so that at its command we cannot but make ourselves act and do what it wills. In fact, it controls us as its instruments, and it produces the effects which we seem to be producing. We are not able, by ourselves, to resist it, and the things it does cannot but be done. We are not permitted, we are not able, to disobey the mistress whom God has given us. When we obey her, we are obeying God who gave us this law." What sin, then, do the limbs or the senses or the things produced commit, since God subjected them to the will in this manner, if they keep doing what God directed them to do? Whatever they do, therefore, is to be imputed totally to the will.

Since this is so, someone may wonder why the limbs and the senses are punished for the fault of the will. But this is not the case. Nothing is, in fact, punished but the will. For nothing is a penalty to anyone unless it is against his will,[23] and nothing experiences punishment except one who has a will. Now the limbs and the senses do not, of themselves, will anything. Just as the will produces its effect in the limbs and the senses, therefore, so it experiences torment or delight in them. But if anyone does not accept this, let him recognize that it is only the soul, with the will within it, which exercises sensation and action in the senses and limbs, and so it is the soul alone which is tormented or delighted in them.[24] It is customary for us, however, to call the actions which an unjust will performs, sins, because in the will by means of which they are performed, there is sin. To some of them we even give names that signify that they are performed without justice, such as "fornicating," "lying." But we understand that it is one thing to consider the action or the utterance itself, and another thing to consider whether it is just or unjust to act or speak. Finally, every essence is from God, and nothing unjust is from Him. Hence no essence is unjust in itself.[25]

FIVE

Evil, which sin or injustice is, is non-being.

Furthermore, injustice, like blindness, is simply non-being. Blindness, surely, is nothing but the absence of sight where it ought to be, yet this is no more a reality in the eye where there ought to be sight than it is in wood where sight is not required. Now, injustice is not the sort of thing that contaminates and corrupts the soul in the way poison does the body, nor does it really do something, as would seem to be the case when a wicked human being does evil deeds. Suppose an untamed beast bursts its fetters and runs around in a rage, or again, suppose a ship is tossed about and is drawn into all sorts of dangers, if the pilot lets go of its helm and leaves it to the winds and the waves of the sea. In such cases, we do say, of course, that the absence of a chain or of a rudder is doing this—not that their absence is something real, or actually does anything, but because if they were present, they would prevent the beast from raging or the ship from foundering. In a similar way, when a wicked man is enraged and is driven into some dangers or other to his soul, which is what evil deeds are, we declare that injustice has brought this about —but not in the sense that it is a real essence, or that it actually performs an action. What we do mean is that when the will, to which all voluntary acts of the whole man are subject, is, in the absence of justice, driven by diverse desires, being capricious and unrestrained and uncontrolled, it precipitates itself and everything subject to itself into many sorts of evils—all of which justice, if it were present, would have prevented from occurring.

From these examples, then, we readily recognize that injustice has no essence, although the states and acts of an unjust will, which, considered by themselves, are something, are customarily called "injustice." By the very same reasoning, we understand that evil is non-being. For even as injustice is nothing but the absence of due justice, so evil is nothing but the absence of due goodness. But no essence, although it may be called evil, is non-being, nor is its being evil equivalent to being something. For any essence, being evil means nothing but lacking goodness which it ought to have. Lacking goodness that ought to be there, surely, is not any kind of being. Hence, for any essence, being evil is not equivalent to being something.

I have given this brief description of evil, that, beyond all doubt, it is always non-being, when it is injustice. Misfortune, surely, is evil, and so individual misfortunes are called evils. At times the misfortune is non-being, such as blindness and deafness; at times it seems to be something, as in the case of pain and sadness.[26] But that justice is rectitude of will preserved for its own sake, and that injustice is nothing but the absence of due justice and has no essence, as well as that every essence is from God and that nothing is from God but good, I think I have adequately shown in that treatise I wrote *On the Fall of the Devil;*[27] but I have treated of justice more fully in the book *On Truth*[28] which I published.

SIX

When God inflicts punishment for sin, however, He is not punishing for nothing.

Some people, when they are told that sin is non-being, are likely to say: "If sin is nothing, why does God punish man for sin, when no one ought to be punished for nothing?" Although their question is insignificant, still, because they do not know what they are asking, some brief answer must be given to them.

Although it is equally true that the absence of justice is non-being, both in a subject in which justice is required, and in one in which it is not required, yet it is right for God to inflict punishment on sinners, not because of nothing, but because of something. The reason is—as I said in the book I mentioned before [29]—that He is exacting from them, against their will, the honor due to Him which they refuse to render willingly, and so that there may be nothing out of order in His kingdom, He keeps them apart from the just in appropriate order. On creatures who are not required to be in the state of justice, however, He does not inflict punishment for an absence of justice, that is, for nothing, because there is nothing that He exacts of them, nor does the right order of the universe demand punishment in their case. Thus, when God inflicts punishment for sin, which is an absence of required justice—which is non-being—He is not at all inflicting punishment for nothing; and it is true that if there is not something real on account of which He must inflict punishment, He absolutely does not inflict it for nothing.

SEVEN

How the human seed is said to be unclean and to be conceived in sins, although there is no sin in it.

From what has been said, it is now evident, I think, that sin and injustice are non-beings, that they exist only in the rational will, and that no essence is properly called unjust except the will. It seems to follow, then, either that an infant has a rational soul—without which it cannot have a rational will—right from the instant of its conception, or else that it is not affected by original sin from the moment of its conception. It is against the common human conviction, however, that an infant has a rational soul right from the moment of its conception. For it would follow that every time a human seed that

has been conceived perishes before it attains to a human figure
—even right after the instant of conception—a human soul is
lost with it, because it is not reconciled through Christ. But
that is simply absurd. This alternative, therefore, ought to be
relinquished entirely.

But if the infant is not in the state of sin from the very
moment of conception, what is the meaning of what Job says
to God: *Who can make him clean that is conceived of unclean
seed? Is it not thou who only art?* [30] And how can David's
statement be true: *. . . I was conceived in iniquities and in
sins did my mother conceive me?* [31] I shall try to find out, then,
how infants are said to be conceived in iniquities and in sins
from unclean seed, even though there is no sin in them from
the very moment of conception.

The fact is that divinely inspired Scripture frequently asserts that something is, when it is not, for the reason that it is
certainly going to occur. Thus, for example, God said to Adam,
regarding the forbidden tree: *. . . In what day soever thou
shalt eat of it, thou shalt die the death,* [32] meaning not that he
was to die bodily on that day, but that on that day he became
subject to the necessity of dying some time. Likewise, because
of the necessity of dying at some time, Paul also says: *And if
Christ be in you, the body indeed is dead, because of sin, but
the spirit liveth, because of justification.* [33] The bodies of those
he was addressing were not dead, surely, but they were going
to die because of sin, since *. . . by one man sin entered into
this world, and by sin, death.* [34] Thus we have all sinned in Adam,
when he sinned, not because we personally committed sin at
that time when we did not yet exist, but because we were
going to be descendants of his in the future, and at that time
it became a necessity that we should sin when we did exist,
because *. . . by the disobedience of one man, many were made
sinners.* [35]

In a similar way, we can understand that man is conceived
in iniquities and sins from an unclean seed, not in the sense
that the uncleanness of sin, or sin, or iniquity, is in the seed,
but in the sense that from the seed itself and from the very
conception from which a human being begins his existence,

he derives the necessity of having the uncleanness of sin, which is exactly the same as sin and iniquity, once he has a rational soul. For even if an infant is generated in sinful concupiscence, still the fault is no more in the seed than it would be in spittle or blood if someone spat out or shed some of his blood with an evil intention. Certainly, blame does not fall on the spittle or blood, but on the evil will. It is obvious, then, both that infants are not in the state of sin from the very moment of conception, and that what I have cited from Sacred Scripture is true. Surely, there is no sin in infants, because they do not possess a will, without which there is no sin in them, and yet it is said to be in them, because in the seed they contract the necessity of sinning when they will eventually be human beings.

EIGHT

In the seed taken from the Virgin there is no sin and no necessity for future sin.

If, then, these things are true, as I think they are, what is derived from a parent for the offspring is without sin, because it has no will. Thus it is obvious that there could be no stain of sin in that which the Son of God took from the Virgin, to be united to His Person. But it has been said [36] that once it has been animated by a rational soul, the seed is derived from the parents with the necessity of future sin. One reason for this, certainly, is that human nature is begotten in infants—as I have said [37]—with the obligation of making satisfaction for the sin of Adam, and, in accordance with what I have supposed,[38] of closer ancestors also, and it is never able to make that satisfaction, and as long as it does not make it, it is in a state of sin. Another reason is that human nature, simply by itself, is not able to possess the state of justice it has abandoned, and the soul which is burdened by the corruptible body [39] cannot even understand that state of justice, which, if it is not understood, cannot be preserved or possessed. Hence, if it can be shown that the seed taken from the Virgin is free of these exigencies, it will be evident that it has not contracted any obligation of sin.

That exigency by which human nature, all by itself, is unable to regain the state of justice, does not belong to that seed. Neither does that exigency by which the corruptible body is a burden to the soul, so that it is unable, without the help of grace, to preserve that state of justice acquired in a complete stage of life, and, in infants, even to understand it. This can easily be shown by the unity in one Person of the nature effecting the union and the nature being united, if, first, that exigency is rejected by which the human nature seems to be bound to satisfaction for the sins of the first parents and of closer ancestors. But there will be no doubt that no obligation falls to the lot of that seed, from closer ancestors, if it can be known to be free from the debt of the first ancestors. With the help of God, then, I shall try, first, to find out how this can be known,[40] since, once this has been made clear, there will be no need to labor hard over other matters.[41]

NINE

Why the sin by which the human race is condemned is to be imputed rather to Adam than to Eve, although he sinned after her and because of her.

With regard to this, I think we ought to inquire, first of all, why the sin for which the human race has been condemned is more often and more particularly imputed to Adam than to Eve, although she sinned first and Adam sinned after her and because of her. For the Apostle says: *But death reigned from Adam unto Moses, even over them also who have not sinned, after the similitude of the transgression of Adam . . .*[42] There are many other texts which seem to reproach Adam more than Eve.

I think the reason for this is that this couple, taken as a whole, is to be understood under the name of its principal member, as a whole is frequently signified by a part. Another reason is that the name "Adam" can indicate Adam together with his rib, even though it had been fashioned into a woman, as we read that God *created them male and female, and blessed them, and called their name Adam, in the day when they were created.*[43] Still another reason is that if not Adam, but only Eve had sinned, it would not have been necessary for the whole human race to die, but Eve alone. Surely, God could have fashioned another woman from Adam, in whom He had created the seed of all human beings, and God's plan [44] could have been brought to fruition from Adam by means of her. For these very reasons, I shall refer to both of them by the name "Adam," unless it will be necessary to distinguish them.[45]

TEN

Why those who were not aware of it bear the burden of Adam's sin

Each and every descendant of Adam is at once a human being by creation and Adam by generation, and a person by the individuality which distinguishes him from others. His existence as a human being is not, indeed, due to Adam, but comes to him by means of Adam. For as Adam did not make himself man, so he did not produce in himself the natural power of propagation; but God who created him man, produced in him such a nature that human beings would be propagated from him. But there is no doubt from what source each and every individual is bound by that debt which we are discussing. It certainly does not arise from his being human or from his being a person. If each and every individual were bound by this debt for the reason that he is a human being or a person, then Adam, before he sinned, would have to have been bound by this debt, because he was a human being and a person. But this is most absurd. The only reason left, then, for the individual's being under obligation is that he is Adam, yet not simply that he is Adam, but that he is Adam *the sinner*. Otherwise, of course, it would follow that if Adam had never sinned, still those who are descended from him would be born with this debt. But that conclusion would be impious.

It is not out of place to repeat here what was already said before,[46] that the reason why every single person is burdened with the sin or debt of Adam is that each one is descended from him, even though he is not aware of Adam's sin. When God made Adam, He produced in him a natural power of propagating his kind, and He subjected this to Adam's power in such a way that he might use it as he willed, so long as he was willing to be subject to God. For he would use it not for bestial and irrational pleasure, but by human and rational choice. As it is proper to beasts to will nothing rationally, of course, so it should be proper to human beings to will nothing without reason. They are always obliged to this, because Adam received this power, and was able to preserve it always. God also gave him this grace, that, just as when He created him without the exercise of the natural power of procreating, or the exercise of a creature's will, He at the same time made him both rational and just, so also, those whom Adam would generate by the exercise of his natural power and his will, would, if he had not sinned, be in the state of justice at the very moment they had rational souls.

The same argument that shows that rational nature was created in the state of justice—which I presented in the little work mentioned before [47]—proves also that those who would have been generated from human nature before sin had occurred, would, of necessity, equally possess the state of justice together with rationality. Surely, He who created the first human being without generation from parents also creates those who come into being through the natural power of generation He created. Every human being, then, if sin had not occurred before, would at the same time be just and rational, like Adam. But because Adam was unwilling to be subject to the will of God, although the natural power of generation itself remained, it was not subject to his will as it would have been if he had not sinned, and he lost the grace he could have passed on to his descendants; and all who are generated by the exercise of the natural power which he had received are born subject to his debt. Human nature was so totally in Adam that none of it existed apart from him. Therefore, since, without any compulsion, it dishonored God by committing sin, with the result that it could not, of itself, make satisfaction,[48] it lost the grace it had received, which it could have preserved always for those generated from itself, and it contracts sin, together with the penalty for sin that goes along with it, every single time it is multiplied by the natural power of generation with which it is endowed.

ELEVEN

Generation from the Virgin is not subject to the law and the merits and demerits of natural generation. There are three courses of realities.

We are now carefully to consider whether this inheritance, so to speak, of sin and of the penalty for sin should justly pass to a man descended from Adam through a virgin. It is, indeed, certain that Adam did not receive the natural power of generating except through a man and a woman together. Surely, it is not a characteristic of human nature, and it is known to be impossible, that a man alone or a woman alone should generate a human being, simply by the exercise of natural power and one's own intention. For just as the slime of the earth [49] had not received the natural power or the will by means of which the first man would originate from it, although it was that out of which God could bring him into existence, so it was not by the activity of a natural power and a human intention that a woman was made from the rib of a man or a man made from a woman alone. Rather, it was God who, by His own power and will, made one man from slime and another from a woman alone, and a woman from a man alone. Although nothing, indeed, begins to be except by the will of God bringing it about or permitting it, yet His power and will, alone, produce certain things, created nature produces certain others, and the will of a creature produces certain things. As a created nature, however, has no power to produce anything by itself, except what it has received from the will of God, so the will of a creature cannot by itself produce anything but what nature helps it or permits it to do. The will of God alone has created the natures of things in the beginning, giving to certain ones powers of volition corresponding to each type, so that the natures and the powers of volition may fulfill their function in the course of things, in accordance with an order assigned to them. It is, moreover, still producing many things, when it produces, out of these natural powers and intentions, what they would never produce in accordance with their own ways of acting and their own intention.

It is the result of God's will alone, for example, when a sea opens up a dry route of travel inside itself; [50] when the dead return to life; [51] when water is unexpectedly changed into wine; [52] when human intellects learn from the Holy Spirit what they have no knowledge of, either by themselves or through another creature; when sinful wills are converted from their own impulses to what is salutary, by the influence of grace alone; when many other things occur which neither a creature nor its desire would bring about through its customary procedure. Nature attracts light things upward, heavy things downward; it makes the earth produce and bring to fruitfulness countless herbs and trees, sometimes following on voluntary cultivation and sowing, sometimes without any exercise of the will preceding; and many other things which we know more readily by sight than by instruction. The things imputed to the will are such as these:

making a journey, constructing, writing, speaking, and the like, which only the will achieves.

Everything that occurs, then, if you think it over carefully, occurs either by the will of God alone, or by nature, in accordance with its God-given power, or by the will of a creature. Since what neither created nature nor the will of a creature, but only God produces, is always a marvel, it is apparent that there are three courses of things, namely: the marvelous, the natural, the voluntary. And the course of the marvelous, certainly, is in no way subject to the others or to their law, but is free and supreme; neither does it slight them when it seems to make them unnecessary, because they have nothing but what they have received from it, nor did it give them anything except as subject to itself. Since the generation of a man from a virgin alone, therefore, is not natural nor voluntary, but marvelous, like that production of a woman from a man alone, and like the fashioning of a man from slime, it is evident that it is never subject to the laws and to the merits and demerits of that generation which both the will and nature—although separately—bring about. For what the free will produces in that matter is different from what nature produces. Still, Adam, derived from what is not human, and Jesus, derived from a woman alone, and Eve, from a man alone—each one is just as much a genuine human being as any man or woman born of both man and woman. Moreover, every human being is either Adam or derived from Adam; but Eve is derived from Adam alone, and all others from Adam and Eve. Now, since Mary, from whom alone Jesus was born, is derived from Adam and Eve, He Himself cannot but be descended from them. For it was thus expedient that He who was to redeem the human race was to be derived and to be born from the father and mother of all.

TWELVE

There would be no rightful reason for Adam's evils to pass on to that Man.

Now, it is also not hard to understand in this way, how the Son of the Virgin is exempt from the sin or debt of Adam. Adam, of course, was created in a state of justice and free from sin [53] and from the debt that has frequently been mentioned, and from penalty for sin. He was also created happy and able always to preserve the state of justice he had received, and through justice, that freedom and happiness I have spoken about. Since, therefore, he did not preserve these blessings for himself, although he could have preserved them forever without any difficulty, he deprived himself of them and subjected himself to their opposites. Accordingly, he became a slave of sin or of injustice, and of a debt he could not pay, and of misery that includes the inability to recover lost benefits. Therefore, as he could not in any other way deprive himself of the benefits which he possessed, and draw to himself evils he did not possess, than by not preserving the blessings for himself when he could, so he could not despoil anyone else of the same blessings and inflict evils upon him, except by not preserving the blessings for him for whom he was able to preserve them.

Now, he could not preserve those benefits for anyone except for those of whose generation he accepted the power, subject to his will. He was not able, then, to transmit the evils previously mentioned, to any person, even though descended from himself, in regard to whose generation neither the natural power of procreating bestowed on him, nor his free will, exercised or could exercise any influence. So the previously mentioned evils of Adam do not, with any reason or rectitude, pass on to the man conceived of the Virgin.[54]

THIRTEEN

Even if He were not God, but mere man, it would still be necessary for Him to be in the same condition as that in which the first man was created.

Similarly, if we carefully explore the wise justice of God by the unaided vision of reason, we understand that it is all too absurd that through that seed any sin or debt of someone else or any penalty should inevitably pass over to that human nature, even if it were not united with the Person of God, but became a mere human being. For that seed is not produced by any created natural power, or by the will of a creature or by a power conferred on anyone; but by the special will of God alone it is selected from the virgin to procreate, by a new power, a human being untainted by sin. The rational mind clearly sees that as it was right for God not to make Adam in any state but that of justice,[55] and not burdened with any debt or any disadvantage, for the very same reason He whom God brings into being in a similar way, by His own will and power, should not be made subject to any evil. For it would be quite inconsistent with the omnipotent and wise goodness of God to make, by His own will, a rational nature of such a sort, from matter in which there is no sin. Whoever does not understand this does not know what is unfitting for God. Hence, even if God made him a mere man, as was said, it would have been necessary for him to be endowed with no less justice and happiness than Adam was, when he was first made.

FOURTEEN

The proposed argument is not refuted by the Scriptural testimony that man is conceived of unclean seed and in iniquities, even though this was properly said of some.

Now, suppose somebody does not mentally grasp what I have said about human seed, that is to say, that there is no sin in it before there is a rational soul,[56] but that it is called unclean with sin and iniquity because of the uncleanness that will occur when it is to be a human being. And suppose he thinks it is unclean in its very conception, because—as I brought up against myself [57]—it is written: *Who can make him clean that is conceived of unclean seed?* [58] and *I was conceived in iniquities; and in sins did my mother conceive me.*[59] I am making no effort here to make him grasp what he cannot grasp, because I have no need of that, but I ask him to give attention to what I shall briefly say.

Surely, those who made these statements wished them to be understood either of every human seed or only of that which is used for generation with a feeling of passion, which would be only that of brute animals, if man had not sinned. But if they were thinking in this way of every seed, then such great men have asserted that the seed taken from the Virgin alone, was unclean; and it would be impious to believe that. So their statements were not written about that seed, but if they meant it in this sense regarding some human seed, they wanted it to be understood only of that which is conceived with passion, as I mentioned. Now this in no way contradicts our argument, which asserts that the seed taken from the Virgin is spotless, although it is descended from the sinful mass.[60]

FIFTEEN

The sinful mass is not totally sinful.

Surely, blindness is not in any part of the human body but the eye, where sight should be—it is not, for example, in the hand or foot—although we may say a man is blind. Similarly, deafness is only in the ear when we say a man is deaf. So also, although the mass of the human race is called sinful, still, as I have said,[61] the sin is in no part of it but in the human will, which we know the seed does not possess in any human conception. Hence, if the things we said before are pondered, we can freely conclude, without any true or probable argument to contradict us, that no reasoning, no truth, no understanding permits the possibility or the necessity of any stain of the sin of the sinful mass having accrued to a man conceived of a virgin alone—even if he were not God—although he has been taken from that mass.

SIXTEEN

Why John and others who, like him, were miraculously conceived, are not for that reason free from sin.

Suppose there are brought up to me, by way of objection, John the Baptist and others who were generated from sterile persons and from those in whom, prior to old age, the natural power of generating had already died out, and of whom it is thought, for a supposedly similar reason, that they must have been born without sin and the penalty for sin, because they were conceived miraculously. Surely, we must understand that this argument to prove that virginal conception is free from every requirement of sin is absolutely inapplicable to them. For it is one thing to do something unheard of and inconceivable and beyond experience in nature, and it is another thing to heal a nature weakened by age or some defect, and to restore it to its proper function. Just as Adam would not have been at all weakened by old age or by any cause at all, if he had not sinned, so the natural power of generating, created in him, and—as we have already said [62]—subject in use to his power, would not be impeded in its course by any fall. In the case of John and similar persons, then, there is nothing exceptional to the nature of Adam, as has been granted in the case of the Son of the Virgin, but what had been weakened in its causes is known to have been repaired. Hence, because those persons were generated by the natural method of propagation conferred on Adam, they never can or ought to be considered the same as the One of whom we are treating, in regard to the miracle of conception, so as to be able to prove that they have been exempted from the bond of original sin.

SEVENTEEN

Why God became man, although He could have made from Adam as many men, sinless but not divine, as would accomplish the same end.

Someone may say: "If a person who was merely human, without being God, could originate from Adam, without any contamination of sin, as you say, then why was it necessary for God to become man, since God could redeem sinners by one such person who would be sinless,[63] or else, by a similar miracle, could create as many human beings as were necessary to complete the heavenly city?"

I have a brief answer to this. God became man for the reason that—as has been shown in the little work frequently mentioned [64]—a man who was not God would not be able to redeem the others. Again, the reason why He did not make as many human beings of that kind as were necessary was that if no one produced by natural generation were saved, it would seem that He had created that natural power in Adam without purpose, and that, as it were, He was correcting what He had not made properly. But it is not congruous with supreme wisdom to act that way in regard to any natural power.

Not long before,[65] I proposed to investigate how the seed taken from the Virgin, in which we have shown there is no sin, can be perceived to be free from the previously mentioned necessities in which I had supposed all other men to be conceived. And I was confident that that seed could be liberated from that necessity by which human nature, of itself, is unable to recover the justice it had abandoned, and from that by which *the corruptible body is a load upon the soul*,[66] and especially in infants. The reason is that that man is God. The condition is that there first be reasonably excluded from Him the necessity of sin and the debt of Adam and of close ancestors. Therefore I began to inquire in what way this could be understood regarding the necessity of the sin and the debt of Adam, so that I might more easily answer my questions, later, regarding the others. And by the overflowing grace of Him, the purity of whose conception we are treating about, we succeeded in proving that He was free from every sin and debt and previously mentioned necessities.[67] Not only that, but we succeeded besides, in proving by intelligible argument that a man so conceived—even if he were not God but simply man [68]—must be endowed with no less justice or happiness than that in which Adam was created. Thus it appeared equally unreasonable that through such a generation he inherit sin or the penalty for sin from any ancestors, and also that God would of Himself make a rational nature unjust or make it miserable without any injustice on its part to deserve that state.

EIGHTEEN

*It was not absolutely necessary that God be conceived of
a virgin in the state of justice, as if He could not be conceived of a sinner; but there was a reason of fitness for this.*

Although it is absolutely true that the Son of God was conceived of a most pure virgin, still it was not necessary that
this occur, in the sense that an offspring in the state of justice
could not reasonably be generated from a sinful parent by a
propagation of this kind. Rather, the reason for it is that it was
fitting that the conception of this man take place in the purest
of mothers. It was fitting, certainly, that that Virgin should
shine with that purity than which no greater, under God, can
be thought of. For to her God the Father was disposed to give
His only Son, begotten equal to Himself, whom from His heart
He loved as Himself, with the result that this One would naturally be, singly and identically, the Son equally of God the
Father and of the Virgin. It is she whose very being the Son
Himself chose to make a mother for Himself, and of whom the
Holy Spirit willed and brought about that the One from whom
He Himself proceeded should be conceived and born. But how
the same Virgin was purified by means of faith before that
conception, I have described where I gave a different account
of this same topic of which we are treating here.[69]

NINETEEN

How this reasoning and the other one given elsewhere
agree and how they differ.

Each one of these two arguments seems to me to suffice, by itself, to answer our question,[70] but both together seem to give abundant satisfaction to a spirit seeking the power of reason and the splendor of action. And although they have the same aim, yet they differ in the following way. The one I have proposed here proves, without any reason to oppose it, that by generation of this kind, God must produce an offspring in the state of justice, in fact, nothing but one in the state of justice, even from the substance of a sinful virgin—because there is no sin anywhere in the nature of a human being but in the will. The previous one, though, proves that, even if sin were in the whole essence of a virgin, still that essence could become pure by faith, for a pure conception of this kind. And in the first case, all necessity of death and of any sort of corruption or labor is evidently excluded from that man; in the other case, though, a question seems to arise about this, but it is resolved by sufficient reason, if it is carefully examined. Hence it is evident from both, that in all things which He suffered, our Lord and Redeemer bore everything only because of His merciful will.

TWENTY

*The one born of a virgin possessed original justice instead
of original sin.*

On the subject of original sin, in my opinion, it has been
sufficiently shown—in accordance with my plan—how it could
not, for any reason, come down from ancestors to a man conceived of a virgin, but rather that he would, by demands of
reason, have to begin existence in a state of justice and happiness. Therefore, since He was born—as we may say—of a just
Father, from the standpoint of His divine nature, and of a
just mother, from that of His human nature, it must be said,
without any incongruity, that He possesses original justice, instead of the original injustice which all other children of Adam
have from their very beginning.

TWENTY-ONE

Why He could not have personal injustice.

With regard to *personal* injustice, however, it would be superfluous to raise the question whether or not it affects Him,
since human nature never existed in Him without the divine
nature, and His soul was never burdened [71] against His will, or
in any way impeded by a corruptible body. Since this very soul,
even that whole human being, and the Word of God, God, always existed as one Person, that Man was never lacking in

perfect justice and wisdom and power. By reason ot His Person, He always possessed these as His own, as God possesses them, although, in regard to His natures, the human one has received from the divine nature whatever it possesses.

I do not deny, however, that there may be another deeper explanation of how God took human nature from the sinful mass without sin, as something unleavened from something leavened,[72] besides the one I have set forth here and the one I presented elsewhere.[73] I would willingly accept this, if it were shown to me, and I would not hold on to my own explanations if they can be shown to be opposed to the truth, although I do not think that likely.

TWENTY-TWO

The magnitude of original sin.

Moreover, original sin cannot be either greater or less than I have said.[74] The reason is that once an infant is rational, the human nature in it does not possess the justice which it received in Adam and which it ought always to have. Inability does not excuse it, either, for not possessing justice, as was said before.[75] Still, I think original sin is not in every regard as grave as I previously supposed.[76] For since I wished to show that it does not affect the Man conceived of the Virgin, I defined it in such a way that nothing could be added to it, so that—as I said [77]—I should not seem to minimize its gravity because of the subject of my inquiry. On this matter I shall briefly make clear what I am thinking at present.

I do not think the sin of Adam passes down to infants in such a way that they ought to be punished for it as if each one of them had personally committed it, as Adam did, although on account of his sin it has been brought about that not one of them could be born without sin, which is followed by condemnation. For when the Apostle says that *death reigned from Adam unto Moses, even over them also who have not sinned, after the similitude of the transgression of Adam*,[78] it is quite evident that he means that there is not imputed to them personally the very transgression of Adam or anything so great, even though in his writing he declares that all children of Adam—except the Son of the Virgin—are *sinners*[79] and *children of wrath*.[80] When he says: *Even over them also who have not sinned, after the similitude of the transgression of Adam*,[81] surely he can be interpreted as saying: "even over those who did not commit *so great a sin as Adam did*, by his transgression." And when he says: *Now the law entered in, that sin might abound*,[82] we are to understand either that sin before the law, in those *who have not sinned after the similitude of the transgression of Adam*, is less than the sin of Adam, or else that if it was not less, then there abounded in them after the law, sin beyond the sin of Adam—and that, when I consider it, I cannot understand. As you have already read, I have set forth my view on the gravity of his sin and the satisfaction for it in *Why God Became Man*.[83] It is true, nevertheless, that no one is restored to the goal for which man was created and for which the power of propagation was bestowed on him, and that no one is rescued from the evils into which human nature has fallen, except through satisfaction for that sin by which it hurled itself headlong into the very same evils.

Someone will say: "If they do not individually have the sin of Adam, how do you assert that no one is saved without satisfaction for the sin of Adam? How does a just God require from them satisfaction for a sin that is not their's?" God does not, indeed, require from any sinner more than he owes, but since no one can make returns for as much as he owes, Christ alone makes payment beyond requirement for all who are saved, as I have already said in the little work frequently mentioned.

It remains to be seen, in still another way, why the sin is less in infants than in Adam, even though it came down to all from him. For *by one man*—that is, by Adam—*sin entered into this world, and by sin, death*.[84]

TWENTY-THREE

How and why it is inherited by infants.

We do not know why it is less, however, if we do not understand why and how it is present in them. Although this was discussed before,[85] to the extent necessary for the subject of our inquiry, still it will not be superfluous to repeat it briefly here. Surely, it cannot be denied that infants existed in Adam when he sinned. But they existed in him causally or materially as in a seed,[86] and they exist personally in themselves, because in him they were the seed itself, in themselves they are individually distinct persons. In him, they were not distinct from him; in themselves, they are distinct from him. In him they were himself; in their own persons, they are themselves. They existed in him, therefore, but not as themselves, since they did not yet exist as themselves.

Someone might say: "That existence by which other human beings are said to have existed in Adam is practically nothing and a vacuous sort of being, and should not be called "existence" at all. Well, he might as well say that that existence by which Christ was seminally in Abraham, in David and in the other fathers—and that by which all things that come from a seed existed in the seeds—was nothing or meaningless or spurious. He might as well say that God made nothing when, in the beginning, He first made within their seeds, all the things that are generated from a seed. He might as well say, too, that this existence without whose reality these objects we see would not be existing, is nothing or meaningless. Surely, if it is not true that those things which nature generates from seeds had some sort of existence in them from the beginning, they would not have being from them at all. But if it is very silly to say this, it was not a spurious or a meaningless, but a real and genuine existence by which all other human beings had being in Adam; and God did not do something meaningless when He gave them existence in Adam. But, as has been said, they did not have existence in him as distinct from him, and therefore it was quite different from the existence they have in themselves.

Although it is established that all of them had being in him, however, still the Virgin's Son alone was in him in a way vastly different from the others. All the others, of course, were in him in this way, that they had their being from him by the natural power of generation, which was subject to his power and his will. That Man alone, however, was not in him in such a way as to originate from him through his natural power or his will. For when Adam sinned, it had already been given to him, with regard to the others, to be the one from whom they were to come, and to be the source of their being. With regard to this Man, however, it had been given to Adam to be the one from whom He was to come, but not to be the source of His being, because it was not in Adam's power that this One be generated from him. But neither was it within his power that this Man might come into being from another essence or from nothing. So it was not due to Adam that this Man might have being in any way. For it was neither in the power of his nature nor in the power of his will that the other should exist at all. Adam did have the nature, however, from which this Man was to be generated, not by Adam's power, but by God's. Among His ancestors, of course, down to His Virgin Mother, the will started generation and nature brought it to fruition, so that the Virgin herself, like everyone else, was brought into her existence from Adam by a process partly natural, partly voluntary. Nevertheless, in this one case it was neither the will of a creature that caused generation, nor nature that brought it to fruition. Rather, the *Holy Spirit* and *the power of the Most High* [87] brought forth a man out of a virginal woman in a marvelous way. With regard to the others, then, it was in Adam, that is, it was within his power, that they might have being from him. But with regard to that Man, it was not due to Adam that He might have being in any way, as it was not due to the slime from which the first man was fashioned, that he had being from it in a marvelous manner, nor was it within the power of the male that Eve, as she was fashioned from him, should have being from him. Nor was it in the power of any of those in whom He had being, from Adam down to Mary, to give Him existence. Still, He was in them, because that from which He was to be taken was in them; just as that from which the first human being was fashioned was in the slime, and that from which Eve was fashioned was in the first man. But He was in them, not by the will or power of a creature, but by the power of God alone; yet He was in them in so much more marvelous a manner and by a far greater favor, because they are mere human beings, and He was made Man-God. In a vastly different way, therefore, than those who are generated by the voluntary and natural process, He was in Adam when Adam sinned. In a certain way, then, Adam produces those whom the human will, by starting generation, and nature, by bringing it to fruition, cause to exist, through a power they have received. This Man, however, no one but God has brought into existence, because although He came from Adam, He was not produced by Adam, but by Himself, just as if He were from Himself.

What, then, could be more apt to manifest the vast extent of the goodness of God and the fullness of grace which He bestowed on Adam, than that the lot of those whose existence was so much in his power that what he was by nature they would be through him, should also be so dependent on his free choice that he could generate them with the same justice and happiness as he enjoyed? This, then, was granted to him. Therefore, since, after having been placed on an eminence of so much grace, he deliberately forfeited the benefits bestowed on him to be preserved for himself and for them, the result was that the children lost what the father deprived them of, by not preserving it, when he could have bestowed it on them by preserving it. This seems to me a sufficient reason why Adam's sin and evils come down upon infants, if we consider pure justice by itself, carefully putting aside our own will, which is a frequent and serious hindrance to the mind in the understanding of rectitude. But just how I think this sin comes down upon them, I shall explain in a few words.

There is a sin that arises from our nature, as I have said,[88] and there is a sin arising from the person. So what arises from the person can be called "personal," and what arises from nature, "natural"—and this is called "original." Moreover, as what is personal passes over to the nature, so what is natural passes over to the person. This can be illustrated. That Adam was accustomed to eat was a requirement of nature, because the nature was created in such a way as to require this. But that he ate of the forbidden tree—it was not a natural will but a personal one, that is, his own, which brought this about. Still, what the person did, he did not do without his nature. It was, of course, the person that went by the name of "Adam"; it was the nature that was called "man." The person, then, made the nature sinful, because when Adam sinned, man sinned. Just the same, it was not because he was man that he was impelled to take what was forbidden; rather, he was drawn by his own desire, which was not required by his nature, but which was given birth by the person. Something like this, in reverse, occurs in infants. The fact that they do not possess the justice they ought to have is the result, surely, not of their personal volition, as with Adam, but of a natural destitution which their nature itself received from Adam. For in Adam, in whom alone the whole of it existed, the nature was stripped of the justice it possessed, and unless it is aided, it lacks it forever. In this way, since the nature has existence in persons and persons do not exist without a nature, the nature is the reason for the persons of infants being sinful. Thus in Adam, the person despoiled the nature of the blessing of justice, and the nature, having been made destitute, makes all persons whom it propagates from itself sinful and unjust, by means of the same destitution. In this way, the personal sin of Adam passes over into all who are generated from him naturally, and in them it is original or natural.

But it is evident that there is a great difference between the sin of Adam and their sin; because he sinned by his own wilfulness, and they sin by a natural necessity which his own personal will deserved. But although no one doubts that an equal penalty does not follow upon unequal sins, the condemnation of personal sin is nevertheless like that of original sin in this, that no one is admitted to the kingdom of God, for which man was made, except by the death of Christ, without which what is due for the sin of Adam is not repaid—although not all deserve to be tormented equally in hell. For after the day of judgment, there will be no angel or human being who is not either in the kingdom of God or in hell. In this way, then, the sin of infants is less than the sin of Adam, and yet no one is saved without that universal satisfaction, by which sin, both great and small, is forgiven. But why there is no satisfaction without that death, and how the salvation of human beings is brought about by means of it—these questions I have raised and answered, so far as God has granted me the power, in the book already mentioned.[89]

TWENTY-FOUR

The sins of ancestors after Adam are not to be reckoned in with the original sin of descendants.

Now, I do not think that the sins of close ancestors belong with original sin. Surely, if Adam had never been able to pass on his own justice to those whom he was to generate, he would never have been able to transmit to them his own injustice. Hence, because no one after Adam was able to preserve his own justice for his offspring, I see no reason why the sins of close ancestors ought to be imputed to the souls of descendants. And then, no one has a doubt that infants do not preserve any rectitude of will for the sake of rectitude itself.[90] In this, therefore, all are equally unjust, that they do not possess any of the justice which every human being ought to have. This deprivation of justice passes down to all from Adam, in whom human nature despoiled itself of that justice. For although in Adam some justice remained in it, so that it preserved rectitude of will in some matters, yet it was so deprived of that gift by which it had been able to preserve justice in itself for future generations, that in no one of them can it reproduce itself in the state of justice. Certainly, in the case of infants, it could not take away from itself more than total justice and total happiness, which is not given to anyone lacking due justice.

That the injustice of the closer ancestors could make this deprivation of justice any greater does not seem possible, moreover, since there cannot be any greater deprivation than this one descending from the sin of Adam into infants. For where there is no justice, no justice can be taken away. Where there can be no deprivation of justice, moreover, there can be no increase of injustice. Hence ancestors who are not in the state of justice cannot increase the injustice in their offspring, beyond the deprivation of justice we have been talking about. Where there is no justice, however, there is nothing to prevent the granting of some justice. It might seem more likely and quite possible, then—if ancestors who are not in the state of justice are said to inflict some injustice on their posterity—that those who are in the state of justice are able to confer some justice on their's. If that were to occur, the infants of the just would possess some justice. If this were true, however, they would be less gravely condemned than the progeny of those in the state of injustice, should they die without baptism; or if they are saved, they would be chosen with some preceding merit of their own. This the apostle Paul denies, though, where he shows, using Jacob and Esau as examples, that no one is saved except by a grace that anticipates the merits of all.[91] Since, therefore, worthy ancestors confer no justice on their infant progeny before baptism, surely those without justice inflict no injustice on their's.

Suppose someone says: "The unrighteous ancestors do not inflict any injustice on their infant progeny from whom they cannot take away any justice, but they do make more grave in them the original injustice which they have from Adam. Hence those who are in the state of justice also make it less grave in their progeny. So, if the infant descendants of just ancestors are less unjust than those of unjust ancestors, they ought the less to be reprobated than the latter." Let him say that, who has the courage and can give some proof. I do not dare to say it, since I see the immature offspring of both the just and the unjust chosen for the grace of baptism and excluded from it, indiscriminately. But if someone says even this much, he cannot prove it. Indeed, just as in this way there is no one more just than one who is simply just, except one who by his will more perfectly strives after what he should, or avoids what he should, so no one is more unjust than simply being unjust, except one who more intensely loves what he should not or condemns what he should not. If, then, it cannot be shown that infants, as soon as they have a soul, have in one individual, a greater or less desire than in another, for what they ought or ought not to desire, then no one can prove that among infants one is born more just or more unjust than another. Likewise, then, it does not seem either that the just, by their worthiness, render original injustice lighter in their infant offspring, or that the unjust, by their unworthiness, render it graver in their's. Hence, if ancestors who are not in the state of justice cannot, by their sin, increase, either in number or magnitude, original sin in their infant offspring, it seems to me that the sins of the ancestors after Adam are not counted in the original sin of infants.

I do not deny that many and great benefits of body and soul accrue to offspring because of the high merits of ancestors, and that, on account of sins of ancestors, children and descendants *unto the third and fourth generation* [92] and perhaps beyond, are scourged with divers tribulations and lose those benefits, even spiritual ones, which they might perhaps have acquired through those ancestors, if they were just. It would take too long to insert examples of these here. But I do say that original sin is naturally equal in all infants conceived, just as the sin of Adam, which is the reason why they are born in it, extends to all equally. [93]

TWENTY-FIVE

How ancestors do injury to the souls of descendants.

If the sins of ancestors sometimes do injury to the souls of descendants, however, I do not think that this occurs by God's imputing those sins to the latter, or by His leading them into some transgressions because of their ancestors. Rather, it occurs because, just as He often rescues the descendants of the just from sins on account of the merits of their ancestors, so He sometimes leaves the offspring of the unjust in their sins because of the demerits of their ancestors. For since no one is free of sin unless God gives deliverance, He is said to "lead into" [94] it when He does not give deliverance, and to "harden" [95] when He does not soften. Certainly, it seems quite a bit more admissible that God abandon the sinful soul to whom He owes nothing but punishment, to his own sins on account of sins of his ancestors, than that He burden it with what is due to others, to be tortured in place of others. Thus, therefore, there is no contradiction in saying both that original sin is the same in all, and that *the son shall not bear the iniquity of the father*,[96] and *everyone shall bear his own burden* [97] and everyone will receive *according as he hath done* in his body, *whether it be good or evil*,[98] and in saying also, that God visits the sins of ancestors on descendants *unto the third and fourth generation*,[99] even if this is to occur in the soul. The same is true of whatever else you read that seems to mean that the sins of ancestors do harm to the souls of their descendants. Surely, the soul of a son does not die for the sin of his father, but for his own sin,[100] and no one is bearing the *iniquity of his father*,[101] when he is left in his own, but he is bearing his own iniquity, and no one is bearing another's burden, but his own,[102] and he is receiving in his body according as he himself, not his father, has done.[103]

But because it is on account of the sins of his fathers that he was not liberated from his own evils, the things he is bearing are imputed to those very sins of ancestors.[104]

TWENTY-SIX

How it is still true that no one bears his father's sins, but his own.

Now, if someone objects that all who are not saved by faith directed toward Christ, are bearing the iniquity and the burden of Adam, wanting to prove by this that infants either ought likewise to bear the iniquities of other ancestors as well, or else are not bound to bear his, let him carefully consider that infants do not bear Adam's sin, but their own. Surely the sin of Adam was one thing, and the sin of infants is another, because they differ in the way described.[105] For the former was the cause, the latter is one result. Adam lacked the justice that was due, not because some one else abandoned it, but because he himself did; infants lack it, not because they forsook it, but because someone else did. So Adam's sin is not the same as the infants'. And when, as I observed before,[106] the Apostle says that *death reigned from Adam unto Moses, even over them also who have not sinned, after the similitude of the transgression of Adam,*[107] he obviously shows that the two are different, by pointing out that the infants' sin is less than Adam's.

When an infant is condemned for original sin, therefore, he is condemned, not for Adam's sin, but for his own. For if he did not have sin of his own, he would not be condemned. Thus, then, he is not bearing Adam's iniquity, but his own, although we may say he is bearing it because the iniquity of the former was the cause of his own sin. This reason for infants being born in sin, which existed in Adam, however, is not found in other ancestors, because in them, as I have said,[108] human nature has not the power of propagating offspring who have the gift of justice. Hence it does not follow that there should be sin in infants because of *their* sin, as there is because of Adam's.

TWENTY-SEVEN

What original sin is. It is equal in all.

I understand original sin, therefore, to be nothing else than what is in an infant, as soon as it has a rational soul, whatever may have occurred in its body, before it was so animated—for example, some disintegration of its parts—or whatever is to occur afterward, either in the soul or in the body. Because of the reasons mentioned before, I think that this is equal in all infants generated in the natural way, and that all who die in that sin alone are equally condemned. Indeed, whatever sin occurs in man over and above this one, is personal; and just as a person is born sinful on account of his nature, so the nature is rendered more sinful by the person, because when any person at all commits sin, man commits sin.[109]

In regard to these infants, I cannot understand this sin I am calling "original" to be anything else than that same deprivation of the required justice, which I described before [110] as the result of the disobedience of Adam, by which all are *children of wrath.*[111] The reason is that the voluntary forsaking of justice, of which nature was the cause in Adam, is a reproach to the nature, and its inability to recover justice does not excuse persons, as has been said.[112] Deprivation of happiness also goes along with this inability, so that as they lack all justice, they likewise totally lack happiness. On account of these two deprivations, they have been left unprotected in the exile of this life, and exposed to the sins and miseries that are unceasingly besetting them everywhere, and assaulting them from every side, except to the extent that they are protected by divine providence.

TWENTY-EIGHT

An answer to those who do not think infants ought to be condemned.

There are those who at heart are unwilling to grant that infants who die without Baptism ought to be condemned simply on account of lack of justice, as I have said.[113] The reason is that nobody is convinced that infants ought to be reprehended for the sin of another person, and that at such an age they are not yet in possession of justice and the use of reason. They also do not think God should judge the innocent any more strictly than human beings judge them. To them we must say that the way God ought to act toward infants is different from the way human beings ought to act toward them. For it is not right for man to demand from nature what he did not bestow on it and what is not due to himself, nor is it just for one human person to accuse another of being born with a fault, since he himself is not born without it, and he is healed of it only through someone else. But it is right for God to exact from nature what He bestowed on it and what is due to Himself in justice.

If you think it over, however, even this sentence of condemnation of infants is not very different from the verdict of human beings. Suppose, for example, some man and his wife were exalted to some great dignity and estate, by no merit of their own but by favor alone, then both together inexcusably commit a grave crime, and on account of it are justly dispossessed and reduced to slavery. Who will say that the children whom they generate after their condemnation should not be subjected to the same slavery, but rather should be gratuitously put in possession of the goods which their parents deservedly lost? Our first ancestors and their offspring are in such a condition: having been justly condemned to be cast from happiness to misery for their fault, they bring forth their offspring in the same banishment. When the cases are similar, therefore, there ought to be a similar verdict, but in the latter case it ought to be all the more severe, since there is less likelihood that their crime could be condoned.

Finally, every human being is either saved or condemned. Now, everyone who is saved is admitted to the kingdom of heaven, and everyone who is condemned is excluded from it. Whoever is admitted, though, is elevated to a likeness with the angels,[114] in whom there never was nor ever will be any sin; and this cannot occur, as long as there is in that person any stain of sin. Thus it is impossible for any human being affected by any sin, even a slight one, to be saved. Therefore, if, as I said,[115] original sin is some kind of sin, it is necessary that every human being born in it be condemned unless it is remitted.[116]

TWENTY-NINE

How the inability to possess justice excuses them after Baptism.

I have said[117] that the inability to possess justice does not excuse the injustice of infants. Now, someone may pose a problem: "Let us grant that in an infant, sin—that is, injustice—exists before Baptism, and there is no excuse for its inability to possess justice, as you say, and that sin is not remitted in Baptism unless it previously existed. Then, since after Baptism, an infant, as long as it is an infant, exists without justice and cannot understand the justice which it is to preserve—provided, of course, justice is the rectitude of the will preserved for its own sake [118]—how is it that the infant does not lack justice even after it has been baptized? Suppose, then, that after having been baptized, it dies in infancy, not immediately after Baptism, while it does not yet know how to have repentance. Because it does not possess the justice it should have, and is not excused by inability, it passes out of this life without justice, as it would have done before Baptism, and it is not admitted into the kingdom of God, since no one is received there without being just. Now this is not what the Catholic Church teaches. But if, in Baptism, a sin that will occur in infancy is forgiven to infants, why not also those which occur in a later stage?"

To this I answer that in Baptism the sins which existed before Baptism are entirely wiped out. So the original inability to possess justice is not imputed as sin to those already baptized, as it was before. Hence, just as the inability could not previously excuse the absence of justice, since it was itself at fault, so, after Baptism, it entirely excuses that absence, because it remains without any fault. Thus it happens that justice, which was required of infants before Baptism, without any excusing cause, is not exacted of them as of obligation, after Baptism. So, as long as they are without justice only because of original inability, they are not unjust, because there is not in them an absence of required justice. For that is not required which is, apart from all fault, impossible. Therefore, if they die in this state, they are not condemned, because they are not in the state of injustice. Rather, they are saved, as being justified both by the justice of Christ who gave Himself for them, and by the justice of the faith of Mother Church, who has faith in their stead.[119]

To the extent of my understanding, I have briefly expressed these conclusions on original sin, not so much making affirmations as trying to draw out consequences, until God will, in some fashion, reveal something better to me. Should someone disagree with me, however, I do not reject anyone's opinion, if it can be shown to be true.

NOTES

ABBREVIATIONS

ACW   *Ancient Christian Writers*, ed. J. Quasten and J. C. Plumpe. Westminster, Md.: Newman Press, 1946—

AHDLMA   *Archives d' histoire doctrinale et littéraire du moyen âge.* Paris: J. Vrin, 1926—

CSEL   *Corpus Scriptorum Ecclesiasticorum Latinorum.* Vienna: Tempsky, 1866—

DDT   *Dictionary of Dogmatic Theology*, ed. by P. Parente, A. Piolanti, S. Garofalo (tr. E. Doronzo). Milwaukee: Bruce, 1951.

DHGE   *Dictionnaire d'histoire et de géographie ecclésiastique.* Paris: Libraire Letouzey et Ané.

DTC   *Dictionnaire de théologie catholique*, ed. A. Vacant et E. Mangenot. Paris: Letouzey et Ané.

PG   *Patrologiae Cursus Completus, Series Graeca*, ed. J. P. Migne. Paris, 1857–1866.

PL   *Patrologiae Cursus Completus, Series Latina*, ed. J. P. Migne. Paris, 1844–1864.

TD   *Theological Dictionary*, ed. by K. Rahner and H. Vorgrimler. New York: Herder and Herder, 1965.

INTRODUCTION

1. Eadmer was a native of Canterbury, born about 1060, and he died there about the year 1130. Since the Norman conquest of England occurred in 1066, he was one of the "Old English" of Saxon stock. He was brought up from infancy in the monastic community at Christ Church. It is probable that he belonged to the English gentry and that his family had been reduced to poverty at the time of the conquest.

Before the end of 1093, when Anselm was consecrated Archbishop of Canterbury, Eadmer lived the quiet life of the monk. But he apparently became a member of Anselm's household, and he accompanied him on his journeys, which were, for an archbishop, more than usually frequent and long. The periodical visits to the manors pertaining to the see of Canterbury were shared by Eadmer, and he went to the continent with Anselm in both his exiles.

From Anselm's death in 1109, Eadmer remained in Canterbury until 1116, and during these seven years did most of his writing. From 1116 to 1119, he set out on travels again with the new archbishop, Ralph, who was appointed as Anselm's successor after a long vacancy.

Besides the *Life of Anselm* and the *History of Recent Events,* Eadmer wrote lives of Saint Wilfrid, Bregwine, Oswald, Dunstan and Odo of Canterbury. (See *PL* 159, col. 709–800). He also wrote, before the year 1115, a meditation called *The Eminence of the Virgin Mary* (*De Excellentia Virginis Mariae Liber, PL* 159, col. 557–580). Another work, *Tractatus De Conceptione B. Mariae Virginis,* written about 1125, was attributed to St. Anselm in certain manuscripts, and is included by Migne in an *Appendix Spuriorum, PL* 159, col. 301–318.

Eadmer was appointed Bishop of St. Andrew's, in Scotland, in 1120. He insisted, however, upon acknowledging Canterbury as the primatial see, and he met strong opposition, so he resigned his position, relinquished his ring and crozier, and returned to Canterbury without ever having been consecrated.

See R. W. Southern, *Saint Anselm And His Biographer,* (Cambridge, England: University Press, 1963) pp. 229–354; also B. Heurtebize, "Eadmer," *DTC,* 4 (1911), col. 1977–1978.

2. The *Historia Novorum,* edited by Gabriel Gerberon, is available in *PL* 159, col. 347–524. M. Rule has provided a later and more reliable edition: *Eadmer, Historia Novorum In Anglia,* in *Rerum Britannicarum Medii Aevi Scriptores,* 81, London, 1884.

Originally, this history comprised four books, which treated of the archbishopric of Lanfranc, the immediate predecessor of Anselm, and reported the public acts of Anselm up to the year of his death. Eadmer wrote these books between 1109 and 1115, and four years later began an addition which increased the work by two books and some insertions, and brought the history of the see of Canterbury up to the death of Ralph, Anselm's successor, in 1122.

It was probably after 1093 that Eadmer started to compile the material for his history, but it was only after Anselm's death in 1109 that he assembled it for publication. His *History* is an account, mainly, of the public events in the lives of Lanfranc, Anselm and Ralph, especially their relations with the pope, the king and their local clergy. It also includes about forty original documents, which are largely the correspondence of pope, king and archbishop.

A good study of the contents and value of the history is given by R. W. Southern, *op. cit.,* pp. 298–313.

3. Unlike the *Historia Novorum,* the *De Vita Et Conversatione Anselmi Cantuariensis Archiepiscopi* is mainly hagiographical. It stresses the personal virtues and the marvelous and impressive achievements of Anselm, but it does give a good factual account of his life too. The text of Gerberon's edition is given in *PL* 158, col. 50–118, and R. W. Southern has provided a new critical edition of the text, *Eadmeri Monachi Cantuariensis Vita Sancti Anselmi Archiepiscopi Cantuariensis,* together with an introduction, English translation and notes (London: Thomas Nelson and Sons, 1962). Southern gives as concluding part of the text itself (pp. 145–151) Eadmer's account of the favors granted through St. Anselm's intercession after his death. This is given by Gerberon (*PL* 158, col. 117 B–120) as a separate supplement to the *Life.* The *Vita Anselmi* is also printed in the Bollandist *Acta Sanctorum,* Aprilis, t. 2, pp. 866–893.

Toward the end of his work, (Southern's ed., Book II, ch. 72, pp. 150–151; Gerberon's, col. 119 D–120 D), Eadmer records that after he had already transcribed on parchment much of his work, Anselm asked what he was copying. Reluctantly the younger monk showed the archbishop what he had put together, and at the time Anselm made some corrections and suggestions. A few days later, however, he ordered Eadmer to destroy the whole work, because he considered himself unworthy of a literary monument. Unwilling to disobey his master, yet unwilling to lose the fruits of his labor and to disappoint posterity, he first copied the work and then destroyed the quires which Anselm had read. He admits that his action was "perhaps not free from the sin of disobedience," since he was knowingly following the letter but not the spirit of the command, and he concludes by asking the prayers of all readers indebted to him, to pray for his forgiveness.

R. W. Southern has a fine critical study of the *Vita* in his *Saint Anselm And His Biographer*, ch. 9, pp. 314–343.

4. 1033 is the year usually given. R. W. Southern, *op. cit.*, p. 3, gives that year without any alternative. P. Richard, "Anselme De Cantorbéry," *DHGE*, vol. 3, col. 464, says the saint was born in 1033, "or, more probably, in the beginning of the year 1034." J. Bainvel, "Anselme De Cantorbéry," *DTC*, t. 1, col. 1327, also gives the two years as possible alternatives; so does R. Roques, in his translation of the *Cur Deus Homo, Pourquoi Dieu S'Est Fait Homme* (Paris: Editions Du Cerf, 1963), p. 12 and note 1.

5. Eadmer, *Vita*, I, ch. 1, n. 2, *PL* 158, col. 51 B; Southern's ed. I, ch. 2, p. 5.

6. This story was preserved, not by Eadmer, but by one of the saint's friends at Bec, possibly Boso. It is included in some, but not all, of the copies of the *Vita Anselmi*. The Latin text is given as an appendix in Southern's ed., pp. 172–173.

7. *Vita*, I, ch. 1, n. 3, *PL* 158, col. 51 D; Southern, I, ch. 3, p. 6.

8. *Ibid.*, I, ch. 1, n. 4, *PL* 158, col. 51 D; Southern, I, ch. 4, p. 6.

9. *Ibid.*

10. *Ibid.*

11. Lanfranc was born at Pavia, about the year 1005. He studied and practiced law, but left his native town to devote himself to learning and teaching. At Avranches, in Normandy, he was employed in a school and became famous as a teacher. Feeling himself called to religious life, he quietly left Avranches, and after some time arrived at Bec, where Herlwin was building a new monastery. He became a monk and devoted himself to biblical studies. Herlwin made him prior and allowed him to open a school there. Within a short time, he attracted scholars from all over Europe, the most celebrated of them being, after Anselm, the future Pope Alexander II.

In 1050, at a council in Rome, he became acquainted with the views of Berengar on the mode of presence of Christ in the Blessed Sacrament, and in refuting them, he formulated the traditional doctrine in a precise way that has since become classical and has been adopted by various councils of the Church.

Lanfranc became abbot of St. Stephen's in Caen, in 1066, the year of the defeat of the English king Harold by Duke William of Normandy, a friend of Lanfranc's. In 1066, too, he declined the archbishopric of Rouen, but in 1070 William the Conqueror prevailed upon him to accept the archbishoric of Canterbury. He brought about a large measure of civil justice and peace in England by his influence upon the king. For example, he effected a separation of civil and ecclesiastical courts, which benefitted both Church and state, and he enacted and enforced beneficial rules of Church discipline. He was also involved in the controversies regarding the relative primacy of Canterbury and York, and regarding the relative authority of pope and king over bishops. In his time, the contest between the ruler of England and the Catholic pope over the right of investiture had its origin, but he had greater success in keeping William the Conqueror reasonable in his appointments than Anselm was to have with the two unruly kings who followed upon their father's throne.

12. Le Bec, or Le Bec-Hellouin, was a monastery founded by Herlwin, about 1039, in the diocese of Rouen, in Normandy. For its history, see B. Heurebize, "Bec (Le)" *DHGE*, vol. 7, col. 325–335.

13. See Eadmer, *Vita* I, 5–7, on the facts of Anselm's first years in religious life. Southern, in his edition, p. 12, note 1, discusses the probable dates of Anselm's arrival at Bec, his profession and his appointment as prior.

14. On these writings, see Introduction, III, 1, 2, 3.

15. A clear and concise yet adequately complete account of the reigns of William Rufus (1087–1100) and Henry I (1100–1135), including their relations with the Church and the archbishop of Canterbury, is given by W. J. Corbett, ch. XVI, "England, 1087–1154," pp. 521–541, in *The Cambridge Medieval History*, vol. 5, *Contest Of Empire And Papacy* (Cambridge, England: University Press, 1957). Specifically on the relations of St. Anselm with the two kings, see especially R. W. Southern, *St. Anselm And His Biographer*, pp. 142–180, of Chapter 4, "Anselm As Archbishop."

16. See Eadmer, *Historia Novorum in Anglia*, ed. by M. Rule, Rolls Series, pp. 27–29, and Southern's ed. of Eadmer, *Vita Anselmi*, p. 63, note 2.

17. See Butler's *Lives of the Saints*, ed. by H. Thurston, S. J., and D. Attwater (New York: Kenedy and Sons, 1956) vol. 2, April 21, p. 139.

18. See Eadmer, *Vita*, Book II, Gerberon, ch. 1, nn. 1–4, *PL* 158, col. 79 C–81 D; Southern, ch. 1–4, pp. 63–66. See also: *Hist. Nov.*, Rule ed., pp. 37–43, and R. W. Southern, *St. Anselm And His Biographer*, pp. 151–155.

19. See Southern's ed. of Eadmer, *Vita*, p. 67, note 2. The two accounts referred to are given in *Vita*, II, 5 (Southern, p. 67) and *Hist. Nov.* (Rule, pp. 43–45).

20. *Vita Anselmi*, Southern's ed. and trans., II, ch. 16, p. 87.

21. See Introduction, Part III, 8.

22. See Introduction, Part IV, A.

23. Eadmer, *Vita Anselmi*, Southern's ed., II, ch. 20, p. 92.

24. *Op. cit.* II, ch. 24, p. 100. See *Hist. Nov.*, Rule's ed., pp. 88–89.

25. *Op. cit.*, II, 29, p. 105 (Southern's ed. and trans.)

26. See Introduction, Part III, 9.

27. See Eadmer, *Vita Anselmi*, II, 38, Southern p. 115 and note 2. See also *Hist. Nov.*, Rule's ed., p. 114; and for the *Acta* of this council, Mansi, XX, col. 961–964.

28. See Eadmer, *Vita Anselmi*, II, 50, Southern's ed., pp. 127–128. On Anselm's relations with Henry, see R. W. Southern, *St. Anselm And His Biographer*, pp. 163–180; also Eadmer, *Hist. Nov.*, Rule's ed., pp. 120–147.

29. See Introduction, Part III, 10.

30. See R. W. Southern, *Saint Anselm And His Biographer*, p. 337.

31. The text is given in *PL* 199, 1009–1040; see Southern, *op. cit.*, p. 338.

32. See Southern, *op. cit.*, p. 339.

33. See Card. De Lambertinis, *De Servorum Dei Beatificatione Et Beatorum Canonizatione*, (1734), lib. IV, pars II, xii, 9; see Southern, *op. cit.*, pp. 342–343.

34. *Epist.* III, 7, *PL* 159, col. 21 A–B.

35. See Eadmer, *Vita Anselmi*, I, 13, Southern's ed. pp. 22–23.

36. See *ibid.*, II, 13, pp. 80–81.

37. See Anselm, *Epist.* III, 152; *PL* 159, col. 184 C–186 A.

38. In *Why God Became Man*, Book I, ch. 11, below, the author says: ". . . the debt which angel and man owe to God . . . is justice or rectitude of will, which makes persons upright or right in heart, that is, in will." See also *Dialogus De Veritate*, ch. 4 and 5, on the "truth of the will" (that is, rectitude) and "truth of action," *PL* 158, col. 471 D–473 C.

39. See Eadmer, *Vita Anselmi*, II, 12, Southern's ed. pp. 79–80.

40. Job, 19.21.

41. See Eadmer, *Vita Anselmi*, II, 8, pp. 69–71.

42. See *Epist.* 37, Schmitt's ed. I, 29, and R. W. Southern, *St. Anselm And His Biographer*, p. 349.

43. See R. W. Southern, *op. cit.*, pp. 14–17.

44. Matt. 1. 19: . . . *Joseph, her husband, being a just man* . . .

45. Sulpicius Severus, *Vita S. Martini*, ch. 27: "nunquam in illius ore nisi Christus, nunquam in illius corde nisi pietas, nisi pax, nisi misericordia inerat." (*CSEL*, ed. C. Halm, p. 137, quoted by R. W. Southern, edit. of Eadmer, *Vita Anselmi*, p. 14, n. 1). Eadmer quotes freely, saying that one can affirm of Anselm what was said of St. Martin: "Eius ori nunquam Christus defuit, sive justitia, vel quicquid ad veram vitam pertinet." (*Vita*, I, 8, Southern, p. 14)

46. See F. S. Schmitt, "Zur Chronologie der Werke des hl. Anselm" in *Revue Bénédictine*, 44, 1932, pp. 322–350.

47. See Eadmer, *Vita Anselmi*, I, 8, Southern's ed. p. 14.

48. Gabriel Gerberon's edition is given by Migne, *PL* 158, as follows: the sixteen homilies, col. 585 A–674 D; the meditations, col. 709 A–854 C; the prayers, col. 855 A–1016 A.

49. See A. Wilmart, "Les homelies attribuées a saint Anselme, *AHDLMA*, 2 (1927), pp. 5–29, and Wilmart's preface to D. A. Castel, *Meditations Et Prières de S. Anselme*, Collection *Pax*, vol. 11, Paris, Maredsous: 1923.

50. *Meditatio De Redemptione Humana*, *PL* 158, col. 762 C–769 B; Schmitt, III, pp. 84–91.

51. See R. W. Southern, *St. Anselm And His Biographer*, p. 36.

52. On the prayers, see Southern, *op. cit.*, pp. 34–47.

53. See editions in *PL* 158, col. 141 D–224 A; and Schmitt, I, pp. 7–87.

54. See *De Veritate*, ch. 1, *PL* 158, col. 468; ch. 10, col. 479.

55. The evolution of the title of the *Monologion* is reported by Anselm himself in the preface to the *Proslogion*, *PL* 158, col. 223–225; Schmitt, I, 93.

56. This translation of *ratio* by "rationale"—the underlying reason or rational foundation—is that of R. W. Southern, in *Saint Anselm And His Biographer*, p. 54, and seems to be the best interpretation of the word in this context, although "grounds" and "basis" are not incorrect.

57. See *Epist.* I, 68, *PL* 158, col. 1138–1139. *Epist.* I, 62, col. 1134 is Anselm's request to Lanfranc. Gerberon's *Epist.* I, 68 is *Epist.* 72 in Schmitt's edition.

58. See *De Fide Trinitatis Et De Incarnatione Verbi*, I, 4, *PL* 158, col. 272 B–273 B.

59. Eadmer, *Vita Anselmi* I, 19, Southern's ed. p. 29; Gerberon's ed., *PL* 158, col. 63; my trans.

60. *Ibid.*

61. See preface to *Proslogion*, *PL* 158, col. 223–225.

62. Eadmer, *Vita Anselmi*, Southern's ed., p. 31.

63. Psalm 13.1 (P.B.V. 14.1) and Psalm 52.1 (P.B.V. 53.1): *The fool said in his heart: "There is no God."*

64. See *Proslogion*, ch. 4, *PL* 158, col. 229.

65. See Eadmer, *Vita Anselmi*, I, 19, Southern's ed. pp. 29–31.

66. *Ibid.*

67. See Gaunilo, *Liber Pro Insipiente, Adversus Anselmi In Proslogio Ratiocinationem*, *PL* 158, col. 241–247, and Anselm's answer, *Liber Apologeticus Contra Gaunilonem Respondentem Pro Insipiente*, col. 247–260.

68. For a good analysis of the argument, and a summary of the defenders and critics of its validity, see E. Gilson, *History of Christian Philosophy in the Middle Ages* (New York: Random House, 1955), pp. 132–134, 618.

69. Gerberon's edition of the text is in *PL* 158, col. 561 A–582 A.

70. For text, see *PL* 158, 467 B–486 C; Schmitt, I, pp. 169–199. An English version is available in *Truth, Freedom and Evil: Three Philosophical Dialogues* by Anselm of Canterbury, ed. and trans. by Jasper Hopkins and Herbert Richardson (New York: Harper and Row, 1967), pp. 91–120, 12–26.

71. The text of this work is given in *PL* 158, col. 489 B–506 C and Schmitt, I, pp. 201–226. A translation into English, with introductory discussion of Anselm's doctrine of will, is found in Hopkins and Richardson, *op. cit.* pp. 121–144, 26–44.

72. *De Libero Arbitrii*, ch. 3 (col. 494).

73. For Gerberon's ed. of the text of this work, see *PL* 158, col. 325 C–360 C; Schmitt's is in vol. I, pp. 227–276. For an English translation and a study of Anselm's doctrine of evil, see Hopkins and Richardson, *op. cit.*, pp. 145–196, 44–78.

74. See *PL* 158, col. 259 C–284 C.

75. See Schmitt, I, pp. 277–290.

76. See R. W. Southern, *St. Anselm And His Biographer*, pp. 79–80, and J. Bainvel, "Anselme De Cantorbéry," *DTC*, vol. 1, col. 1336–1337.

77. For texts, see *PL* 158, col. 285 A–326 B; Schmitt II, pp. 177–219. See also Eadmer, *Hist. Nov.*, Rule ed. pp. 105–106; and Anselm, *Epist.* 239, Schmitt III, 160; *Epist.* 240, Schmitt III, 53.

78. For text, see *PL* 158, col. 507–542; Schmitt II, pp. 245–288. See also Eadmer, *Vita Anselmi*, II, ch. 64, Southern's ed. p. 140 and note 3.

79. See Southern, *Saint Anselm And His Biographer*, pp. 217–221, and his ed. of the *Vita Anselmi*, pp. 74n., 95n, 120n.

80. See Southern, *op. cit.*, pp. 221–226 and his ed. of Eadmer's *Vita*, pp. 13 n. 2, 21 n. 1, 36n, 55n, 91n, 95n, 101n.

81. See Eadmer, *Vita Anselmi*, II, ch. 66, Southern's ed., p. 142 and note 1. The problem was apparently the same one that long bothered St. Augustine: whether the human soul is created or "generated" by the souls of parents. See Southern, *St. Anselm And His Biographer*, p. 206.

82. See Eadmer, *Vita Anselmi*, II, 29, Southern's ed. p. 107 and note 2.

83. See *Epist.* III, 25, *PL* 159, col. 56.

84. See *Epist.* IV, 55, *PL* 159, col. 232–233.

85. See J. Bainvel, "Anselme de Cantorbéry," *DTC* I, col. 1331, and Southern's ed. of Eadmer, *Vita Anselmi*, p. 107, note 2.

86. Boso was born at Montivilliers, in the diocese of Rouen, in 1065. Eadmer, in his *Vita Anselmi* (Gerberon's ed., I, ch. 6, n. 53, *PL* 158, col. 70 B–80 A; Southern's ed., I, ch. 34, p. 60), tells us that as a youth of acute intelligence, concerned about certain perplexing problems and unable to find anyone who could solve them for him, Boso came to Bec to consult Anselm. After speaking with the abbot and laying bare the perplexities of his heart, he was given all the answers he had been looking for, and he found certitude on fundamental matters of faith for the first time. Impressed by Anselm's holiness and his inspiring conversations, he felt attracted to the monastic life. But he was tempted and spiritually harried to such a degree that he almost lost his sanity. After some days he manifested his disturbance to Anselm and the abbot merely said: "May God take care of you!" and dismissed him. Boso told Eadmer that at that moment he experienced peace of mind and heart and never went through the same experience again. (*ibid.*)

He was clothed in the monastic habit at Bec in 1088, when he was twenty-three years old. His elder brother Gilbert had already made profession there, and his younger brother Renaud was to join later.

When St. Anselm became archbishop of Canterbury, he invited and urged Boso to come from Bec to assist him. He needed help with his theological writings, especially the *De Incarnatione Verbi* and the *Cur Deus Homo*. When the archbishop was unable to attend the council called by Pope Urban in 1095, it was Boso whom he sent to represent him. Boso became ill at the council, and was forced to remain on the continent for some time to recuperate.

Boso served Anselm mainly, it seems, as stimulator in his theological inquiries, by asking questions. He was witness of some, at least, of the saint's miracles, and is one of the sources of Eadmer's accounts of them. It is possible that Anselm's own story of his unhappy experience with an early teacher was preserved by Boso. (See Introduction, Part I.) After Anselm's second exile, he again asked Boso to come to England, and the young scholar was with him when he wrote his last treatise on predestination, grace and free will. Their mutual high regard was expressed by Anselm in a letter: "As I am sure that you always desire to be with me, so you ought not to doubt that I desire to be always with you." (*Epist.* III, 22, *PL* 159, col. 49)

Boso became prior of Bec in 1115, and abbot in 1124. He sought to be spared this promotion, because he did not want to disobey the pope by giving homage to the king of England, nor to offend the king by refusing the oath of allegiance. At first, Henry I refused to accept Boso's election, but he changed his mind later and acknowledged Boso as abbot without requiring him to pay homage to the royal throne. The king admitted that there was not a holier person nor a more capable counselor in his realm than Boso. No other abbot of Bec ever received such gifts and such privileges from royalty as he did.

Boso died on June 24, 1136. He left no writings that can be attributed to him with certainty, although one treatise in the form of a letter, whose theme is the defence of the monastic way of life, has been attributed to him by some. The letter was in editions of Anselm's works prior to Gerberon's. Boso's glory in literature and theology remains that of sharing in the production of Anselm's writings, especially the *Cur Deus Homo* and the *De Conceptu Virginali*. See the *Vita Bosonis* (probably by Milo Crespin) in *PL* 150, vol. 723–732; Ph. Schmitz, "Boson (8)," in *DHGE*, 4 (1939), col. 1322–1324; R. W. Southern, *St. Anselm And His Biographer*, pp. 82–83, 202.

87. The *De Casu Diaboli* (*PL* 158, col. 325–360), *De Libero Arbitrii* (*PL* 158, col. 489–506) and *De Veritate* (*PL* 158, col. 467–486) are such dialogues.

88. ". . . Hic est ille Boso cum quo disputans (Anselmus) composuit librum qui dicitur *Cur Deus Homo*."—Milo Crispin, *Vita Venerabilis Bosonis, PL* 150, 726 B.

89. Eadmer, *Vita Anselmi* I, 34 (Southern's ed. p. 60) refers to Boso as *ingenio acer*, and Milo Crispin, *op. cit.*, 725 A, makes it superlative: ". . . Erat autem acutissimi ingenii, et quod subtiliter intelligebat luculento sermone proferebat."

90. See p. 168, below.

91. See *Why God Became Man*, II, ch. 17, near end.

92. See Eadmer, *Vita Anselmi*, II, 44, Southern's ed., p. 122 and note 1.

93. St. Thomas, *Summa Theologiae*, III, qu. 1, art. 3.

94. This is the title given in the article "Satisfaction of Christ," *Dictionary Of Dogmatic Theology*, ed. P. Parente, A. Piolanti, S. Garofalo (1951) p. 253.

95. J. McIntyre, *St. Anselm And His Critics* (Edinburgh: Oliver and Boyd, 1954), p. 117 and 198.

96. *Op. cit.*, p. 117.

97. *Op. cit.*, pp. 197–198.

98. *Op. cit.*, p. 198.

99. ". . . Summa quaestionis fuit, cur Deus homo factus sit. . . ," II, ch. 18, Schmitt, 126, 23.

100. ". . . Qua ratione vel necessitate Deus homo factus sit. . . ," I, ch. 1, Schmitt 48, 2 f.

101. See F. S. Schmitt, "Die Wissenschaftliche Methode in Anselms *Cur Deus Homo*," *Spicilegium Beccense* (Paris, J. Vrin, 1959, pp. 349–370) p. 351.

102. See Introduction, Part III, no. 8.

103. See R. W. Southern, *St. Anselm And His Biographer*, pp. 77–82.

104. See J. Rivière, "D'un singulier emprunt à S. Anselme chez Raoul de Laon," *Revue Des Sciences Religeuses*, 16, 1936, 344–346.

105. See R. W. Southern, *op. cit.*, pp. 87 f., 357–361.

106. See Gislebertus Crispinus, *Disputatio Judaei Cum Christiano*, *PL* 159, col. 1005 A–1036 D.

107. *Why God Became Man*, Book II, ch. 22.

108. See R. Roques (ed. and trans.), *Anselme De Cantorbéry, Pourquoi Dieu S'Est Fait Homme*, (Paris, Cerf: 1963) pp. 72–74.

109. St. Paul, I Cor. 1.20–21: . . . *Hath not God made foolish the wisdom of this world? For, seeing that in the wisdom of God, the world, by wisdom, knew not God, it pleased God, by the foolishness of our preaching, to save them that believe.*

110. *Ibid.*, 2.4.

111. See E. Gilson, *History of Christian Philosophy in the Middle Ages*, (New York: Random House, 1954), pp. 9–10.

112. Tatian, *Address To The Greeks*, 2; *Ante-Nicene Fathers Of The Church*, (Edinburgh, 1867) III, 7. The Greek text is in *PG* 6, col. 803–888.

113. Tertullian, *De Carne Christi*, ch. 5, *CSEL*, 70, 200.

114. St. Augustine, *Contra Academicos*, III, ch. 20, n. 43; *CSEL* 63, 80.

115. See Introduction, p. 15, above.

116. *Why God Became Man*, I, 1.

117. *Commendatio Operis Ad Urbanum Papam II*, in S. Anselmi Opera Omnia II, pp. 39–41, ed. F. S. Schmitt.

118. See *PL* 158, 259 C–261 C.

119. See F. S. Schmitt, "La lettre de saint Anselme au pape Urbain II a l'occasion de la remise de son *Cur Deus Homo* (1098) in *Revue des Sciences Religieuses*, 16, 1936, pp. 129–144. When Dom Schmitt reprinted the text of the *Cur Deus Homo* with his German translation, *Warum Gott Mensch Geworden* (Munich, Kosel--Verlag, 1956), he did not prefix the letter to Pope Urban.

120. See *Why God Became Man*, preface, I, 10 and II, 1.

121. F. S. Schmitt, "Die Wissenschaftliche Methode In Anselms *Cur Deus Homo*," *Spicilegium Beccense*, I. Congrès international de IXe centenaire de l'arrivée d'Anselme au Bec, (Paris: J. Vrin, 1959) p. 358.

122. See *Why God Became Man*, I, ch. 1, 4.

123. See J. McIntyre, *St. Anselm And His Critics*, pp. 51–55.

124. See Aristotle, *Categoriae*, X, 12a, 32; *Analytica Priora*, 27, 70 a; Cicero, *De Inventione*, II, c. 29; Marius Victorinus, *De Rhetorica*, 10.

125. See A. M. Jacqúin, "Les 'Rationes Necessariae' de saint Anselme," in *Mélanges Mandonnet*, (Paris: 1930) t. 2, pp. 67–78.

126. See *Why God Became Man*, I, 4.

127. *Ibid.*, I, ch. 10.

128. F. S. Schmitt, *art. cit.*, p. 370.

129. *Ibid.*

130. "Atonement" is an original English word made up of "at" and "one," and meaning "being in agreement," or "bringing into agreement." Hence it signifies the act or state of satisfactory reparation or of reconciliation. In Christian theology, the word designates the effect of Christ's incarnation, sufferings and death, namely the reconciliation of human beings with God, after human sin occurred.

131. "Redemption" literally means "a buying back." It is not precisely synonymous with "atonement," but is generally richer and more inclusive, so that atonement or expiation is part of the redemption. The two words

are commonly taken, however, to refer to the same acts of Christ, and the word "redemption" is more common in Catholic theological writings.

132. Rom. 5.12.

133. See Gen. 3.15.

134. Gal. 4.4–5.

135. Titus, 2.14. See also Eph. 5.25–28.

136. John 10.17–18.

137. Rom. 6.3–4.

138. See Jean Rivière, *The Doctrine of the Atonement*, tr. Luigi Cappadelta (2 vols., St. Louis: B. Herder, 1909) II, part V, *The Rights of the Devil*, pp. 111–240.

139. *Why God Became Man*, I, 7.

140. See St. Anselm, *Meditatio XI, De Redemptione Humana*, PL 158, col. 764.

141. Origen, *In Rom.* 5.3, PG 14, col. 1026; see also *In Exod. Hom.* 6.9, PG 12, col. 338.

142. See St. Gregory of Nyssa, *Orat. Catech. Magna*, 22–24, PG 45, 60–66.

143. See St. Gregory Nazianzen, *Orat.* 45.22, PG 36, col. 653.

144. See St. John Damscene, *De Orthodoxa Fide*, 3.27, PG 94, col. 1096.

145. See St. Ambrose, *Epist.* 41, 7–8, PL 16, 1115; also *In Luc.* 7.114–117, PL 15, 1727–1728.

146. As examples may be cited: St. John Chrysostom, *In Joan. Hom.* 68, 2–3, PG 59, col. 372–373; *In Rom. Hom.* 13.5, PG 60, col. 515; and St. Cyril of Alexandria, *In Joan.* 6, PG 73, col. 894.

147. See St. Augustine, *Serm.* 263.1, PL 38, 1210; *Serm.* 134.5.6, PL 38, 745.

148. See *De Trinitate*, 13.10–16, PL 42, 1026; Rivière, *op. cit.*, pp. 146–149; Eugene Portalié, S.J., *A Guide To the Thought of St. Augustine* (Chicago: Regnery, 1960), pp. 167–170.

149. *dicere solemus—Cur Deus Homo*, I, 7.

150. See J. Rivière, *op. cit.*, pp. 202–209.

151. See *Why God Became Man*, I, ch. 11.

152. *Ibid.*, I, ch. 12.

153. *Ibid.*

154. *Ibid.*, I, ch. 13.

155. See Book I, ch. 16–19.

156. *Ibid.*, I, ch. 20.

157. *Ibid.*, I, ch. 15.

158. *Ibid.*, I, ch. 25.

159. *Ibid.*, II, ch. 6.

160. *Ibid.*, I, ch. 20.

161. *Ibid.*, I, ch. 21.

162. On this theory, see: J. Rivière, *The Doctrine Of The Atonement*, trans. L. Cappadelta (St. Louis: B. Herder, 1909), vol. 2, ch. 17, *The Doctrine of Satisfaction—St. Anselm's System*, pp. 14–43; R. W. Southern, *St. Anselm And His Biographer* (Cambridge, England: University Press, 1963), pp. 97–121; John McIntyre, *St. Anselm And His Critics*, pp. 56–116, 154–204.

163. David Smith, *The Atonement in the Light of History and the Modern Spirit* (London: Hoder and Stoughton, no date) p. 85.

164. See Introduction, Part IV, D.

165. J. Rivière, *op. cit.*, vol. 2, p. 34, cites as proponents of this criticism: A. Ritschl, *Die Christliche Lehre von der Rechtfertigung und Versöhnung,* 3 t., 4 ed. (Bonn: 1895–1903); J. Lichtenberger, "Redemption," art. in *Encyclopedie des Sciences Religieuses* (Paris: 1881); A. Sabatier, *La Doctrine de l'Expiation et Son Evolution Historique* (Paris: 1903).

166. Hilary of Poitiers, *In Ps.* 52.12, *PL* 9, col. 344.

167. See J. McIntyre, *St. Anselm And His Critics,* pp. 46, 82–95; R. W. Southern, *St. Anselm and His Biographer,* pp. 107–114.

168. See *Why God Became Man,* Book II, ch. 5 and 17.

169. *Ibid.,* Book I, ch. 12 and 13.

170. See St. Thomas Aquinas, *Summa Theologiae,* III, Qu. 46, art. 2, c.

171. *Ibid.*

172. *Ibid.*

173. *Sum. Theol.,* III, Qu. 46, art. 1, c.

174. *Sum. Theol.,* III, Qu. 46, art. 2, c.

175. *Ibid.,* ad 3.

176. *Ibid.,* c.

177. St. Thomas Aquinas, *Compendium Theologiae,* I, ch. 200.

178. See Emile Mersch, S.J., *The Theology Of The Mystical Body,* trans. C. Vollert, S.J. (St. Louis: B. Herder, 1951) pp. 249–252.

179. *Why God Became Man,* II, ch. 18.

180. *Why God Became Man,* I, ch. 10, 13, 21.

181. *Ibid.,* II, ch. 7.

182. *Ibid.,* I, ch. 11.

183. St. Anselm's words are: "Non est aliud peccare quam Deo non reddere debitum." (*Ibid.*) Some critics have found fault with the conception of sin given in that sentence and implied throughout the whole work, as being "too commercial" and "too quantitative." While *debitum* can be translated "debt," and while we can speak of man having "debts" to God, the charge of unworthy implications being made by Anselm is totally unfounded. See. J. McIntyre, *St. Anselm And His Critics,* pp. 71–76.

184. *Why God Became Man,* I, ch. 12 and 15.

185. *Ibid.,* I, ch. 21.

186. *The Virgin Conception And Original Sin,* ch. 1.

187. *Ibid.,* ch. 3.

188. See: Eugene Portalié, S.J., *A Guide To The Thought Of St. Augustine,* trans. by R. J. Bastian, S.J. (Chicago: Regnery, 1960), pp. 208–211; A. Gaudel, "Peché Originel," in *DTC* 12, (275–606), col. 436.

189. *The Virgin Conception And Original Sin,* ch. 27.

190. *Ibid.,* also ch. 4 and 7.

191. See J. Bainvel, "Anselme De Cantorbéry," *DTC,* t. 1, col. 1346–1347; also *Dictionary Of Dogmatic Theology,* (ed. P. Parente, A. Piolanti, S. Garofalo; Milwaukee: Bruce, 1951) s.v. "Innocence," p. 145; A. Gaudel, *art. cit.,* col. 435.

192. See St. Thomas Aquinas, *Summa Theologiae,* I, Qu. 95.

193. See *The Virgin Conception And Original Sin,* ch. 2.

194. *Ibid.,* ch. 1.

195. *Ibid.,* ch. 23.

196. *Ibid.,* ch. 7.

197. See *Monologion,* ch. 1–2, *PL* 158, col. 144 A–147 A.

198. *De Fide Trinitatis Et De Incarnatione Verbi*, ch. 2, *PL* 158, col. 265 B.

199. *The Virgin Birth And Original Sin*, ch. 7.

200. *Ibid.*, ch. 11.

201. *Ibid.*, ch. 13.

202. *Ibid.*, ch. 18.

203. *Why God Became Man*, II, ch. 16.

204. See R. W. Southern, *St. Anselm And His Biographer*, p. 295. On the whole question of St. Anselm's position and influence regarding this privilege of Mary's, see M. Jugie and X. Le Bachelet, "Immaculée Conception," *DTC* 7, col. 995–1004.

205. The *Tractatus De Conceptione B. Mariae Virginis* is given among the spurious works attributed to St. Anselm, in Migne, *PL* 159, col. 301 C–318 D.

206. See R. W. Southern, *op. cit.*, p. 295 and note 4.

207. Correctly attributed to Eadmer, *De Excellentia Virginis Mariae Liber* is found in Migne, *PL* 159, col. 557 C–580 C.

208. *Op. cit.*, ch. 3, *PL* 159, col. 561 C.

209. *Tractatus De Conceptione B. Mariae Virginis*, *PL* 159, col. 305 B.

210. *Ibid.*, col. 305 D.

211. *The Virgin Conception And Original Sin*, ch. 18.

212. For brief descriptions of these works, see Introduction, III, 2 and 3.

213. *Meditatio XI, De Redemptione Humana*, *PL* 158, col. 763 A.

214. See *ibid.*, col. 769 A.

215. See *ibid.*, col. 763 C–765 A.

216. Franciscus Salesius Schmitt, O.S.B. (Ed.), S. *Anselmi Cantuariensis Archiepiscopi Opera Omnia* (Edinburgi, apud Thomam Nelson et Filios, MDCCCCXLVI), vol. 2, *Cur Deus Homo*, pp. 39–133; *De Conceptu Virginali Et De Originali Peccato*, pp. 135–173.

WHY GOD BECAME MAN

[Submission of the Work to the Scrutiny of Pope Urban II]

1. This presentation of Anselm's writing to the Holy Father for approval is put prior to the *Cur Deus Homo* by F. S. Schmitt, in his critical edition, *Sancti Anselmi Opera Omnia* (Edinburgi: apud Thomam Nelson et Filios, MDCCCCXLVI), vol. 2, pp. 39–41. Schmitt gives it the heading: *Commendatio operis ad Urbanum Papam II*. Gerberon (in the reprint of *PL* 158, col. 259–261), makes it a preface to the *Liber De Fide Trinitatis Et De Incarnatione Verbi*. Schmitt's inclusion of it with the *Cur Deus Homo* gives occasion to difficulties and disputes regarding the setting and method of the whole treatise; see Introduction, p. 40 above. Nevertheless, most authorities agree that Schmitt's judgment of the place of the *Com-*

mendatio is correct. See, for example: Anselme de Cantorbéry, *Pourquoi Dieu S'Est Fait Homme,* trad. et notes de René Roques (Paris: Cerf, 1963), p. 194, n. 1; John McIntyre, *St. Anselm And His Critics* (Edinburgh: Oliver and Boyd, 1954), p. 3. Curiously, however, Schmitt does not include the *Commendatio* in the edition of his German translation, *Warum Gott Mensch Geworden* (München: Im Kösel-Verlag, 1956).

2. See Acts 15.3, where St. Peter speaks of God's having cleansed the hearts of Gentiles by faith.

3. Again in *Why God Became Man,* Book I, ch. 1, Anselm refers to the purpose of this theological inquiry as finding delight in the understanding and contemplation of what Christians believe.

4. In *Why God Became Man,* Book I, ch. 1, Boso likewise declares it "a matter of negligence if, after we have been confirmed in the faith, we make no effort to understand what we believe . . ." On the position of St. Anselm regarding the use of natural reason in developing revealed truth, see the Introduction, Part IV, D.

5. Job 14.5.

6. Matt. 28.20.

7. St. Anselm is quoting the text *Nisi credideritis, non intelligetis,* a version of Isaias 7.9 which St. Augustine often quoted and appealed to (e.g., in *Sermo* 91, c. vii, n. 9; *PL* 38, 571). The Vulgate translation of St. Jerome, however, gives the text: *Si non credideritis, non permanebitis,* rendered in the Douay version: *If you will not believe, you will not continue.*

[Preface]

8. There have been several opinions offered (see René Roques, *Anselme De Cantorbéry: Pourquoi Dieu S'Est Fait Homme,* Paris, Cerf, 1963, Introd. pp. 53–64), but there is no solid evidence to indicate just what these "first parts" of the treatise comprise, by whom they were copied, or when or where.

9. An obvious cause of the saint's "tribulation of heart" was the opposition of William Rufus and the consequent exile of Anselm (see Introduction, pp. 4–7), but he might himself be referring to the very elevation to the archbishopric.

10. Anselm commonly attached great importance to this presentation of preface and chapter headings with the text of his books. At the end of the prologue to his *Monologion* (Schmitt, I, p. 8, 21–26, *PL* 158, 144 A–B) he likewise asks copyists to be careful to place that preface at the beginning of the book. At the end of the preface to the *De Veritate,* he also asks (Schmitt, I, p. 174, 3–7, *PL* 158, 468 B) that with this work copyists will also join *De Libertate Arbitrii* and *De Casu Diaboli* in all future editions.

BOOK ONE

1. A similar importunity of friends is given by the author for the writing and publication of the *Monologion*. See *Monologion,* Prologus, Schmitt I, p. 7, 2; *PL* 158, 142 C–143 A.

2. I Peter 3.15.

3. See Introduction, Part IV, A, and note 86.

4. See Introduction, part IV, D.

5. See Ecclus. 3.22: *Seek not the things that are too high for thee, and search not into things above thy ability; but the things that God hath commanded thee, think on them always, and in many of his works be not curious.*

6. See Matt. 10.8: *Freely have you received; freely give.*

7. An unfinished little work on these questions has been discovered and attributed to Anselm. See F. S. Schmitt, "Ein neues, unvollendetes Werk des hl. Anselm von Canterbury: De potestate et impotentia, possibilitate et impossibilitate, necessitate et libertate," in *Beiträge zur Geschichte der Philosophie und Theologie des Mittelalters,* 33(3), 1936. Objection to the authenticity of the work has been made by H. Weisweiler in a review in *Scholastik,* 13, 1938, pp. 103–105.

8. Psalm 44.3 (Douay)

9. In I, ch. 4, below, Boso throws against Anselm's "arguments from fitness" the very objection Anselm is here afraid of, and under a similar metaphor of inept pictorial art.

10. This is only a genial disclaimer of learning on the part of Boso and his associates, not an indication of limitation of the intended audience. In the first paragraph of this first chapter, Anselm himself says that the questions have been put by both the learned and unlearned, and that the solutions which this study of his proposes will be intelligible *to all.*

11. This is a clear indication that Anselm is concerned with theology, not philosophy. Anselm's word which I have translated "manifests" is *revelet;* he does not, of course, refer to a revelation in the strict sense. But this sentence is enlightening for showing that Anselm takes both revelation in the strict sense and "understanding" in the light of reason, as coming from God.

12. Again, the author indicates that he does not shrink God's wisdom and magnitude to the size of the human intelligence.

13. On the identity of these "unbelievers" see Introduction, Part IV, C.

14. For sources in which such objections have been made by Jews, see: Gilbert Crispin, *Disputatio Judaei Cum Christiano De Fide Christiana, PL* 159, col. 1005–1036; and F. Vernet, "Juifs (Controverses avec les)," *DTC* 8(2), 1925, col. 1870–1914, esp. col. 1876–1889. Regarding objections made by some Mohammedans, see E. Fritsch, *Islam und Christentum im*

Mittelalter, Beiträge zur Geschichte der Muslimischen Polemik gegen das Christentum in arabischer Sprache (Breslau, 1930).

15. See Rom. 5.19: *. . . As by the disobedience of one man, many were made sinners, so also by the obedience of one, many shall be made just.* Pope St. Leo the Great (*Sermo* 25, c. 5; *PL* 54, 211) comments: "One person, obeying the devil to the extent of collusion in evil, deserved the death of all in himself; the other Person, obeying the Father to the limit of the cross, brought about the life of all within Himself."

16. The parallel between Eve, who influenced the first man to sin, and Mary, who brought forth the One who vanquished sin, is very common among the Fathers. See, for example, Tertullian, *De Carne Christi*, c. 17, *PL* 2, 827 f.; Justin, *Dial. Cum Tryph.*, 100, *PG* 6, 710–711; Irenaeus, *Adv. Haer.* III, 22.4, *PG* 7, 958–959; V, 19.1, *ib.*, 1175–1176; Ambrose, *Expositio In Lucam*, II, n. 28, *CSEL* 32, p. 56; *PL* 15, 1643; Augustine, *Sermo* 237, c. II, n. 2, *PL* 38, 1108.

17. This parallel is expressed in the preface of the Passion, in the Roman Missal: ". . . Satan, who became a victor over us through a tree, is himself conquered on a tree, through Christ our Lord."

18. *. . . non de massa peccatrice . . .* St. Paul (Rom. 9.21) says: *. . . Hath not the potter power over the clay, of the same lump, to make one vessel unto honor and another unto dishonor?* His Greek word *phyrama*, there translated "lump," was commonly translated by St. Augustine as equivalent to the Latin word *massa*. He generally uses it in a pejorative sense of the human race, as in phrases such as "massa damnata," "massa perditionis," and "massa peccati." See, for example, *Sermo* 26, c. 12, n. 13, *PL* 38, 177; *Sermo* 22, c. 9, n. 9, col. 153. St. Anselm is taking the phrase and the notion from St. Augustine.

19. See Luke 20.36: *Neither can they die any more, for they are equal to the angels and are the children of God, being the children of the resurrection.*

20. Gilbert Crispin, in his *Disputatio Iudaei Cum Christiano* (*PL* 159, 1022 f.) similarly argues that since "a person is committed to the service of the one by whom he is redeemed from slavery," it would not be fitting for man to be redeemed by angel or man, but only by the God-Man.

21. See Rom. 5.8–9: *. . . God commendeth his charity towards us, because when as yet we were sinners according to the time, Christ died for us. . . .*

22. In his *De Agone Christiano*, ch. 11, *PL* 40, 297, St. Augustine refers to the objections against God's power and wisdom that are spoken of here, and, after admitting that God could have devised another plan, curtly comments that if He had, He would have incurred the stupid displeasure of the objectors just the same.

23. On the view of the "rights of the devil," so completely rejected here, see Introduction, Part IV, E.

24. See St. Paul, Col. 2.14.

25. The interpretation of the text of Col. 2.14 which Anselm here rejects was accepted by St. Ambrose in *De Virginitate* 19, 126, *PL* 16, 314, and some other Fathers.

26. Ps. 77.39 (Douay)

27. John 8.34.

28. The opposition to reason of Christian doctrines and Christian in-

terpretations of Old Testament texts has been charged commonly by Jews through the centuries prior to the time of Anselm. See B. Blumenkranz, *Juifs et Chrétiens dans le Monde Occidental,* (Paris: 1960), especially pp. 213–289. The Mohammedan Algazel or Al Ghazali (1059–1111), a contemporary of Anselm, says explicitly that Scriptural texts are to be tested by the norm of reasonableness, and if they are contradictory of reasonable evidence, they are to be interpreted as allegories or metaphors. On that score, he rejects the incarnation of the Son of God. See E. Fritsch, *op. cit.,* pp. 102–138.

29. The tenth century author of *Altercatio Ecclesiae Contra Synagogam,* edited by B. Blumenkranz in *Revue du moyen âge latin* (Strasbourg), 10, 1954, has represented the synagogue as addressing the Christian Church in precisely the fashion indicated by Anselm, or by Boso. "Was it possible for me to think," the text reads, "that this same individual (Christ) whom the princes of my people treated with so many insults, bound to a cross and finally gave over to death, is the one who was promised to me, who ought to free me and save me, and to elevate my kingdom above all the kingdoms of the world forever? How could he free me or save me, if he could not save himself from death? I could not see in him, could I, that power which David foretold: . . . *He shall rule from sea to sea, and from the river unto the ends of the earth . . . And all kings of the earth shall adore him, all nations shall serve him* (Ps. 71.8 and 11)?" The criticism of the Mohammedan Al Ghazali is directed largely against the doctrine of the Divine Trinity, and the impossibility of the incarnation of a Divine Person is deduced from the opposition between the Father's Will and Christ's will, as expressed in Matt. 26.39. See E. Fritsch, *loc. cit.*

30. See Matt. 3.17: *And behold a voice from heaven, saying: This is my beloved Son, in whom I am well pleased.*

31. See chapter 6, above.

32. This dilemma was used quite frequently by Mohammedan critics of Christianity. See E. Fritsch, *op. cit.,* pp. 128–130.

33. Here, and frequently in his works, Anselm quite obviously means by "God the Father," or simply "the Father," not just the First Person, but the Triune God, Father, Son and Holy Spirit.

34. Phil. 2.8–9.

35. Heb. 5.8.

36. Rom. 8.32.

37. John 6.38.

38. John 14.31.

39. John 18.11.

40. Matt. 26.39.

41. Matt. 26.42.

42. See John 14.31: *And as the Father hath given me commandments, so do I.*

43. See John 18.11: . . . *The chalice which my Father hath given me, shall I not drink it?*

44. See Phil. 2.8: *He humbled himself, becoming obedient unto death, even to the death of the cross.*

45. See Heb. 5.8: *And whereas indeed he was the Son of God, he learned obedience by the things which he suffered.*

46. Anselm's word is *scientia,* which can mean "knowledge" in gen-

eral, or "certain, intellectual knowledge" (i.e., what we commonly call "science" in English). It can also mean "knowledge imparted by the Holy Spirit," as it does, for example, in the Vulgate, in I Cor. 12.7: *alii quidem per Spiritum datur sermo Sapientiae, alii autem sermo scientiae;* and in Rom. 15.14: *repleti omni scientia* . . . While Anselm could mean natural intellectual knowledge, obtained independently of the senses, he seems rather to mean that which results in Christ's human intellect as a result of the union of His human nature with the Divine Person.

47. Phil. 2.8.

48. Phil. 2.9.

49. The Vulgate gives the Latin verbs *bibet and exaltabit,* so that the verse would be translated: *He shall drink . . . shall he lift up . . .*

50. See Luke 10.22: *All things are delivered to me by my Father.*

51. See John 16.15: *All things whatsoever the Father hath are mine.*

52. Luke 2.52.

53. See below, II, ch. 13.

54. John 6.38.

55. John 7.16.

56. Rom. 8.32. Directly and exactly, Anselm is quoting the first antiphon for Lauds on Good Friday: "Proprio Filio suo non pepercit Deus, sed pro nobis omnibus tradidit illum."

57. Matt. 26.39.

58. Matt. 26.42.

59. John 14.31.

60. John 18.11.

61. Phil. 2.8.

62. See John 14.31: *But that the world may know that I love the Father: and as the Father hath given me commandments, so do I. . . .*

63. See John 18.11: *. . . The chalice which my father hath given me, shall I not drink it?*

64. See Rom. 8.32: *He that spared not even his own Son, but delivered him up for us all, how hath he not also with him given us all things?*

65. Phil. 2.8.

66. Heb. 5.8.

67. James 1.17.

68. John 6.44.

69. See John 14.31 and 18.11.

70. See Rom. 8.32.

71. Rom. 8.32.

72. Phil. 2.8.

73. Heb. 5.8.

74. The same principle is expressed in *De Casu Diaboli,* ch. 28, Schmitt I, p. 276, *PL* 158, col. 360 B.

75. See John 18.11.

76. Isaias, 53.57.

77. John 10.17–18.

78. This question, which has been discussed in the last three chapters, will be taken up again in Book II, chapters 10, 11, 16, 17.

79. Again, the names "God" and "Father" here designate the Holy Trinity. See note 33, above.

80. See Book I, ch. 6 and ch. 8.

81. This is the end of the preliminary objections of the unbelievers. As their representative, Boso has been quite blunt and severe in his criticism of the Christian conception of salvation.

82. See Book I, ch. 3.

83. This principle is also expressed in the *Epistola De Incarnatione Verbi,* 10, Schmitt, II, p. 26, or the *Liber De Fide Trinitatis Et De Incarnatione Verbi,* cap. 5, *PL* 158, 276 C.

84. Regarding the force of the exclusion of the Incarnation, and the character of the assumptions being accepted here, see Introduction, Part IV, D.

85. See Ps. 35.11: *Extend thy mercy to them that know thee, and thy justice to them that are right in heart.*

86. The notion of *rectitudo,* identified with *iustitia* ("righteousness"), is central in the teaching of St. Anselm. It has no small part to play in the doctrine of the Saint on original sin. He also finds a close relation between truth and rectitude. "The power of thinking that something exists or does not exist has been given to us so that we may think that thing to exist which really does exist, and that thing not to exist which does not really exist. Therefore, he who thinks that to exist which does, is thinking as he ought; hence his thought is right. So if thought is true and right for no other reason than that we think that to exist which does exist, or think that not to exist which does not, truth is the same as rectitude."—*De Veritate,* cap. 3, Schmitt, I, p. 180; *PL* 158, 471 C. In *De Libertate Arbitrii,* cap. 3, Schmitt, I, p. 212; *PL* 158, col. 494 A, he says that the only purpose for existence of a rational nature is to preserve rectitude of will for its own sake.

87. Anselm regularly speaks of order as a requirement of the kingdom of God, and of sin as a violation of that order.

88. See Matt. 6.12: *And forgive us our debts, as we forgive our debtors.*

89. See Rom. 12.19: *Revenge not yourselves, my dearly beloved, but give place unto wrath, for it is written: Revenge is mine, I will repay, saith the Lord.* (Matt. 5.39; Deut. 32.35; Heb. 10.30).

90. See Rom. 13.1: *Let every soul be subject to higher powers. For there is no power but from God, and those that are ordained of God.*

91. See also *Monologion,* cap. 16, Schmitt, I, p. 30; *PL* 158, col. 165 B: ". . . It is the same to say of the supreme being that He is just and that He is justice . . ."

92. The thoughts of St. Anselm here on the propriety of God's punishment of sin reflect the attitude of St. Augustine, in, for example, *Enarr. in Ps.* 7, n. 19, *PL* 36, 108; *Epist.* 140, cap. 2, n. 4, *CSEL* 44, (3), p. 157 f.; *PL* 33, col. 539; *De Libero Arbitrio,* III, 9, 26, *PL* 32, 1283 f.

93. This reflects the opinion of Tertullian, *De Pudicitia,* cap. 2, *CSEL* 20, p. 224; *PL* 2, col. 1036: "Omne delictum aut venia dispungit aut poena, venia ex castigatione, poena ex damnatione."

94. Precisely the same thought, expressed in almost exactly the same words, occurs again at the beginning of chapter 19, indicating, it might seem, that Anselm considered himself at precisely the same place in his argument as he was when he introduced this long discussion of the replacement of angels by human beings in heaven. At the end of chapter 18, also, Boso speaks of returning to the subject from which they have

digressed. This whole topic of the replacement of angels by human souls, however, tedious and inconclusive as it seems in this context, was taken seriously by Anselm because it had been traditionally taken for granted.

95. See Book I, ch. 10.

96. II Cor. 9.7. See also Ecclus. 35.11: *In every gift show a cheerful countenance, and sanctify thy tithes with joy.*

97. On the substitution, in heaven, of human souls for fallen angels, see Augustine, *De Civitate Dei*, XIV, 26, *CSEL* 40, pars II, p. 54 f.; *PL* 41, col. 435.

98. See Book II, ch. 21.

99. Here the author is talking about moral truth, or "truth of the will," which he distinguishes from logical truth and truth of action. This "truth of the will" he identifies with rectitude. He derives the notion and the term from John 8.44: (The devil) *was a murderer from the beginning, and he stood not in the truth, because truth is not in him.* See Anselm's *Dialogus De Veritate*, cap. 4, *PL* 158, 471 D–472 A.

100. See *De Casu Diaboli*, ch. 2, 3, 24, Schmitt, I, p. 235–237, and 271–272; *PL* 158, col. 328 A–332 A, 356 A–357 B.

101. See Book I, ch. 16.

102. See Gen., ch. 1–3.

103. The author is dependent here upon St. Augustine, *De Genesi ad litt.*, 4, 33, *CSEL* 28, p. 131 ff.; *PL* 34, col. 317 f.; John Scotus Eriugena, *De Divisione Naturae*, Book 5, *PL* 122, col. 1006 ff.

104. See St. Augustine, *De Civitate Dei*, 11, ch. 9, *CSEL* 40, pars I, p. 524; *PL* 41, col. 324 f.

105. Ecclus. 19.1. See also: St. Augustine, *De Genesi ad litt.*, 5, cap. 23, *CSEL* 28, p. 167 ff.; *PL* 34, col. 337 f.

106. See Book I, ch. 16.

107. St. Anselm uses the term "gentibus" here, obviously referring to the pagans in the first century of the Church. He does not, therefore, mean the same as those called "pagani" in Book II, ch. 22, who appear to be Mohammedans.

108. Acts 10.35.

109. See II Peter, 3.13: *But we look for new heavens and a new earth according to his promises, in which justice dwelleth;* and Apoc. 21.1: *And I saw a new heaven and a new earth . . .*

110. See St. Augustine, *De Civitate Dei*, 20, cap. 14, *CSEL* 40, pars II, p. 461; *PL* 41, col. 679.

111. The "birthday" (*natalicia*) of a saint is the day on which the saint died and presumably entered heavenly life. On the origin and use of this term, see: A. C. Rush, C.SS.R., *Death And Burial In Christian Antiquity* (Washington: Catholic University Press, 1941), ch. 4.

112. Anselm is again echoing St. Augustine, *De Civitate Dei*, 22, ch. 30, n. 3, *PL* 41, col. 802: ". . . the first immortality, which Adam lost by sinning, was an ability not to die; the ultimate one will be an inability to die. . . ."

113. Here the saint is implicitly denying the Immaculate Conception of the Blessed Virgin. See Introduction, Part IV, F.

114. Deut. 32.8.

115. The reading is that of the Septuagint: kata arithmon aggelon

theou. Chief among the interpreters to whom St. Anselm refers is St. Gregory the Great, *Hom. in Ev.* 34, n. 11, *PL* 76, col. 1252: ". . . that heavenly city is composed of angels and men, and we believe that only as many of the human race ascend there as would equal the number of chosen angels who remained there, in accordance with the text: *I have appointed the bounds of people according to the number of the angels of God* (Deut. 32.8, translated from a variant text used by Gregory).

116. See the "Submission of the Work to the Scrutiny of Pope Urban II," preceding the preface.

117. See Gal. 3.7: *Know ye, therefore, that they who are of faith, the same are the children of Abraham.*

118. See Luke 20.36: *Neither can they die any more, for they are equal to the angels and are the children of God, being the children of the resurrection.*

119. See John 6.71–72: *Jesus answered them: Have I not chosen you twelve? And one of you is a devil. Now he meant Judas the Iscariot, the son of Simon, for this same was about to betray him, whereas he was one of the twelve.*

120. Deut. 32.8.

121. *Ibid.*

122. In Book I, ch. 2 and ch. 10, Anselm states that the rule to be applied to test truth, when clear authority from Scripture is lacking, is to accept the conclusion that is backed by "sounder reasons."

123. See Book I, ch. 16.

124. See the beginning of ch. 16 and note 94.

125. Matt. 6.12.

126. See Book I, ch. 12.

127. See Book I, ch. 10.

128. This thought is also expressed by St. Anselm elsewhere, e.g.: in chapters 7 and 24 of the present book, and also in *De Casu Diaboli*, ch. 1–3, Schmitt, I, pp. 233–240; *PL* 158, col. 325 C–332 A, where it is a development of I Cor. 4.7: *. . . what hast thou that thou hast not received, and if thou hast received, why dost thou glory as if thou hadst not received it?*

129. See Matt. 7.12: *All things, therefore, that you would that men should do to you, do you also to them. For this is the law and the prophets.*

130. See Book I, ch. 12.

131. Gal. 5.6. St. Anselm gives the text: *quae per dilectionem operatur*, whereas the Vulgate has: *. . . per caritatem . . .*

132. Ezech. 18.27. Anselm's reading differs from that of the Vulgate, which is rendered in the Douay-Challoner translation: *And when the wicked turneth himself away from his wickedness, which he hath wrought, and doeth judgment and justice, he shall save his soul alive.* See also Ezech. 18.22 and 33.16.

133. See Book I, ch. 10, the preface and the "Submission" which precedes the preface.

134. See Book I, ch. 12.

135. See Ps. 50.7: *For behold I was conceived in iniquities, and in sins did my mother conceive me.* The theme of this section of Anselm's work had already been developed by St. Augustine, *De Libero Arbitrio*, III, ch. 10, nn. 29–31, *PL* 32, 1285–1287.

136. This reflects the classical formula for happiness given by Boethius, *De Consolatione Philosophiae*, Book 3, pros 2, *CSEL* 67, 49; *PL* 63, 726 f.: ". . . Non est aliud quod aeque perficere beatitudinem posset quam copiosus bonorum omnium status, nec alieni egens, sed sibi ipse sufficiens."

137. See Book I, ch. 21.

138. See Book I, ch. 14.

139. The word used here is *homuncio*, which the Saint often uses to describe fallen humanity. See, e.g., *Proslogion* 1, Schmitt, I, 97; *PL* 158, 225 B; *De Casu Diaboli* 10, Schmitt I, p. 247; *PL* 158, col. 338 B.

140. See Ps. 35.7–8: . . . *Men and beasts thou wilt preserve, O Lord! O how hast thou multiplied thy mercy, O God!* . . .

141. See Book I, ch. 19 and ch. 20.

142. See Eph. 2.4: *But God, who is rich in mercy* . . .

143. Anselm is implying, here, that "unbelievers" are just as convinced as Christians that there must be some way for human beings to be saved from sin and to attain happiness. Since they cannot find that way without Christ, they ought to accept Him as Redeemer.

144. *Insipiens* is Anselm's word.

145. See Book I, ch. 16–18.

146. See Book I, ch. 4.

147. See Book I, ch. 19–20.

148. See *Monologion*, ch. 64, Schmitt, vol. I, p. 75; *PL* 158, col. 210 B–C, where he expresses the opinion that one who is investigating an incomprehensible subject-matter, such as the Holy Trinity, ought to be satisfied if his reasoning brings him far enough to recognize that this reality actually exists. He goes on there, as here, to insist that the inability to give a complete explanation of *how* it exists and acts does not mitigate the certitude a person may have of the existence of that reality.

149. See Book I, chapters 1 and 2.

150. See Book II, chapters 5 to 18; also the Preface of the work.

151. See Book II, ch. 19.

152. See Book II, ch. 20.

BOOK TWO

1. In *Monologion*, ch. 68, Schmitt I, p. 79; *PL* 158, col. 214 C, Anselm similarly maintains: ". . . The rational creature was created for this purpose: to love the Supreme Essence above all other things that are good, as this Essence is itself the Supreme Good. Indeed, it was created to love nothing except that Essence, unless it be a means to that Essence. For that Essence is good through itself, and nothing else is good except because of it."

2. See *Monologion*, 69, Schmitt I, p. 80, 2–4; *PL* 158, col. 215 C–D: ". . . It is absolutely absurd to suppose that any nature that forever loves

Him who is supremely good and supremely powerful, forever lives in misery."

3. The theme of man's being destined to happiness, by means of love of God who is man's sovereign good, is a traditional one. Anselm's originality, here, is less in his conclusion than in his rational "demonstration" that justice is due to human beings precisely because they are rational. The argument is not fully satisfactory, however, because of lack of clear definition of "justice" as something supernatural.

4. See Book I, ch. 9.

5. See Book I, ch. 19.

6. See Book I, ch. 18, and also the Preface.

7. See Book I, ch. 4.

8. See Book I, ch. 16–18.

9. See Book I, ch. 19.

10. See Book I, chapters 11 to 15, and 19 to 24.

11. See Book I, ch. 4.

12. St. Anselm here uses the expression *sanctae conversationis*. Although the term can mean simply "a pious way of life," it more commonly was understood to designate monastic life under vows.

13. See Book I, ch. 21.

14. See Book I, ch. 16 and ch. 19.

15. Ps. 65.20.

16. This paragraph contains a brief but exact and comprehensive summary of the various alternative descriptions of what occurred in the Incarnation. Adhering to the path of theological reasoning alone, Anselm eliminates all those alternatives rejected at Chalcedon and in other Councils. See St. Leo the Great, whose formulas of faith are found in *PL* 54, cols. 755 A–781 A and in Mansi, *Sacrorum Conciliorum Amplissima Collectio*, V, 1271 D–1290 A. See also the formulas of Chalcedon, in Mansi, *op. cit.*, VII, 111 A–118 B.

17. The formulation of faith called *Symbolum Athanasianum* or *Quicumque,* formerly recited in the prayer of prime on certain Sundays, is being referred to by Anselm; especially the proposition: ". . . Sicut anima rationalis et caro unus est homo, ita Deus et homo unus est Christus." Philosophically, the union of the Divine Word with human nature is not of the same kind as the union of the human soul with matter, for the latter two principles constitute one nature. The same formulation of faith excludes that, regarding the hypostatic union. But the point being made is simply that there is *unity* in both cases, although it is a unity of Person with two natures, in the case of Christ, and a unity of nature in that of man.

18. This chapter is remarkable for incorporating the traditional distinctions and precise statements on the Incarnation which Catholic authority had settled, without, however, quoting the Councils or appealing to the Councils at all. It is a good example of synthetic theological reasoning, showing the necessity of certain conclusions, once the correct principles are accepted and pondered.

19. St. Anselm's title of this chapter is very similar to that of St. Augustine, in *De Trinitate,* 13, ch. 18, n. 23, *PL* 42, col. 1032–1033: "Why God took human nature from the race of Adam, and from a virgin."

20. See Book I, ch. 5.

21. The present two paragraphs present an answer to the objection of Book I, ch. 5. Anselm sees a close resemblance between the pattern of circumstances surrounding the fall of man and the pattern of details of the restoration. In this he is greatly influenced by St. Augustine and other Fathers. He is concerned, however, not merely with factual correspondences between the two events, but with "necessary reasons" discoverable by rational analysis, not just accepted by faith.

22. This sentence suggests the striking words of St. Bernard (*Hom.* 2.1: Super "Missus Est."): ". . . The only birth worthy of God was that which made Him the son of the virgin, as the only motherhood worthy of the virgin was that which made her mother of God." Also relevant and well expressed is the comment of St. Thomas Aquinas: "Christ was born of a woman to show that His body was a real human body. He was born of a virgin to show He was also divine." (Sum. Theol. III, qu. 28, art. 2, ad 2).

23. See Book I, ch. 4.

24. See Book I, ch. 3.

25. On the fitness of a holy virgin being the mother of the God-Man, see *The Virgin Conception And Original Sin,* ch. 18.

26. See Book II, ch. 18.

27. See II Cor. 4.4: . . . *Christ, who is the image of God;* Col. 1.13–15: . . . *the kingdom of the Son of His love, . . . who is the image of the invisible God.* . . .

28. The arguments given here have been advanced previously in *Epist. De Incarnatione Verbi,* 10, Schmitt, II, pp. 24–28, or *Liber De Fide Trinitatis Et De Incarnatione Verbi,* ch. 5, *PL* 158, col. 276 A–278 A.

29. See Book II, ch. 2.

30. John 8.55.

31. See *Proslogion,* 7, Schmitt I, p. 253; *PL* 158, col. 230 B–D, where Anselm similarly, but with more rhetorical fervor, shows that to be capable of corruption, lying, making true things false, and the like, would really amount to being capable of perverseness and wrong-doing, and thus would really be an incapability of resisting evil.

32. See *De Casu Diaboli,* ch. 18, Schmitt, I, 263; *PL* 158, col. 350 A, whose chapter heading is: "How the evil angel made himself unjust and the good one made himself just."

33. See Book II, ch. 5. In insisting that the only possible source of what might be called "necessity" in God is His own unchangeableness, Anselm is following St. Augustine, in *Opus Imperfectum Contra Julianum,* I, cap. 101, *PL* 45, col. 1117.

34. Here again, Anselm is relying upon St. Augustine, *op. cit.,* I, c. 96, *PL* 45, col. 1112.

35. See I Cor. 15.42: *So also is the resurrection of the dead. It is sown in corruption; it shall rise in incorruption.*

36. Anselm is right in saying that "mortality" does not pertain to the *essence* of human nature, and that if it did, no human being could ever be immortal. Scholastic philosophers, however, consider mortality to be *natural* (not "essential") to man, in the sense that it flows from human nature as a property of its generic, corporeal essence. Bodily immortality, such as was offered to Adam and the human race conditionally, is con-

sidered by all Scholastics to be a "preternatural" gift. Anselm makes no distinction of natural, supernatural and preternatural states.

37. The "philosophers" who put "mortal" into their definition of man are generally pagan Greeks and Romans who did not know, by revelation, of the special gifts enjoyed by Adam and Eve. St. Augustine testifies to this: "Man has been defined by the ancient wise men in this way: man is a mortal, rational animal." (*De Ordine*, II, cap. 11, n. 31; *PL* 32, col. 1009). Augustine himself uses that definition as a correct one in his *De Quantitate Animae*, ch. 25, n. 48; see J. M. Colleran (tr.), *St. Augustine: The Greatness of the Soul and The Teacher*, ACW, 9, Westminster, Md.: Newman, 1950, pp. 71–73, and p. 205, n. 58. Anselm is obviously not satisfied with it as a definition.

38. See John 10.17–18: *Therefore does the Father love me, because I lay down my life, that I may take it up again. No man taketh it away from me; but I lay it down of myself. And I have power to lay it down; and I have power to take it up again. This commandment have I received of my Father.*

39. See Book I, ch. 21; Book II, ch. 6.

40. See Book I, chs. 20 to 23.

41. See Book II, ch. 10.

42. On these "fitnesses" or "suitabilities," see Book I, ch. 3 (end) and ch. 4; Book II, ch. 8 (end); also Introduction, Part IV, D.

43. See Heb. 4.15: *For we have not a high priest who cannot have compassion on our infirmities, but one tempted in all things like as we are, without sin.*

44. See Baruch 3.38: *Afterwards, he was seen upon earth and conversed with men.*

45. See Book I, ch. 9.

46. See Book I, ch. 21.

47. *Ibid.*

48. I Cor. 2.8.

49. St. Augustine, *Tract. In Ioan.* 92.1, *PL* 35, col. 1863, speaks of the blood shed by Christ on the cross as blotting out the very sins which caused the shedding of that blood. See also St. Leo the Great, *Sermo* 54.2, *PL* 54, col. 320.

50. See Book II, ch. 22.

51. See Book I, ch. 17, and note 18 in Book I, regarding the phrase "the sinful mass." See also *The Virgin Conception and Original Sin*, introductory paragraph.

52. See *The Virgin Conception and Original Sin*, ch. 21.

53. See Ps. 50.7.

54. St. Anselm here again is rejecting the Immaculate Conception of the Blessed Virgin, and he is following St. Augustine, *Contra Iulianum Pelag.*, 5.15, *PL* 44, col. 813, in the matter. See Introduction, Part IV, F.

55. Rom. 5.12.

56. See the Submission to Pope Urban and Book I, ch. 2.

57. In the *Roman Missal*, the priest is directed to recite this prayer as he mixes a few drops of water with the wine to be offered and consecrated: "O God, who wonderfully created and still more wonderfully renewed the dignity of the substance of man. . . ."

58. See Book I, ch. 2.

59. See Book II, ch. 6.

60. Repeatedly Anselm has pointed out that inability to know exactly *how* and *why* something is true should not make us doubt of the necessity of the truth itself. See Book II, ch. 15. In Book I, ch. 25, he calls a person an *insipiens* who doubts about a truth or a fact which has been established with logical necessity, simply because he has not arrived at an understanding of the *cause* of this fact or the *reason* for this truth.

61. Boso is reviving the opposition between "fitness" and "necessity" to which he had recourse in Book I, ch. 3.

62. See Book II, chapters 5, 10, 11; Book I, chapters 8, 9, 10.

63. See Book II, ch. 10.

64. See Book I, chapters 8, 9, 10; Book II, chapters 5, 10, 11.

65. See Book II, ch. 7.

66. Anselm's Latin sentence is: "Nimis haeres in nihilo, et ut dici solet, quaeris nodum in scirpo." The second phrase is obviously proverbial, and was considered a common expression even in ancient times. Ennius, *Saturarum Fragmenta*, 46, indicates this: ". . . quaerunt in scirpo, soliti quod dicere, nodum." Similarly, Plautus: ". . . nodum in scirpo quaeris." (*Menaechmi*, act 2, sc. 1, line 247; Loeb Classical ed. II, 390); and Terence (*Andria*, act 5, line 94, Loeb. ed. I, 102).

67. See Book I, ch. 1.

68. See Book II, ch. 5.

69. See Book II, ch. 7 and ch. 9.

70. See Book II, ch. 5.

71. See Book II, ch. 7.

72. Is. 53.7 (as rendered in the Vulgate).

73. See Aristotle, *De Interpret.* 9, 18a, 28 to 19b, 4; Boethius, *In Lib. Arist. De Interpret.*, ed. la, I, *PL* 64, col. 329 ff. edit. 2a, III, col. 495 ff.

74. See John 10.18.

75. See Book I, ch. 2.

76. *The Virgin Conception and Original Sin*, in the beginning of which this insistence of Boso will be recalled, is the fulfillment of Boso's request.

77. See Book I, chapters 3 to 10.

78. See Book I, chapters 3, 8, 9, 10.

79. Analogous examples may be found in *De Veritate*, 8, Schmitt I, p. 188; *PL* 158, col. 477 B, C.

80. See Book II, ch. 11; Book I, chs. 8, 9, 10.

81. See John 16.15: *All things whatsoever the Father hath are mine.*

82. See Book II, ch. 18.

83. See Luke 6.47–48: *Everyone that cometh to me and heareth my words and doth them, I will shew you to whom he is like. He is like to a man building a house, who digged deep and laid the foundation upon a rock. And when a flood came, the stream beat vehemently upon that house; and it could not shake it; for it was founded upon a rock.*

84. See Book I, ch. 2.

85. See Book I, chapters 6 and 7.

86. See Book I, ch. 24.

87. See Book I, ch. 17.

88. See Book II, ch. 8, beginning.

89. See John 8.44: *You are of your father, the devil; and the desires of the devil you will do. He was a murderer from the beginning; and he stood not in the truth, because the truth was not in him. When he speaketh a lie, he speaketh of his own; for he is a liar, and the father thereof.*

90. This sentence neatly expresses the tremendous ambition Anselm had in composing his treatise: to establish or safeguard the whole of revelation, in both Testaments, by showing that the central teaching on the God-Man is reasonable, and, on the assumption of God's willing it, is "necessary." He showed that same desire to unify and simplify complex problems and their solutions in *Proslogion,* where he sought a single argument that, of itself, without other corroboration, would establish the existence of a Supreme Being, about whose attributes conclusions could be readily and directly drawn by deduction. See Prooemium to the *Proslogion,* Schmitt I, p. 93; *PL* 158, col. 223 B–C.

91. See Book II, ch. 9.
92. See Book II, ch. 16.
93. See Book II, ch. 15.

THE VIRGIN CONCEPTION AND ORIGINAL SIN

1. See *Why God Became Man,* Book I, ch. 1.
2. See *ibid.,* Book II, ch. 17, near end.
3. See *ibid.,* Book II, ch. 1.
4. This same distinction of personal and original sin is made by St. Augustine, *De Peccatorum Meritis Et Remissione,* Book I, ch. 10 and 11, *CSEL* 60, p. 12.
5. On St. Anselm's notion of "justice" see Introduction, Part IV, F.
6. On the "ultra-realism" reflected here and frequently throughout the book, see Introduction Part IV, F.
7. See *Why God Became Man,* Book I, ch. 20 to ch. 23.
8. Wisdom 9.15.
9. Exod. 20.5.
10. See *Dialogus De Casu Diaboli,* ch. 16, Schmitt I, p. 259; *PL* 158, col. 349 B.
11. See *Dialogus De Veritate,* ch. 12, Schmitt I, pp. 191 ff.; *PL* 158, col. 480 C–484 A, in which Anselm gives this definition of *iustitia.*
12. See St. Anselm's *Tractatus De Concordia Praescientiae Et Praedestinationis Necnon Gratiae Cum Libero Arbitrio,* Qu. I, c. XI, Schmitt II, pp. 278 ff.; *PL* 158, col. 534 A–537 A.
13. Gal. 5.17.
14. Rom. 7.25 and 23.
15. Rom. 8.1.
16. Rom. 7.22.
17. *Ibid.*

18. Rom. 7.23.

19. I Esdras, 7.21.

20. Josue 8.31.

21. See Num. 25.7–11. Phinees, a descendant of Aaron the priest, slew public and notorious sinners in the name of God and turned God's wrath away from the children of Israel. He is also mentioned in Ps. 105.30.

22. See Eph. 5.3: *But fornication and all uncleanness or covetousness, let it not so much as be named among you, as becometh saints.*

23. See *Why God Became Man*, Book II, ch. 12.

24. In saying that it is only the soul, with the will within it, that exercises sensation and muscular action, Anselm seems to be following a view of St. Augustine that sensation is a direct operation of the soul alone, occasioned by a physical effect (*passio*) on the body, produced by the action of an external material thing. See J. M. Colleran (tr.), *St. Augustine: The Greatness Of The Soul and The Teacher, ACW*, vol. 9, Westminster, Md.: Newman Press, 1960, p. 208 ff., note 73. The principal point being made in the present context, however, is that responsibility and guilt pertain to the will, which is a power of the spiritual soul, and not to the corporeal powers. This point remains true, regardless of the parenthetical remark that seems to imply that the soul is directly operative, or that sensation is a purely spiritual operation.

25. See *Dialogus De Casu Diaboli*, ch. 7, Schmitt I, pp. 244–245; *PL* 158, col. 335 A–336 B.

26. See *ibid.*, ch. 26, Schmitt I, p. 274; *PL* 158, col. 358 B–359 A.

27. See *ibid.*, chapters 9–11, 15, 16, 19, 26, Schmitt I, p. 246 ff.; *PL* 158, col. 337 A–359 A.

28. See *Dialogus De Veritate*, ch. 12, Schmitt I, p. 191 ff; *PL* 158, col. 480 B–484 A.

29. See *Why God Became Man*, Book I, ch. 14; also ch. 12.

30. Job 14.4.

31. Ps. 50.7.

32. Gen. 2.17.

33. Rom. 8.10.

34. Rom. 5.12.

35. Rom. 5.19.

36. See ch. 7.

37. See ch. 2.

38. See *ibid.*

39. See Wisdom 9.15: *For the corruptible body is a load upon the soul* . . .

40. See ch. 9 ff.

41. See ch. 24 ff.

42. Rom. 5.14.

43. Gen. 5.2.

44. See *Why God Became Man*, Book I, ch. 16.

45. This chapter nine reflects the thinking of St. Augustine regarding the attribution of original sin to Adam alone. He says, for example, that Eve "was understood to be in Adam, because of unity of flesh." Again, "generation begins with the male," and the Apostle intended to show that sin entered into the progeny of the first couple, by generation. (See Augustine, *Contra Julianum Opus Imperfectum* II, ch. 173, *PL* 45, col.

1216). Augustine also (*ibid.*, ch. 194, col. 1225) gives the interpretation that "the two are included in the singular number" because of the words of Christ regarding husband and wife: *Therefore now they are not two, but one flesh* (Matt. 19.6).

46. See ch. 2.

47. See *Why God Became Man*, Book II, ch. 1.

48. See *ibid.*, Book I, ch. 22.

49. See Gen. 2.7: *And the Lord God formed man of the slime of the earth, and breathed into his face the breath of life; and man became a living soul.*

50. See Gen. 14.21–23.

51. See John 11.1–45.

52. See John 2.1–11.

53. See *Why God Became Man*, Book I, ch. 22.

54. The teaching of Anselm in this chapter is based upon St. Augustine, *Sermo* 152, n. 9, *PL* 38, col. 824.

55. See ch. 10.

56. See ch. 3.

57. See ch. 7.

58. Job 14.4.

59. Ps. 50.7.

60. On the "sinful mass," see *Why God Became Man*, Book I, ch. 17, note 18.

61. See ch. 3.

62. See ch. 11.

63. See *Why God Became Man*, Book I, ch. 5.

64. See *ibid.*, Book II, ch. 6.

65. See ch. 8 of the present book.

66. Wisdom 9.15.

67. See chapters 11–12.

68. See ch. 13.

69. See *Why God Became Man*, Book II, ch. 16.

70. See the untitled preface to the present essay.

71. See Wisdom 9.15: *For the corruptible body is a load upon the soul* . . .

72. See *Why God Became Man*, Book II, ch. 16.

73. See *ibid.*

74. See ch. 2.

75. See *ibid.*

76. See *ibid.*

77. *Ibid.*

78. Rom. 5.14.

79. See Rom. 5.8–9: *But God commendeth his charity towards us, because when as yet we were sinners according to the time, Christ died for us.*

80. Eph. 2.3.

81. Rom. 5.14.

82. Rom. 5.20.

83. See *Why God Became Man*, Book I, ch. 21 ff.

84. Rom. 5.12.

85. See ch. 10.

86. This causal and seminal pre-existence of the whole human race in

Adam was pointed out frequently by Fathers of the Church. St. Ambrose, for example, wrote: "Adam existed, and we all existed in him; Adam was lost, and all were lost in him" (*In Lucam*, Book VII, n. 234, *CSEL* 32, p. 387; *PL* 15, 1852 B). St. Augustine is more explicit: "God, indeed, created man virtuous, being the author of natures, not of vices; but once man was depraved by his own will and justly condemned, he gave birth to offspring who were depraved and condemned. We were all, surely, in that one man, since all of us were that one man, who fell into sin because of a woman who was made from him prior to sin. There did not yet exist, there was not apportioned to us individually, the form in which we were individually to live; but there already existed a seminal nature from which we would be propagated." (*De Civitate Dei*, Book 13, ch. 13, *CSEL* 40, Part I, p. 632; *PL* 41, col. 386).

87. Luke 1.35.

88. See ch. 1.

89. *Why God Became Man.*

90. This is Anselm's definition of "justice" given and discussed in *Dialogus De Veritate* ch. 12, Schmitt I, pp. 191 ff.; *PL* 158, col. 480 B–484 A.

91. See Rom. 9.10–13.

92. Exodus 20.5.

93. There is reflected here the thought of St. Augustine: "It is said, not without probability, that offspring are under debt by the sins of their ancestors, not only of the first human beings, but also of their own parents, of whom they were directly born. . . . For in that one sin which passed down to all men, and is great enough to change human nature and bring it to the necessity of death, many sins are to be found. There are also other sins of the immediate parents which, although unable to change nature, still bind the children under guilt, unless unmerited grace and God's mercy come to their aid." (*Enchiridion De Fide, Spe et Caritate*, ch. 13, n. 46, *PL* 40, 254 f.). Also pertinent to the message of this chapter is the teaching of St. Gregory the Great: "We contract original sin from our ancestors; and unless we are delivered by the grace of Baptism, we also bear the sins of the ancestors. The reason is that we are one being with them. The sins of ancestors fall upon their offspring since, because of the fault of the ancestor, the soul of the offspring is stained by original sin. Again, the sins of ancestors do not fall upon their offspring, because when we are freed from original sin by Baptism, we no longer have the sins of ancestors, but only those we ourselves commit." (*Moralia*, Book 15, ch. 51, *PL* 75, 1110).

94. See Matt. 6.13: *. . . and lead us not into temptation . . .*

95. See Job 23.16: *God hath softened my heart;* and Exodus 4.21: *I (God) shall harden his heart;* and Rom. 9.18: *He (God) hath mercy on whom he will. And whom he will, he hardeneth.*

96. Ezech. 18.20.

97. Gal. 6.5.

98. II Cor. 5.10.

99. Ex. 20.5.

100. See Deut. 24.16: *The fathers shall not be put to death for the children, nor the children for the fathers, but everyone shall die for his own sin.*

101. Ezech. 18.20.

102. See Gal. 6.5: *For everyone shall bear his own burden.*

103. See II Cor. 5.10: *For we must all be manifested before the judgment seat of Christ, that everyone may receive the proper things of the body, according as he hath done, whether it be good or evil.*

104. The author is influenced, in the thoughts of this chapter, by St. Augustine, *Quaestiones In Heptateuchum,* Book 5, ch. 42, *PL* 34, col. 765.

105. See ch. 23.

106. See ch. 22.

107. Rom. 5.14.

108. See ch. 10.

109. On the "ultra-realism" underlying this statement, see the Introduction, Part IV, F.

110. See ch. 23.

111. Eph. 2.3.

112. See ch. 2.

113. See ch. 23.

114. See Luke 20.35–36: . . . *They that shall be accounted worthy . . . of the resurrection from the dead shall neither be married nor take wives. Neither can they die any more for they are equal to the angels and are the children of God, being the children of the resurrection.*

115. See ch. 23.

116. In proposing the opinion expressed here in ch. 28 and before in ch. 23, that unbaptized infants are "condemned," or positively punished in hell, St. Anselm is following St. Augustine. Although Augustine admits there is a graver condemnation imposed on those who have added personal sin to original injustice, he nevertheless maintains that original sin not only separates the unbaptized from the "kingdom of God" and the beatific vision, but that it also deprives them of "salvation and eternal life." See *De Peccatorum Meritis Et Remissione,* I, ch. 12, *CSEL* 60, p. 16; *PL* 49, col. 117. Hence, he continues, the unbaptized infants undergo a very "mild" or "mitigated" (*mitissima*) eternal punishment, but it would be mistaken and deceptive to say that they are not condemned. (*Ibid.,* ch. 16; p. 20; col. 120). He is emphatically clear in saying that if they are not adopted into the people of God by Baptism, they are "estranged from salvation and from the light, and will remain in perdition and in darkness." (*Ibid.,* ch. 27, n. 41; p. 40; col. 132). See also *Contra Julianum Pelagianum,* III, ch. 5, *PL* 44, col. 707 f.

St. Augustine's principal concern, it may be noted, was to refute the Pelagians' denial of the transmission of original sin and its consequences, to the descendants of Adam. The Pelagians maintained, as a corollary, that human infants are born in identically the same state as Adam was in, before his fall, and that even if they are not baptized when they die, they reach eternal life and the happiness of the beatific vision. See P. Parente et al., "Pelagianism," *DDT,* p. 211; R. Hedde and E. Amann, "Pélagianisme," *DTC,* t. 12, col. 675–715. In opposing the Pelagian "naturalism" and the denial of the need for grace, Augustine went too far in insisting that infants without sanctifying grace deserved eternal punishment, however mitigated. Greek Fathers, however, fairly commonly spoke of the exclusion of unbaptized infants from heaven and the beatific vision, without any punishment, because there is no deliberate personal sin, and without any pain of loss, because they have no knowledge of the beatific vision or of anything supernatural. This tradition became more widespread and generally accepted, later, than the Augustinian tradition.

"Limbo" (*limbus*—border) is the name commonly given to the place and state of those who deserve neither heavenly happiness nor eternal damnation. It was especially during the Scholastic period of theology, after the lifetime of Anselm, that this doctrine of "Limbo" found its full acceptance. See, for example, the *Supplementum IIIae Partis Summae Theologiae S. Thomae Aquinatis,* Qu. 69, art. 4–7; this is not actually the work of St. Thomas himself, but was compiled by Reginald of Piperno or some other follower of Thomas, and it does bear testimony to the acceptance in the thirteenth century, of this doctrine of Limbo.

There has been no formal decision of the teaching authority of the Church on the matter, and no proof of a consensus of early theologians. In the twentieth century, there has been renewed theological investigation of the question of the lot of unbaptized infants, in the light of what is known of the will of God for the salvation of all, and of the efficacy and extent of "Baptism of desire." See K. Rahner and H. Vorgrimler, "Limbo," *TD,* pp. 262–263.

117. See ch. 2.

118. See *Dialogus De Veritate,* ch. 12, Schmitt, I, pp. 191 ff.; *PL* 158, col. 489–494.

119. As in the matter of the state of unbaptized infants (see ch. 28 and note 116) Anselm is the pupil of St. Augustine, so is he also in regard to the state of those who are baptized. Although he so forcibly says that the unbaptized are to be punished, Augustine maintains in the same book that baptized infants will be brought to a state of perfection in the Light that eternally illumines the souls of the saved. For sins alone bring about a separation between God and human beings, and sins are remitted by the grace of the Mediator through whom we are reconciled to our Creator. See *De Peccatorum Meritis Et Remissione,* I, ch. 19, n. 25; *CSEL* 60, p. 25; *PL* 44, col. 123.

In discussing what benefit infants gain from the sacrament of Baptism, when they die after receiving it but before they are able to appreciate the faith and exercise acts of virtue, Augustine gives it as "a pious and reliable belief" that the faith of those who have them baptized benefits the infants. He gives as an example the benefit of restoration to life of the widow's son because of his mother's faith. From this he argues that it is even more probable that the faith of a Christian adult can help an infant who cannot exercise faith by himself. See *De Libero Arbitrio,* Book III, ch. 23, n. 67; *PL* 32, col. 1304.

OTHER MAGI TITLES OF LASTING VALUE

Raissa's Journal   *Presented by Jacques Maritain*
Jacques Maritain: Homage   *John Howard Griffin and Yves R. Simon*
Louise Imogen Guiney   *Henry G. Fairbanks*
Approach to Philosophy   *D.J.B. Hawkins*
Twentieth Century Philosophy   *Bernard Delfgaauw*
Studies in the Psychology of the Mystics   *Joseph Marechal*
The Grace of God, the Response of Man   *J.P. Mackey*
Freedom or Tolerance?   *Enda McDonagh*
The Great Dialogue of Nature and Space   *Yves R. Simon*
Science and Common Sense   *W.R. Thompson, Fellow of the Royal Society*
Five Oriental Philosophies   *Thomas Berry*
Contemporary Philosophy of Religion   *J.P. Mackey*
The Philosophy of Language   *Robert G. Miller*
Freedom   *Mortimer Adler*
The Philosophy of Karl Rahner   *Joseph Donceel*
The Theology of Karl Rahner   *Gerald A. McCool*
Wisdom: A Manifesto   *Maritain, Journet, etc.*
Art of Prayer   *Ferdinand Valentine, O.P.*
Aquinas Scripture Series:
Commentary on Paul's Galatians
Commentary on Paul's Ephesians
Commentary on Paul's Philippians and First Thessalonians
Commentary on the Gospel of St. John, Part I

524186

Send for a complete list of titles in philosophy, theology and related fields to the publisher: **Magi Books, Inc., Buckingham Dr., Albany, New York 12208, U.S.A.**